ON YES MAN

"Danny Wallace's account of the year during which he vowed never to say no is seizure-inducingly funny."
—Anneli Rufus, *East Bay Express*

"*Yes Man* is a breezy, charming read. . . . It seems to be [Wallace's] simple contention that in our increasingly mechanized world, living by serendipity is both an act of rebellion and a pretty good way to seek happiness. And I can say yes to that."
—Neal Schindler, *Seattle Weekly*

"No wonder Jack Black has already optioned film rights to *Yes Man*."
—Whitney Pastorek, *Entertainment Weekly*

"Experience what it's like when you open yourself up to all possibilities in Wallace's latest book, *Yes Man*." —*Morning Call* (Allentown)

"I am a total sucker for the dry British brand of verbal farce, and that is definitely one of the reasons I liked this book. . . . It's probably the kind of book you would say no to. But suppose, just once, you said yes. Go to parties, volunteer for projects, buy this book just because I said so." —Jon Carroll, *San Francisco Chronicle*

On Danny Wallace

"Danny Wallace does things that few people would and writes about them in ways that few people could. He's as funny as Bill Bryson used to be." —*Independent on Sunday* (London)

"It's no mystery how Wallace attracts people: He is immediately likable and casually brilliant, his voice reminiscent of that of the late Douglas Adams." —MSNBC (TV)

"He is a little odd, but ultimately, he is harmless."
—*De Standaard* (Amsterdam)

"Having met him, I can confirm that he is both a great philanthropist and (in the nicest possible sense) an idiot. But he has changed the world."
—*Financial Times* (London)

"Beautiful, heartwarming, inspiring, and original."
—*Time Off* (Queensland)

"Hillarious and brilliant." —*Bookseller* (UK)

"One goofball with something vaguely approximating a mission."
—*Onion*

"One cannot help but wonder whether he has stumbled upon the future shape of spirituality." —*Daily Telegraph* (London)

"He is responsible for over 100,000 good deeds done."
—*Khaleej Times* (Dubai)

"The new Jesus? No."—*Aftenposten* (Oslo)

"Wallace is a Generation X legend."—*Wisconsin State Journal*

by Danny Wallace

SIMON SPOTLIGHT ENTERTAINMENT
New York • London • Toronto • Sydney

ALSO BY DANNY WALLACE

Are You Dave Goreman? (with Dave Goreman)

Join Me!

Random Acts of Kindness

SIMON SPOTLIGHT ENTERTAINMENT
A Division of Simon & Schuster, Inc.
1230 Avenue of the Americas, New York, NY 10020
Copyright © 2005 by Danny Wallace
This Simon Spotlight Entertainment trade paperback edition December 2008.
SIMON SPOTLIGHT ENTERTAINMENT and colophon are trademarks of
Simon & Schuster, Inc.
For information about special discounts for bulk purchases, please contact
Simon & Schuster Special Sales at 1-800-456-6798 or business@simonandschuster.com
Manufactured in the United States of America
10 9 8 7 6 5 4 3 2 1
Library of Congress Cataloging-in-Publication Data has been catalogued for
the hardcover edition as follows:
Wallace, Danny.
Yes man / by Danny Wallace.
1. Wallace, Danny. 2. Conduct of life. 3. London (England)—Biography. I. Title.
CT788.W319A3 2005
920.0421—dc22
2005007752
p. cm.
ISBN-13: 978-1-4169-0066-5 (hc)
ISBN-10:   1-4169-0066-7 (hc)
ISBN-13: 978-1-4165-9553-3 (pbk)
ISBN-10:   1-4165-9553-8 (pbk)

CONTENTS

For my mum and dad,
and for Sammy

"The wise man can pick up a grain of sand and envision a whole universe.
But the stupid man will just lie down on some seaweed
and roll around until he's completely draped in it.
Then he'll stand up and go, 'Hey, I'm Vine Man!'"
—*Jack Handey*

PROLOGUE

In Which We Set the Scene

It was nearly midnight. I was standing in the rain, outside the house of a rich banker in Las Vegas.

I checked my pockets. I had everything I needed. The photos. The keys to the car. The silver pocket watch.

Most important, I had the gun.

Because I had been asked to kill a man.

And I had said yes.

Ahem.

I wasn't, really. And I hadn't, really.

I mean, when was the last time *you* were asked to kill a man? It very rarely happens to me. And I'm not sure I could even do it, to be honest. If you asked me today whether I would kill a man for you, I'd most likely flat out refuse, and even if I asked for more details, my decision would still most likely be not to do it.

"No," I'd say. "Surely you can resolve your issues with this man another way?"

And you'd see my point, and say yes, and I'd suggest you beat him at chess instead, and you'd walk away shamefaced yet impressed by my wisdom.

Nope. I can honestly say I have never killed a man. Not on purpose, anyway. And the only reason I forced you to imagine me on the verge of undertaking a messy assassination in Las Vegas was to give you an idea of how my life *could* have gone. How this story *could* have started. Me, standing in the rain, charged with a terrible and sinister mission, gun in hand. I mean, I *hate* rain. And I'd look *rubbish* with a gun. I wouldn't *dare* be out on my own after midnight in Las Vegas. I rather frown upon murder. And I really don't know *where* a silver pocket watch comes into all this.

So thankfully the real story doesn't start this way. But the real story did take me to some strange places, meeting some strange people, doing some strange things. And the real story takes place over the course of several months; not so long ago. Several months which changed not just my life, but my entire *way* of life and my entire *attitude* to life.

I should just say thanks to all those people I've written about in the next few hundred pages. Their names are real, apart from those few cases where I've changed a name or detail to save anyone from any obvious embarrassment, or, in one rather central and vital person's case, just because they thought it would be cool and so asked. There is also, I'm afraid, the odd occasion where I've moved an event to a slightly different time or place . . . but this is for your own good. I don't want you falling asleep on me. I've got some very important things to say.   ·

I wrote this book after keeping a diary. Some of that diary I have written more on than other bits, some I didn't include at all, and some has made it in word-for-word. I recommend keeping a diary. Diaries are cool.

And lastly do me a favour. While you read this book—however long it takes you, and wherever you end up doing it—make a note of all the times you could have said yes to something. And think about where that yes could have led you. It might come in handy one day.

You look lovely today, by the way.

Danny Wallace
St. Petersburg, January 2005

SELECTED EXTRACTS FROM THE DIARY OF A YES MAN

January 12

I have started this diary to record all that is going on in my life. All so that one day I will be pleased I had recorded the things that have happened to me, for posterity. If you are a historian from the future, please, save your thanks. Your time will be better spent reading up on my thoughts and philosophies.

So, with pen in hand, I say to you, Life: I am ready! Throw at me what you will!

January 19

Nothing yet.

CHAPTER 1

In Which the Story Begins

It is quite incredible how a bus—a simple, red, London bus—can change your life.

There were other reasons for why what happened eventually happened, of course. I'm not saying it was all about the bus. But the bus was pretty high on the list. Or, more accurately, the man sitting next to me on the bus. Here he is, right now, flicking through his *Evening Standard*, checking his cheap, black watch, mere moments after uttering a sentence that, quite without him knowing, has had the most unexpected effect on me.

It's like one of those moments in a cartoon, when a second of complete and total revelation hits an unenlightened fool, a moment in which they're bathed in a golden light from the heavens above; their face a picture of comfort; the only sound the chorus of a thousand angels.

Of course, real life isn't quite like that. I'm on a crowded bus in the East End of London, for a start, and so the only thing I'm bathed in is an unpleasant mist of sweat and coughs.

But it's still an epiphany. And I'm still smiling from what I've heard, smiling from what I've learned. I start to wonder whether anyone else is feeling the same. So I sneak a chance to glance around. To see if one of my fellow passengers has been struck by the man's simple message; his message of hope and optimism and all the things I hadn't realised I'd been losing sight of.

But no one has. Not that I can see, anyway. That's okay, though. There's time for them.

Because this man next to me . . . this man has changed *everything*.

"Maybe it was Jesus," said Ian, putting his pint down on the table. We were in the Yorkshire Grey, and Ian was a bit drunk. "Or maybe it was Buddha! I'd love to meet Buddha. He looks like a right laugh.

What did this bloke look like? If he had a beard, it was probably Jesus, and if he had a belly, it was probably Buddha."

"He had a beard, but it wasn't a Jesus beard."

"A belly, then?" he said with what looked like real hope in his eyes. "Did he have a Buddha belly?"

"I'm fairly sure he wasn't Buddha, either. This was an Indian bloke. His name was Medhi, or something."

"'Medhi' sounds a bit like 'Jesus.'"

"No, it doesn't. And it wasn't Jesus. What would Jesus be doing in Bethnal Green?"

"Sorry, go on. So there was this bloke on a bus last week, who wasn't a deity or a son of God, and then there was also your diary?"

Yes. There was also my diary. High up on the list, right under the bus, was my diary. A diary I had only started because I was afraid I would forget all the wonderful things I was doing. All the dazzling, crazy, hazy times. The important times, the carefree times, the times I'd look back on as the times of my life. Only when I flicked through it did I realise there was nothing to forget. Or, rather, nothing worth remembering.

Things had been different last year. Last year was a year of adventure. Of fun. Of friends. Six months into a new year I'd slowly begun to realise that all my stories were about last year. All my memories, too. I'd been cruising on past glories, dining out on better times. Well, that's not strictly true. Not true at all. I'd been dining *in* on them.

In my mind I was one of London's young, thrusting urbanites. In my mind I was always on the go, always had somewhere to be, always in the thick of things. I thought I was like something out of an advert. I probably even thought I had a moped.

I couldn't have been more wrong. Especially about the moped.

I'd ended up talking to the man on the bus quite by chance.

We'd been standing, me and this man, waiting for the Central Line train to take us from Holborn to the East End, when the announcement had spluttered and stuttered its way over the tannoy. It was a security alert. We were being asked to leave. Our journeys home had just gained an hour. We'd be shunted and squeezed onto buses outside and driven home, very slowly during rush hour, on a rainy, rainy London night.

The man and I had raised our eyebrows at each other and smiled in a "what's the world coming to" way. We'd started to walk up the stairs and out of the station, like the good, old-fashioned, obedient British citizens we were.

"Nice weather for this!" said the man as we jogged through a slanting rain and flashed our travel cards at the bus driver. I ha-ha'ed, probably a little too ha-hard, and we joined the seething masses on board the bus.

"Where are you headed?" I'd asked.

"Aldgate," he'd replied.

The man, as it turned out, was a teacher.

And he was about to teach me.

"So, what did he teach you?" said Ian.

"I'll tell you in a minute."

"Tell me now. I want to know what kind of wisdom he imparted on you that's caused you to summon me here."

"I didn't 'summon' you here."

"You sent me an e-mail saying that your entire life had changed and that you wanted to meet up."

"That's hardly summoning. I was more saying 'Do you fancy a pint?'"

"Great. I do. Thanks."

I sighed, stood up, and went to get us a round.

Now that I think about it, my downward spiral had probably started after I'd been dumped by my girlfriend last autumn. It was a shock to the system, a body blow that had really changed things.

But don't go thinking I'm all hung up on an ex-girlfriend. This isn't one of those stories of obsession and regret and of trying to get back together. I've never been someone who would have made an effective stalker, for one thing, lacking as I do both the necessary energies and a decent pair of binoculars.

It's just that being dumped suddenly puts time into perspective. I'm

not saying my three years with Hanne were wasted, because they
weren't; they were great and warm and loving. I'm just saying that at
the end of any relationship you take a long, hard look at the years that
have gone by and say "What now?"

So I did three years of growing up in two weeks. I returned to the
world of freelance employment as a radio producer at the BBC. I got
a mortgage. And a pension. I started to shop at Habitat and IKEA. I
experimented with new and exciting pastas. I learned how to iron. I
even bought a plant.

Most of these were small changes. But soon, quite without my
knowing, I developed a certain satisfaction for staying in. For potter-
ing about and tinkering with things. For slouching, and napping, and
channel hopping. Soon that was all I wanted to do. And so I became
the man who could wriggle out of any prior engagement. Who could
spot an invitation coming a mile away and head it off at the pass. The
man who'd gladly swap a night down the pub for just one whiff of an
episode of *EastEnders*. The man who'd send an e-mail instead of
attend a birthday. Who'd text instead of call, and call instead of visit.
I became the man who'd mastered the white lie. The man who always
had an excuse. The man who always said no.

And I was perfectly happy. Perfectly happy to be me, myself, and
ironing. Perfectly happy until that night on that bus, next to that man.

"Okay. So, there was a man," said Ian. "And you sat next to him. So
far this isn't really what you'd call a classic anecdote."

"But it's what he told me that was important, Ian."

"Yes, it sounds it. But *what* did he say?"

It was my friends who'd noticed it first. They'd noticed I'd changed,
or that I just wasn't around as much as I was, or that I was just saying
no a lot more often. I was too tired, or there was something I wanted
to watch, or I just felt like being alone. I couldn't put my finger on it.
The weird thing was, it didn't make me sad. Not while it was happening, anyway. It only made me sad when I finally realised the effect
it was having on my friendships; on the friends I was letting down or
annoying or disappointing or even losing.

But at the time I just didn't notice it. The sad fact is, saying no had become a habit.

"Aha! I knew it!" said Ian, pointing his finger slightly too close to my face. "I *knew* you were always making excuses!"

"I know. And I'm sorry."

"That night when you said you couldn't come out because you'd won a competition to meet Lionel Richie, was that an excuse?"

"Yes."

"How about that time you couldn't come out because you said you'd accidentally reversed all your leg joints?"

"That was quite obviously a lie. And I'm sorry. But there will be no more excuses. Honestly, Ian, I'm a changed man."

Ian had become concerned that I wasn't going out enough anymore. So he'd decided to take matters into his own hands. Every couple of days there'd be another idea, or invitation, or suggestion for a night out. He'd send me e-mails, and text me, and leave grumpy messages on my answerphone.

"Danny," he'd say. "I know you're there. How do I know you're there? Because you're *always* there. You're not picking up because you're scared I'll invite you out, which I'm going to do anyway. We'll be at the pub at eight. I look forward to receiving your standard text message, saying you can't make it, and you're sorry, and we should have fun. Bye."

And then I'd get all hoity-toity and text him, and write I'M NOT IN ACTUALLY. I'M OUT. BUT I CAN'T MAKE IT, SO I'M SORRY AND HAVE FUN. And then I'd realise that he'd left the message on my home phone, and that to have heard it I would have to have been in. And then I'd blush, and he'd text back and call me a wanker.

But then one evening Ian had bumped into Hanne and shared his concerns. That Friday night she'd turned up unannounced at nine or ten o'clock, carrying a bottle of wine.

"So what's going on?" she said, using her hand to brush some stale rice off the sofa and taking a seat.

"How do you mean?"

"You. What's happened to you?"

"Nothing's happened to me, Hanne."

"Well, I suppose that's true."

"Eh?"

"What I mean, Dan, is that *nothing's* happened to you. Nothing does, anymore, apparently. Your friends are worried. Where have you been for the past six months?"

"Here," I said, confused. "I've been right here!"

"Precisely. You've been here. Where were you on Steve's birthday?"

"I was . . . busy!" I lied, trying desperately to remember what excuse I'd used that time. "I went to a women-and-war exhibition."

I never said they were good excuses.

"Okay. And where were you when everyone else was at Tom's stag night?"

"Again, busy. I'm very busy, Hanne. Look at me."

I don't know why I asked Hanne to look at me. It's not as if I looked particularly busy. I was just a man standing up.

"You're no more busy than your friends. We've all got jobs, Dan, but we all find time to do other things, too. You've cut yourself off, and we're concerned. You don't have fun anymore."

"I do! I have loads of fun! And I have loads of fun new hobbies!"

"Like what?"

I struggled to find an answer. Of course I had fun! Surely I did! I just couldn't think of any examples right now. Hanne had put me on the spot, that was all. But there must be *something* I enjoy doing.

"I . . . enjoy toast," I said.

"You enjoy toast," said Hanne, who, because she is Norwegian, likes to be matter-of-fact about things.

"Yes, but not just toast," I said defensively. "Other things, too."

"Like what?"

My mind raced. What else was fun?

"Theme parks."

"Right," said Hanne. "So you've been eating toast and going to theme parks, have you?"

"Yes."

"For six months."

"On and off."

"You hate theme parks," she said. "So, which theme parks?"

"What?"

"Which theme parks have you been going to?"

I think she may have been on to me. I looked around the room, desperate for inspiration.

"Shelf . . . Adventure."

"Sorry?"

I cleared my throat. "Shelf Adventure."

Hanne took a sip of her wine. So did I. Of *my* wine, I mean, not hers. Taking a sip of *her* wine would have spoiled the atmosphere.

"So, you were making Shelf Adventure up too! I *knew* it!" said Ian.

"Of *course* I was making Shelf Adventure up! How many adventures can you have with a shelf?"

"I couldn't find a *thing* about it on the Internet. Hanne knew you were lying too, you know."

"I guessed that she probably had," I said.

"And then what happened?"

"Is this about us, Dan?" said Hanne, getting her stuff together in the hallway. "Because we split up?"

I didn't know what to say. So I didn't say anything at all.

"It just seems like you're doing all the things that I would once have loved you to do . . . the job, the mortgage, the staying in more. You're not doing this . . . for *me*, are you?"

I smiled gently. "No, Hanne. Don't worry."

"Because you know that now we've split up, you can do all the things that used to annoy me? You can come home drunk whenever you like, and you can do as many stupid boy projects as you want."

"It's not about us, Hanne . . ."

"Because you know that just because you've changed doesn't mean we're going to get back together, don't you?"

"I know."

if you *did* buy handwash for the bathroom."

w," I said.

you can't mend a relationship with a garlic crusher."

"Is that a Norwegian proverb?"

"No. I'm referring to the new garlic crusher in your kitchen."

"I didn't even know it was a garlic crusher. And no, I know you can't mend a relationship with a garlic crusher. To be honest I don't even know how you crush a garlic with one."

"Okay, then," said Hanne, opening the door to leave. "But, listen. You should make more of an effort. Because you're not just saying no to your friends—you're saying no to yourself."

I paused for a second to place the quote. *"Dawson's Creek?"*

"Yep," said Hanne.

"Bye."

"Bye."

"Look, Dan," said Ian. "Will you just tell me what this fucking bloke on the bus said to you, or should I make another appointment?"

"Okay, I'll tell you."

I put my pint down on the table and looked Ian in the eye. "He said: 'Say yes more.'"

I picked my pint up again and took a sip. I raised my eyebrows to show Ian he should be impressed, but for some reason he still appeared to be waiting for more. That's the problem with the MTV generation. Never satisfied.

"Is that it?" he said. "'Say yes more'?"

"Yep," I said, smiling. "That's it."

The sentence had tripped off the man's tongue like he'd been saying it all his life.

"Say yes more," he'd said.

"Say yes more," I'd repeated. Three little words of such power.

"The people without passion are the ones who always say no," he'd said moments before, and I'd turned, stunned, to listen.

"But the happiest people are the ones who understand that good things occur when one *allows* them to."

And that was that.

That was all it took to turn my life on its head. A few choice sentences from a complete and utter stranger. A stranger on a bus. And a bearded stranger, at that. This went against everything I held as true. If there was one lesson that had been drummed into me as a kid, it was never listen to a bearded stranger. I felt like Danny, from the movie *Karate Kid*, sitting next to Mr. Miyage. One minute we'd been idly chatting about this, about that, and about what we'd done with our weeks, and the next this thin and bearded man had dropped a philosophical bombshell.

I couldn't work out whether it was just coincidence. Whether his words were really intended for me, whether they truly reflected on our conversation, or whether they were just the throwaway ramblings of some bloke on a bus. If I'd been in another mood, I might just have laughed them off, or buried my head in my newspaper, or politely ignored them. But with my friends' concerns, and everything that had happened—or, in a way, everything that *hadn't* happened—the words took on a strange and important resonance.

"That is the stupidest bloody thing I have ever bloody heard," said Ian, ever the diplomat. "Some drunk bloke on a bus mutters something oblique, and you claim it's changed your life? Bollocks. How come you never listen to me when I'm drunk?"

"Because when you're drunk, you usually talk about us buying a caravan and moving to Dorset."

"Oh, we should, though, just think of the . . ."

"And anyway, he wasn't drunk. We'd been talking about what we'd been up to in the week. He seemed very interested."

"And what did you tell him?"

"I told him I'd been staying in a lot. Not doing much. Having early nights."

"And that was all?"

"Pretty much."

And it was. The simple fact of the matter was that this man would probably have had no idea of the impact of his words. I surely was just someone who wanted to make a decision, who deep down *wanted* to make a change. His words were just the catalyst that kick-started me into action. I wish I could claim that he was a shaman or some kind of spiritual figure, sent into my life at that time to push me over the edge. And as much as I'd like to believe that, the fact is he was probably just a bloke on a bus. But chatty. And wise.

"He doesn't sound much like Jesus to me," said Ian. "Apart from the beard."

"I never said he was Jesus!"

"Or Buddha, for that matter. Buddha would've probably just smiled a lot. Or taken you to a nice restaurant. That's the thing about Buddha; he knows how to have a good time."

"Ian, listen. It wasn't Jesus. Or Buddha. It was just some bloke on a bus."

"So, why are you taking him so seriously?"

"Because he was right. And *you* were right. And Hanne was right. But the thing is, none of you knows *how* right you were!"

"So, what are you saying? Just that you're going to start saying yes more? That's hardly an announcement."

"I'm going to say yes to *everything*."

"Everything? What do you mean, everything?"

"I mean, I'm going to say yes to everything from now on."

Ian looked shocked. "When do you start?"

"That's just the thing," I said, finishing my pint and looking him dead in the eye. "I already have."

CHAPTER 2

In Which Daniel Becomes Increasingly Excited

This was it.

This was bloody *it*.

I didn't know what "it" was yet, but by God it was this, and that was enough for me.

It had been just ten minutes since the man on the bus had uttered his words of wisdom, and I was excited. And inspired. And slightly out-of-breath, because sometimes when I'm excited and inspired, I tend to leap up stairs, when I should realise that I live on the fourth floor and such exertions do not become me.

But my red face and now-dampened forehead didn't matter, because the thing is, what the man on the bus had said to me made complete and utter sense. I know it sounds odd, and I know it might seem meaningless to you, but to me those three words had . . . *done* something. It was like the man had known me in a way I hadn't even known myself. Which is quite a disquieting idea unless it turns out that the thing you didn't know about yourself was quite glamorous, like you were a matador or you once freed some slaves, in which case you'd be quite grateful to whoever pointed it out.

But what he'd shown me about myself wasn't glamorous. It was worrying. It was something I had to change. And luckily he'd shown me the way.

I was smiling, now. Grinning as I walked through the door of my flat, flicked the kettle on, and reached for a mug. Had I been a more feminine man, I dare say I'd have probably skipped about a bit as well, although as I suspect I'd make quite a *sensible* feminine man, I would not have done this around boiling water, and I would certainly have put the mug down first.

I paced the kitchen, thinking and rethinking the night's events, and then, just before the click of the kettle, I realised something.

I could see.

Not just what was around me.

But what I'd been doing wrong.

And how I could turn it around.

I was on the verge of something. But sometimes to look forward, you have to look back. So, I went and got my diary. And even though I suspected it would be the case, I was nevertheless shocked at what I saw.

I saw nothing. Well, virtually nothing.

Nothing apart from missed opportunities. And blank spaces. And things I'd scribbled out, or hadn't gone to, or said I couldn't make. Acres of white lies.

I'd missed birthdays. I'd missed barbecues. I'd missed various parties. I'd missed dinner with friends, I'd missed nights down the pub, I'd missed Tom's stag do. God, Tom's stag do. I bet that had been *legendary*. I bet they'd all got together and painted his privates blue and handcuffed him to the buffet car of a train. Suddenly *I* wanted to do that. *I* wanted to paint a man's privates blue and handcuff him to buffet cars!

But not just that, I wanted to do *all* the things I'd missed out on. I wanted to turn the clock back and shout yes to all the things I'd mumbled no to. Not just the big nights or the main events or the frantic celebrations, but to the little things. The normal things. The things that sometimes matter the most.

I scanned and rescanned my diary. Hanne had been right. Ian had been right. Everyone had been right . . . except me. As I flicked my way through the months that had flown by, I realised with horror that probably the most excitement I'd had was on April 18, when I'd gone to PC World to buy a new printer cartridge. Suddenly that didn't seem like enough. I mean, yeah, at a push I could probably scrape a short anecdote out of it, but still . . . It was hardly one to save for the grandchildren, was it?

And hang on—*what* grandchildren? I was already twenty-six, and there wasn't even a *hint* of a grandchild down the pipeline! Who was I going to tell all my stories to when I was old? Who was I going to impress with my tales of short, uneventful walks to PC World, and me worrying that there wasn't going to be the right kind of printer cartridge in stock, but it being all right because in the end there actually was?

And who was going to *give* me grandchildren? Well, my kid, obviously, but who was going to give me one of *those*?

My ambition had turned to panic. Who knew what I had already missed out on in life? Now I would never know what *might* have happened, who I *might* have met, what I *might* have done, where I *might* have ended up, how different life *could* have been. And my friends . . . how many connections had I lost?

I was angry at myself. I had wasted half my year. Half a year *gone*. Thrown away. Swapped for toast and evenings in front of the telly. It was all here—or, rather, it *wasn't*—in black and white, and blue and red. Every dull nonentry was a sharp slap in the face.

I had to get back out there. I had to start living life rather than just living.

I would say yes more. Saying yes more would get me out of this rut. It would rekindle my love for life. It would bring back the old me. The me that had died a little the day I'd been dumped. I just needed a little kick-start. A little fun. A chance to live in a completely different way. I could treat it like an experiment. A study in my own behaviour. A study in positivity and opportunity and chance.

This was serious. This went beyond what Hanne would have called a "stupid boy project," because now . . . now I was dealing with a whole new *way of life*.

My mind was racing. This could work. But how should I approach it? How would I say yes more?

I decided I needed to tackle the problem quickly and efficiently. If I could spend just a day on this, surely that would be all I'd need? I'd go out to whatever was happening, hang out with whoever wanted to, and let life just lead the way. I'd surrender myself for twenty-four hours, answer everything with a yes, and let opportunity and chance boot me out of this midtwenties crisis.

A day. Yes. A day. A day of relentless positivity. What harm could that do? A day of saying yes. Yes to anything. Anything and everything.

A day of being a Yes Man.

• • •

"Hello, can I speak to Mr. Wallace, please?"

"Yes!"

"Hello, Mr. Wallace. I'm phoning from Mark 1 Double Glazing in London. Would you have a moment to talk about double glazing, sir?"

"Yes!"

"Have you ever thought about having your house or apartment equipped with double glaze at all?"

"Yes!"

"Can I ask you, would you be interested in a free, no-obligation quote for double glaze on your property, Mr. Wallace?"

"Yes!"

"Okay . . . Well, what we can do is, we can certainly send one of our representatives around to your place of residence. Is there a particular time or day that's good for you?"

"Yes."

"Uh-huh . . . and . . . when would that be?"

"You suggest a time."

"Right. How are you fixed for Tuesday, Mr. Wallace?"

"Yes, Tuesday. Yes."

"Two o'clock?"

"Yes."

"Okay, let me just make a note. . . . So, that's Tuesday, at—"

"Um . . . I should warn you, though. My windows are already double glazed."

"You're what, sorry?"

"I already have double glaze throughout my flat."

"Right . . . so . . . Sorry, I don't . . ."

"I'm just saying, I've already got plenty of double glazing, but you shouldn't let that put you off. Life should be all about taking opportunities, you know? The best things that ever happened to us happened because we said yes, just like the man on the bus told me. I realise that now."

"Well, wait a second . . . Why would you want a quote?"

"Sorry?"

"Why would you want a quote on double glazing, when you've already got double glazed?"

"Well, you asked, and—"

"Just seems like a bit of a waste of everyone's time, Mr. Wallace . . ."

"I just thought it might be nice. Maybe you could come round and tell me what you think of the double glaze I've already got. We could have some tea. You could still give me a quote if you like."

"I have to go now, Mr. Wallace, okay?"

"Yes."

And that is how my Yes experiment started—confusing a cold-caller with my unnerving desire to discuss all aspects of double glazing.

I'd woken up only minutes before and was now lying in bed with a grin on my face and a head full of thoughts. What should I do? Where should I go? How should I begin?

But that wasn't up to me. None of it was. I had to see how things went. I had to go with the flow. I got up and switched my computer on, willing it to provide me with all the opportunities I'd been batting away only a day before. I had a few e-mails and quickly scanned through them.

One was from Hanne. Could we have a chat? Yes.

Another was from my good friend Wag. Did I fancy a pint sometime? Yes.

Another was from a complete stranger. Would I like a bigger penis? Ye—hang on. Who was this from?

Would you like a bigger penis? New Penis Patch Technology now means thousands of men just like you can . . .

Oh. Spam. Still, I'd rather it was a piece of spam than a suggestion from an ex-girlfriend. My cursor hovered over the Delete button, an instant reaction formed by thousands of similar unsolicited e-mails in the past, but then I realised that wasn't the spirit.

So I said yes. And I laughed. Then I clicked on the link, added my credit-card information, and ordered the Amazing Penis Patch.

I filled the kettle and scratched around in the cupboard, looking for something to eat. I found a small box of Cocoa Pops and was absolutely delighted.

I walked back to the computer, hoping that in the five minutes since I'd written back to Hanne and Wag, they'd replied with suggested times and places. But they hadn't. So, I decided to take matters into my own hands. I sat down at my computer and drafted an e-mail. When I'd done that, I sent it to every friend I felt I'd let down, or said no to, or hadn't seen in too long.

This is what I wrote:

```
To: Mates
From: Danny
Subject: Me, you, and us
Hey there. Listen. It's been too long. That's my fault,
and I'm sorry. But I've changed. I'm going to be more like
the old me now. So, if you fancy meeting up . . . let me
know.
    Your pal (I hope),
    Danny
```

I felt oddly cleansed. But then I decided to up the ante. I phoned Hanne.

"Hey, Hanne, it's Danny."

"Hey, Dan. You got my e-mail?"

"I did. And yes, I would *love* to meet up for a chat."

"Okay . . . in town for a coffee? Today?"

"Yes."

"Fourish?"

"Fine."

"I'll meet you by Covent Garden Tube station. Is that okay?"

"Yes, absolutely. I'll see you there."

Great! That was easy! I had just successfully organised a meeting with my ex-girlfriend. If there were such a thing as the Grown-up Scouts, I'd probably get a badge for that.

Next I phoned Wag.

"Wag! Waggle! Wagamama!"

Sadly this is not me saying that. This is how Wag chooses to answer the phone sometimes.

"Hey, Wag . . . I got your e-mail. I do indeed fancy a pint some-time. When and where do you recommend?"

"Coool . . . How about today?"

"Yes."

Oh, hang on, though. I started to realise that blindly saying yes to everything could well have its complications. What would I do if he suggested four o'clock for a coffee at Covent Garden?

"How about seven for a pint at the Horse and Groom?"

Thank God Wag was a bloke.

"Done," I said.

This was all going very well. Very well indeed.

Arrangements for the day made, I pootled down to the corner shop to buy milk and a newspaper or two. I was already starting to feel like a new man, which probably explains why I also bought a pot of yoghurt and some freshly squeezed orange juice. It was the kind of feeling that usually ends up with me considering going to the gym, or getting a dog and walking it a bit, and doing all the things that blokes in catalogues do. It was a feeling I hadn't had in quite some time.

Back upstairs I sat down with my tea and my newspapers and looked up at the clock. Midday. Just four short hours before I had to be anywhere.

I started to leaf through the *Guardian* before realising that I was kidding myself, and picked up the *Sun* instead. I wish I was the type of person who could read the *Guardian* before reading the *Sun,* but even as a kid I'd want to eat the chocolate mousse before I attempted the healthy stuff.

I amused myself with a piece about a young Scottish man who'd tried to take his kite out in a storm and ended up flying for three quarters of a mile, before I turned the page and saw, in a small box at the top of the page:

DO YOU HAVE AN INVENTION?

I bristled with excitement. Now, technically, no, I didn't have an invention. I had no invention at all. But this tiny advert was an opportunity. An opportunity to try my hand at something new. I could invent something! Maybe that's why I was put here on Earth! To be an inventor!

I tore the ad out and read it again. It had been placed by the Patents & Trademarks Institute of America, and it was offering to help new inventors get their brilliant inventions off the ground. Ace! All I had to do was phone them up and ask for an information pack. Five minutes later I'd done just that and had been assured my information pack was on its way to me.

I finished off my copy of the *Sun*, picked up the *Guardian*, put it down again, and decided to head into town a little earlier than I'd planned.

I could always buy the *Mirror* on the way.

It was a sunny day, and it felt like a different city. Even my walk to the Tube station, under deafening railway arches and down sparse streets, pavements broken up by tufts of dying grass and puddles of spit, had a certain beauty about it.

But now here I was, walking from Leicester Square up to Covent Garden and feeling quite proud to be a Londoner.

"Cup of tea, please," I said to the man in the café.

"Sugar?" he said.

"No thanks."

"Fifty pence, please," he said, putting my polystyrene cup in front of me.

I reached for my change and realised I'd made a huge error. An error which I hope you will find excusable, based as it is on twenty years of habitual tea drinking.

"Sorry, you asked me if I wanted sugar . . ."

"Yeah," he said. "You said no."

"I know. But . . . could you ask me again?" I slid the tea back toward him.

"Eh?"

"Could you ask me again if I want sugar, please?"

The man frowned slightly, but then obliged. He picked up the cup and said, "Sugar?"

I cleared my throat.

"Yes, please," I said.

"How many?"

Now it was my turn to frown.

"I don't know. I don't take sugar."

Now we were both frowning at the same time.

"Just give me whatever you think's reasonable," I said with a shrug.

The man took a spoon and, without even breaking eye contact, slowly and carefully put three heaping teaspoons of sugar into my tiny cup.

"Okay?" he said.

"Yes," I said. "Thank you very much."

Now, I realise that this sugar-based story probably reaches new lows in terms of contemporary European storytelling, and that as you read this, half of you is probably tempted to turn back a few pages in order to enjoy a banker like the PC World story once more, but this meant something. I've been drinking tea for a long time. A lot of it. And this was the first time I have ever consciously asked for it with sugar. It represented a lot to me: I was willing to change even the most basic, ground-in aspects of my daily routine. It was a discovery that excited me.

I left the shop, sugared tea in hand, and wandered farther toward Covent Garden, pausing only to watch a juggler drop his balls, and a small child run off with one of them. It was this that was distracting me when I was pounced upon.

"Excuse me, sir, do you have two minutes?"

"Yes," I said, instantly and with joy in my heart. I turned to see a short woman with curly, ginger hair and a bright green bib on.

"Great! Can I tell you a little bit about Help the Aged?"

Ten minutes later I'd agreed to sign up to their Adopt-a-Granny scheme and had directed a few quid of my monthly earnings toward some deserving old woman's upkeep. Mainly because she kept beginning her sentences with the words "Would you be interested in . . ." and I kept saying "yes." Thanks to me, some old granny would now never have to worry about where the next mint was coming from. I said good-bye to the little, bubbly lady and walked on toward the Tube station. But then I heard a voice to my right.

"Excuse me, sir, do you have two minutes?"

I turned to see a tallish man with a long nose and a green bib. A green bib with the words "Adopt-a-Granny" on it.

"Er, well, yes, but . . ."

"Great! Can I tell you a little bit about Help the Aged?"

"So you're late because . . ."

"I was adopting some grannies."

"I should have guessed," said Hanne, and we started to walk to a nearby café. "It is, after all, why *most* people are late these days."

Since we'd split—which is my nice way of saying "since she'd dumped me"—Hanne and I had remained very good friends. We'd started off having lunch every week, and sometimes we'd catch a quick drink, if we could, but lately we'd been seeing a lot less of each other. That was fair enough, I'd reasoned. After all, Hanne had been concentrating on making great waves in her career, and I, of course, had been eating toast.

"How's Lizzie?" asked Hanne, and I smiled.

Since the break up, neither Hanne nor myself had been in another relationship. I'd come close, with a girl called Lizzie. A *fantastic* girl called Lizzie. But Lizzie, of course, had left. Not because we'd split up. But because ten days after we'd met she'd had to go back to where she'd come from. Australia. About as far away as it's possible to get. We were still in e-mail contact, and there was even the odd phone call, but we both knew as much as we liked each other, it was an impossible situation.

"You liked her, didn't you?" said Hanne.

"Yeah," I said. "I did. She was cool."

Hanne had been a great girlfriend. And an even better ex-girlfriend. She was supportive of the whole Lizzie thing when I'd told her. And, even better, she'd never put me in a similar position. There's a time after every split up when you genuinely hope the other person will find it so hard to get over you that they'll book themselves straight into the nearest nunnery. . . . Hanne hadn't gone quite that far. But as yet neither had she brought out the jealous ex-boyfriend in me.

"I know things never really got off the ground with you and Lizzie," she said. "But you'd have *liked* them to, wouldn't you?"

"Well, yeah," I said. "I would."

It was nice of Hanne to care, I thought.

"And you and I have been apart for quite a while now, haven't we?"

"Yes . . . I mean . . . I suppose we have."

Suddenly it felt like Hanne had brought this up out of more than concern. It was like she was building up to something. In fact, I could tell she was, because she'd started to play with her napkin, and she wasn't looking me in the eye. If you're ever having dinner with Hanne, look out for this, because it may mean you won't make it to dessert.

"I know there's no need to ask you this, Dan . . . but the thing is . . . I'd just feel better if I said this to you now, to get it out in the open, you know . . ."

Oh. Oh my. Hanne was about to ask if we could get back together!

"I don't know why I'm so nervous asking you this. . . ."

Blimey! She was! She was about to ask to get back together! How did I feel?

"I know your answer already, Dan, but I just want to hear it from you. . . ."

She had real love in her eyes, now . . . Yes, it was fairly well hidden, but that's probably what she loved about me most—that I just knew these things.

". . . and you must be completely honest with me about this. . . ."

God, this must be hard for her, realising she'd made the biggest mistake of her young life, knowing she'd have to plead with me to get me back . . .

"It's okay, Hanne," I said. "You can talk to me about anything."

She squeezed my hand.

"Would you mind," she said, "if I started seeing someone else?"

Oh.

"There. Said it," she said, and sat back in her chair with a smile.

She'd met someone else. Jesus. What should I say? I had to smile and say well done, clearly. But oh, God—she was asking me for my blessing. The girl I'd been out with for three years before she dumped me was asking for my blessing.

Who had she met? Or had it gone further? Oh no. Hanne was

engaged, wasn't she? And she was probably pregnant, too. And he was probably an *amazing* bloke. He was probably a baron or something! I bet he was a millionaire. I always knew Hanne would end up with a millionaire. A millionaire who was dashing and had a castle and who, when offered an Amazing Penis Patch at a party, would just laugh heartily as if the very idea was the silliest thing he'd ever heard.

"Danny?" said Hanne. "What are you thinking?"

I snapped back into reality.

"I was just wondering if he was a baron."

Hanne smiled.

"He's just a guy I met through Cecilia. But I like him. He reminds me of you a little. Just less . . . work."

"Well . . . that's . . ."

"I know, I know. You're cool with it. I mean, of course you are."

And I was. I *was* cool with it. In fact, the more Hanne talked about him, the more cool with it I began to feel. If this whole Yes thing had been about starting again, then surely this was one of the best things that could have happened.

"Danny? You're not saying much." She looked concerned. "Do you *mind* that I want to start seeing someone else?"

I was about to shake my head, smile, and say, "Hanne, that's the best thing ever. Go forth and make this bloke yours."

But suddenly I realised what she'd just said—or, rather, the *way* in which she'd said it—and my stomach churned slightly.

"Sorry?" I said, playing for time, but it was already too late.

"I said, you don't mind that I want to start seeing someone else, do you?"

Hanne smiled sweetly. It was short-lived.

"Yes."

Her eyes narrowed. "Yes, what?"

"Yes to what you just said."

"Yes, you don't mind, or yes, you do?"

I think I looked a bit scared now. "Yes."

Hanne's mouth dropped open. "Yes, you mind? You *mind* that I want to start seeing someone else?"

Oh God.

"Yes."

Now, clearly, this was a *stupid* thing to say. And the fact that Hanne kept repeating the question, and I kept saying yes to it, wasn't helping matters.

"I'm shocked," she said.

"I'm just trying to be more *positive*, you see," I tried.

"But this isn't positive! It's negative! *Very* negative! How can you say that? How can you say you mind, when I was so cool about you and Lizzie?"

"Well . . . it depends on *how* you ask me, you see . . . If you said, 'Will you give me your blessing to start seeing this bloke?,' then I would *definitely* have said yes . . ."

"Oh, so I need your blessing, do I? Oh, I see. So it's a power thing? I need your blessing before I can start seeing this guy?"

"Hanne, please, stop asking me questions. . . ."

"I don't need your blessing for *anything*! Do you understand?"

Aha! A way out!

"Yes! Yes, I understand!"

"And you accept that?"

"Yes! Absolutely! Yes to that."

"Good. So . . . I'll ask you again," said Hanne. "Do you have any objections to me seeing this man?"

I took a deep breath.

"Yes."

I'll be honest. The meeting with Hanne hadn't gone quite as well as it could've. I imagine that if the Grown-up Scouts *did* exist, they'd have asked for their badge back.

I started to wish that I'd refined my scheme somewhat. Saying yes to everything anyone asked me was suddenly starting to feel like asking for trouble. And not telling anyone what I was up to could also bring its own problems—not as bad as the problems I'd face if word *did* get out, but still . . .

I started to feel like maybe a drink would be a good idea.

I phoned Wag.

"Listen," I said. "Do you fancy meeting up a bit earlier?"

• • •

"So," said Wag, putting his pint down, "you're late."

"Sorry," I said, slightly out of breath, and sitting myself down.

I was twenty minutes late for meeting Wag, because on my way out of the Tube, a man sitting on the steps had asked me if I could spare any change. I'd said yes and had handed him what I could spare. Five minutes later another man I was walking past asked me whether I could spare any change. But I'd given all my spare change to the first man, so I had to go to a cashpoint to get some money out, and then find a shop to buy something from so that I would have some change, which I could adequately call "spare," to give to the second man. And after I'd done that I'd bumped into the first man again, who didn't recognise me and asked me whether or not I had any spare change at all.

Wag just looked at me.

"Why didn't you just say no?"

Good question. I tried to change the subject.

"Nice tie," I said.

"I'm not wearing a tie."

There was an awkward silence.

"So, did you get me a pint?" I asked.

"Yes," said Wag. "But I drank it."

"Oh."

"Your round."

"Right." I went to get the beers.

Wag and I sat in the corner of the Horse & Groom and quietly sipped at our pints. He's a good friend of mine who shares a love of table football and intellectual chitchat. I'd met him a couple of years ago at a wedding, and we'd been hanging out ever since.

We'd discussed this and that already. His burgeoning musical career, for one thing. He was about to set off for Germany with the boy band Busted, after he had just returned from a tour of the same country with Right Said Fred (though for some reason he always forgets to tell people about this). We'd also touched upon some of his odd ideas about life. For example, he is a firm believer that his haircut—the mullet—will one day be regarded as the height of style and cool, and all he has to do is wait. For another, he truly and deeply believes that one day men too will bear children, despite the widely hailed success of the current system.

"What you've got to understand, Danny," he said, "is that you obviously have a problem with moving on. You nearly managed it with that Lizzie girl, but it didn't work out. And because of that, you resent Hanne for trying to move on with her own life. Am I getting close?"

He was getting nowhere near to being close, to be honest, but I played the game and nodded. Wag looked delighted.

"I'm good!" he said. "Aren't I good?"

I nodded again, and said, "Yes."

"Deep down, this is all to do with Lizzie," he said. "Let me break it down for you . . ."

And this is where I started to drift off . . .

It sounds like a cliché, but I started to fall for Lizzie the moment she had gotten her purse out and showed me a picture of a big prawn.

"This one's my favourite," she'd said. "Look at the size of it."

It was the day after Boxing Day, and we were with mutual friends in a small pub just off Brick Lane.

"It certainly does look like a very big prawn," I'd said.

"Show him that other one you've got," Rohan had said, the man who'd brought us all there. "The one of the Big Egg."

"Aw, Danny doesn't want to see that," Lizzie'd objected. "It's just a picture of a big egg."

But I did. I really did want to see a picture of a big egg.

So, Lizzie delved deeper into her bag.

"This Big Egg isn't actually there anymore," she'd said. "It used to be in Geelong, near where I'm from, but protestors had it removed."

I had had a look at the Big Egg. Just like the prawn, it was pretty big. Only a bit more eggy and less obviously prawnlike.

"You probably think it's a bit weird, me having photos of Big Prawns and Big Eggs in my bag," she'd said.

But I didn't. I had thought it was the coolest thing on Earth.

• • •

"And that, my friend, is why you will never get married. Not to a woman, anyway."

"Sorry, what?"

"Were you listening to a thing I just said?"

"Yes."

"So, what did I say?"

I had absolutely no idea. "Something to do with a woman?"

Wag made a tsk noise and raised his eyebrows.

"Sorry," I said. "It was just . . . you know. I was thinking of Lizzie."

"Oh," said Wag. "Right."

"I suppose today with Hanne made me think of Lizzie. When she left, it was just another reason to stay in and lay low—dumped by my girlfriend, then left by a fantastic girl I hadn't even had the chance to properly date."

"At this rate they'll be ditching you before you've even met them," said Wag helpfully. "They probably already are. Right this moment, all around the country, dozens of girls are probably dumping you left, right, and centre and not even having the good grace to tell you about it. They're probably keeping your favourite CDs, too."

"Thanks for that, Wag."

He smiled a "that's okay" smile. Wag was in high spirits tonight, and so we drank and laughed and drank some more. Mainly because he kept saying, "D'you fancy another pint?" and I kept saying yes.

"So . . . do you have pictures of any other big things?" I asked as we left the pub and walked up Brick Lane. "Or is it just prawns and eggs?"

"Not with me," Lizzie'd said. "But I can get you some, if you like. There's a picture I've got of the Big Pineapple . . ."

"That sounds perfect," I'd said. "A picture of a big pineapple would be perfect."

Lizzie had smiled.

"Okay. Are you around tomorrow? Are you coming to Rohan's for New Year's?"

"Yes. I definitely am."

I made a mental note to ask Rohan where and when it was, and whether it was all right if I turned up after all, having already said no to the invite. As usual.

"Cool. Well, I'll bring a picture of the Big Pineapple," Lizzie'd said, climbing into her taxi.

"And if you're lucky," she had said, just before closing the door, "I'll bring a picture of a big cow as well . . ."

I think it's fair to say that I'd never looked forward to seeing a picture of a big cow quite as much.

"Right," said Wag, when the bell finally sounded for last orders. "Let's go to a club, yeah?"

"Yes," I said with all the assurance of a man quite certain of his decision.

Wag balked. "What?"

"Yes. Let's go to a club. Yes."

"A club?"

"Yeah."

Wag looked confused. The pints had taken their toll, but my faith and enthusiasm in what I was doing had grown.

"What club?"

"Eh?"

"What club are you on about?"

"It was *your* idea," I said. "You said, 'Let's go to a club.'"

"Did I?"

"Yes! You always do!"

"Well . . . only because I don't expect you to agree! Since when have you wanted to go to a club? Why do you want to go to a club?"

"Because you asked, Wag. Come on. It's Saturday night. We're in the middle of London. This is what we're *supposed* to do at twenty-six."

"But . . . it's nearly eleven at night! What's gotten into you?"

"I told you! Life is for living! Sometimes the biggest risk is never taking one!"

Wag looked worried.

"You said let's go to a club, mate. I said yes. You know what we have to do now," I said.

• • •

"So . . . all these pictures of big things," I had said tentatively. "Is that, like, a hobby of yours?"

"No, no," Lizzie'd said, smiling. "My brothers send them to me. As a joke. And it's not 'big things.' It's 'Big Things.' Capital *b*, capital *t*."

"How do you know I didn't use capitals?" I'd said.

"I just do," she'd replied.

"Big Things," I had said, trying somehow to make sure I'd said a capital *t*.

"My brothers sent them to me. To remind me of home. They think it's funny. I think it's geeky."

"I think it's . . . cool," I had said, and immediately wished I hadn't.

"Big Things are dotted all around Australia. For some reason it's quite an Australian thing."

"To build huge concrete representations of . . ."

Lizzie'd handed me another picture.

"A rolling pin?" I'd said.

"Yep. Rolling pin, bananas, barrel, lobster, koala . . ."

"Ah," I'd said. "Now, a big koala makes sense. I mean, that's Australian."

"Yeah, the Big Koala." She had laughed. "Imagine how proud that makes us feel. There's even a Big Ned Kelly."

"Wow," I'd said. "A Big Ned Kelly. I would *love* to see a Big Ned Kelly."

"You should get yourself an Aussie girl, then," she'd said, and she had smiled in a way that made me feel a bit, well, fizzy.

Yes. Fizzy. Shut up.

"I suppose I should," I'd said, suddenly slightly flushed.

I've just realised I'm making it sound like Lizzie and I have only just met. But the fact is that's how it felt. In reality we'd known each other for a number of months, but only in the way that friends-of-friends usually do. Lizzie had gone out with a friend of mine for a while, but we'd never hung out; never got to know each other. We always had to be somewhere else with other people, doing other things, and suddenly I realised that I didn't really know her at all. And suddenly I really wanted to.

"So what would you build, then," she'd said, "if you had to build a Big Thing for me to take a picture of?"

I thought about it. Whatever I said had to be good. This was the kind of thing girls asked you when they were checking you out. It was a sort of basic psychology test. If I said something like "a lovely big puppy," then that would be good. Saying something along the lines of "a really huge knife" or "a giant smiling knocker" . . . well . . . that would clearly be quite bad.

What do girls like? And what do girls like that I like?

"I . . . would have to say . . . ," I had said, reaching desperately for girl-friendly ideas, "a baby."

Lizzie had just looked at me.

"A baby?" she had said, flatly.

I'd clearly just made my answer too obvious. She had known instantly why I'd chosen a baby. Because that, in my mind, is what a girl would want to hear.

"Hang on, though, because it's not just a baby."

"What is it, then? A two-in-one thing? Both a baby *and* a bottle opener?"

"No. It's a . . . special kind of baby."

Lizzie had raised her eyebrows, waiting for my elaboration.

"It's a Chinese one."

Lizzie had somehow managed to raise her eyebrows even farther than they were already. I wouldn't have thought it possible.

"A Chinese baby?" she'd said.

"A *massive* Chinese baby," I had corrected her.

"Sorry," she'd replied, but I'm not sure that she was. "A *massive* Chinese baby?"

"That's correct," I'd said firmly, like I'd thought it through. "A massive Chinese baby."

"And why would you build a massive Chinese baby?" she had said in a tone which I hoped was gentle amusement but could just as easily have been the way experienced therapists talk to disturbed children.

"Well . . . there's nothing cuter than a Chinese baby," I'd said, which I thought was fair enough. "I mean, that's not to say other Chinese people aren't cute too. Well, no, that sounds patronising . . ."

Lizzie had folded her arms.

". . . What I mean is, Chinese babies are cute, and so are . . . well . . . Chinese pensioners, now that I think about it. But, you know, anything in between I can take or leave, to be honest . . ."

Suddenly this wasn't going so well. But I was sure I could rescue it.

"Let's face it," I'd said. "People would come from miles around to see my massive Chinese baby."

What the hell was I saying?!

I stopped speaking immediately and stared into my drink.

Lizzie spoke next.

"Um . . . well, I think that if there . . ."

But I wouldn't find out what Lizzie thought. Because suddenly Rohan was there with fresh cans of lager and a bowl of little carrots, and he sat down next to us, and we started to talk about London and Australia and how much Lizzie was looking forward to going back, and not one more word was said about massive Chinese babies for the rest of the evening.

The rest of the year, in fact.

It was twenty past three in the morning, and Wag and I were as drunk as we've ever been.

We'd ended up, somehow, sitting in the corner of a club in Soho, talking to three Australian lads in town on holiday. I was using all the Australian knowledge I had to impress them.

"So you've got a Big Pineapple, haven't you?" I said. "And a Big Prawn. And you've got that Big Ned Kelly, too."

But the men were looking at me blankly.

"You know . . . those sculptures you've got all over the place? You must've seen them. The Big Barrel and the Big Mosquito? The Big Worm? The Big Orange? I've never been over there, but I've seen pictures that this girl I was sort of seeing showed me, and it sounds *amazing*."

I was still getting blank looks. I decided I probably just hadn't said enough Big Things. So I continued.

"The Big Can. The Big Cod. The Big Carrot. The—"

"Big, Boring Bastard," said Wag, and everyone laughed.

"I am talking about Australian culture here, Wag," who was annoying me now, so I'll tell you his real name is actually Wayne. "It is important that these gentlemen know that we in the United Kingdom are taking an interest."

"But they're Austrian," said Wag.

"I'm terribly sorry. I thought you were Australian. Why did I think you were Australian?"

Everyone just sort of shrugged.

"But I've been talking to you about Australia and being Australian for about . . ."

"Twenty minutes," said one of them. In an Austrian accent. It was then that I noticed his T-shirt had the word "Austria" on it.

"Yes. Twenty minutes," I said. "Well, I hope you've at least learned a little something about Australia from our conversations. Good day to you and welcome to our country."

Wag and I sauntered gracefully away from the Austrians, or as gracefully as it's possible to saunter while still swaying quite a lot and bumping into people, and stood at the edge of the dance floor.

"Drink?" said Wag.

"Yes!" I nearly shouted, correctly identifying a Yes moment. "Yes, yes, yes!"

I was pointing in the air and jabbing my finger with every "yes" and continued doing so long after Wag had gone to the bar.

It was probably this that attracted the man wearing the sombrero.

At first I assumed he was a Mexican, but slowly began to realise that a real Mexican probably wouldn't be wearing a sombrero in a London nightclub. And he'd probably have a real mustache, not a stick-on one. A Mexican with a stick-on mustache would be like a super Mexican, because he'd have two mustaches, and that'd be cool, because a super Mexican could probably use his poncho as a cape, and then I realised I was saying all this to the man's face.

"Tequila?" he said by way of a response, revealing himself to be a novelty tequila seller. He revealed what at first glance appeared to be a gun holster but was actually holding a whole bottle of the stuff. "It's one pound a shot."

Now, I have developed, over the years, an amazing ability to avoid tequila. A number of unfortunate escapades have happened to me as a result of drinking it, and as a result I have an almost subconscious ability to say no whenever the word is mentioned.

"Yes!"

The man poured me a shot, and I downed it.

"Another?"

I looked a lot less keen this time.

"Yes," I said without the previous exclamation mark and with a slightly sickly feeling in my stomach. To be perfectly honest I'm fairly sure I'd had more than enough to drink already. I downed my second shot and smiled at the Mexican, willing him to walk away. Either he got the gist, or he thought I was coming on to him, because he walked away very quickly indeed.

I tried to focus my eyes on the dance floor. Ah, that looked like fun. I was suddenly convinced I was a very good dancer indeed, certainly as good as that lady in the blue top, or that one in the green. And they were *very* good. Especially the one in the blue top. She was brilliant! But she'd be no match for me. Maybe I should instigate a dance off with her. Sure, she looked like she knew what she was doing with her arms and legs and head and stuff, but mere physical fitness and coordination and probable classical training was no match for my artistic flailings. I could do what she was doing; I was convinced of it. But unlike the classically trained, my dancing had no respect for so-called boundaries; I wasn't afraid to break the rules. I'd probably scare the blue-top lady, or her mate in the green, or even that big friend of theirs—the one staring me straight in the eyes and now walking right up to me. That was probably why he was coming toward me, in actual fact. To tell me they all knew what I was thinking, and that I was right—I *was* the rightful Lord of the Dance! Then we'd probably all go back to their place, and I'd show them some of my moves, and we'd all be great mates, and . . .

"Are you looking at my girlfriend?" said the man, suddenly inches away from me and not looking like the happiest bloke in the world.

"Huh?" I said brilliantly.

"Are you looking at my girlfriend?"

I smiled and tried to stifle a little tequila burp.

"Am I looking at your girlfriend?" I said in what I hoped was a *very* amusing voice.

The man wasn't amused.

I suddenly realised he was serious. My instinct told me to say no. No to whatever he was suggesting. It was a definite No moment.

"Who's your girlfriend?" I asked as if showing a willingness to undertake detailed research was going to make things better.

"Blue top," he said.

Oh. Her.

"You make a lovely couple," I tried.

"So are you looking at her?"

This was awkward. Every part of my being was screaming at me to make peace with this man, to say no and walk away, but it was *obvious* I had been looking at her, and anyway, I already knew what I had to say . . .

"Yes," I said.

The man looked a little shocked by this. He looked back at his girlfriend, and then at me again.

"Right," he said. "So . . . you're looking at my girlfriend."

"Yup," I said, trying a little half-smile.

He smiled back. This wasn't going too badly, I suppose. Maybe he was still going to hail me as the Lord of the Dance.

But then, slowly . . .

"Do I look like the sort of idiot who'd let you look at my girlfriend?"

Uh-oh. He was upping the stakes. Quite considerably. He was asking me to call him an idiot. To his face. To his big, manly face.

"Yes."

I was now cringing slightly and trying my hardest to make my answer sound like a question rather than a statement.

The man smiled again. I was hoping it was a smile of acceptance and gratitude, like I'd told him exactly what he'd always wanted to hear.

He took another small step toward me. I could smell him.

"Are you looking for a fucking smack in the mouth?" he said.

It's about now that I should have feigned a heart attack or fainted or run away or broken down in tears or renounced my position as the Yes Man. I should have shouted for Wag or pretended I was in the FBI or begged for forgiveness. But I didn't. I saw this as a challenge. A challenge to who I was, and what I wanted to achieve. How serious was I about this? How much did I care? I tensed up, closed my eyes, and said . . .

"Yes."

Jesus. I had just said, yes, I am looking for a fucking smack in the mouth. And I wasn't. I rarely am.

I was now bracing myself for the impact. I could already feel the punch before it even happened. I turned my head slightly, hoping he'd miss my nose and not smash my glasses, or my cheekbone, or anything else he could possibly smash, or crack, or bruise, or burst.

But nothing happened.

I opened my eyes.

He was just standing there, looking at me, watching me flinch.

I watched him, watching me flinch.

And then he spoke.

"You fucking psycho."

I blinked a couple of times.

And then he pushed my shoulder, turned, and walked away.

My God.

I had survived. I had survived a punch-up in a nightclub! Fair enough; there hadn't been any actual punches. But I had survived nonetheless! I had been the Yes Man, and I had stared death in the face, and I had come out of it unscathed!

Wag was suddenly by my side. He'd clearly been watching from some distance away.

"Do you want to leave, right now?" he said.

"Yes, I do," I said, and we left, right then.

"I'm sorry for what I was saying earlier," I'd said. "You know . . . about massive Chinese babies."

I'd managed to catch up with Lizzie a little after midnight in the first few minutes of a brand-new year.

"What—That? Well, as a matter of fact, I agree. There's almost nothing cuter than a Chinese baby."

"You agree?" I had said, like I'd have walked away if she'd said she preferred German ones.

"Of course I do. Listen, if I'm not married with kids by the time I'm thirty-five, just get me drunk and take me down to China-town."

I laughed more out of shock than anything else.

"So, what've you been up to lately?" she'd said.

"Not much, if I'm honest," I'd said.

Lizzie made a concerned face.

"Why?" she had said, but I didn't want to talk about it.

"So, listen . . . Is that true, what you were saying to Rohan earlier? About going back to Australia?"

"Yep. In ten days. I'm starting a new job. So, it's back to the Aussie summer. Beats the British rain. What happened to white Christmases? I'd wanted to see my first snow."

"You haven't seen snow?" I had asked.

"Terrible, isn't it? I've never seen snow, and you've never seen a Big Ned Kelly," she said. "And people complain about wars, eh?"

And we laughed, and an hour later, and I still don't know how, we had kissed.

Outside the club I started to laugh.

And laugh and laugh and laugh.

I was utterly exhilarated. I am not, by nature, a fighter. And yet I'd nearly got into a fight. A fight! Me! And I'd *won*!

"I just won a fight, Wag! With a man twice my size!"

"You *didn't* win a fight. And he *wasn't* twice your size. He was about an inch taller than you."

"He was massive! And I won!"

"You did not win. He just decided not to hit you, that's all. What did you say to him, anyway?"

"I told him I was looking at his girlfriend and that he was an idiot and then I dared him to punch me!"

"You did what?"

"That's right! I said, 'Yes, I am looking at your girlfriend. Punch me if you dare, you big idiot!'"

"You *said* that?"

"Kind of, yes! Well, no, not really. But I was taken with the moment, Wag! It was brilliant! I was taken with the moment and look at me—I'm still here!"

Wag did as I asked and looked at me.

"You're a drunk man who escaped a beating."

"I know! It's great!"

We walked to where we'd find a night bus but a dodgy old Volvo pulled up alongside us.

"Minicab?" said the man inside.

"Do I *look* like a minicab?" I said, and nearly wet myself laughing. Neither Wag nor the driver seemed to find it quite as amusing as I did.

"I'm going to take this cab," I said to Wag.

"You sure?"

I shrugged. "He asked."

"What are you doing later in the week?" he said.

"Whatever you want."

As the cab raced alongside the Thames, I was excited. And enthralled. And I felt like a little kid on the verge of something thrilling. At one point we overtook a night bus, and I found myself craning round to take a look at the passengers inside. Part of me was hoping I might catch a glimpse of the man who'd unwittingly kickstarted all of this, and if I did, I'd stop the cab and get out, and jump on the bus to tell him how I was changing, and what I'd already done, and how I'd had the best day ever. And all thanks to him! Him and his three, simple words.

I got home, made a cup of tea, and switched my computer on. I was happy, and tired, and ready for bed.

I brushed my teeth while I checked my e-mails. There was one from my friend Matt.

Danny! How's about breakfast tomorrow? Nine thirty? Camden?

I looked at my watch. Tomorrow was now today. It was getting on for 6 a.m. To get to Camden I'd have to be up again in just a couple of hours, and I suspected I might be in line for quite a hangover.

I started to write back to Matt . . .

> Matt,
> Had a bit of a late one, mate. Can we raincheck?

But then I stopped in my tracks. Writing those words felt empty. Hollow. Like I'd learned *nothing*. Sure, my day of yes was over, but . . . *one* more yes couldn't hurt, could it?

So one by one I deleted each of the letters I'd written, and I replaced them, slowly, drunkenly, with the letters: Y-E-S

By lunchtime I was certain I'd made the right decision.

Here I was, among friends, in a light and breezy café, my hangover nursed by reading the papers and drinking coffee and sharing jokes and laughing. For the first time in months I felt warm and cosy and like I was *part* of something.

I'd made one small change in my life, and already things were improving. And all I'd had to do was let them happen.

And that was when I'd phoned Ian and told him to meet me at the pub that night, so I could tell him all about the decision that had revolutionised my life . . .

Because I could feel it.

I was The Yes Man.

CHAPTER 3

In Which Daniel Lifts Up His Head and Beholds the Sun

Not much had been said for the past minute or two. We were just sitting there—two men, staring into space, considering it all. The events of the past few days were obviously a lot for Ian to take in. This was pretty philosophical stuff.

"Ian?" I said.

Nothing. Just a blank stare.

"Ian, did you hear all that?"

I tried to steal one of his peanuts, and he seemed to stir.

"Right . . . two things," he said, pointing his finger in the air. "Number one, at the end of that little tirade, you just called yourself the Yes Man."

"Yeah."

"Well, you can't. It's entirely wanky. What were you going to do, make yourself a little cape?"

"It was just a figure of . . ."

"Or did you see yourself as some kind of Dice Man for the day? Eh? Which is it? Superman or Dice Man?"

"Well . . ."

"Because you can't go about being Dice Man. What if you'd got asked to murder someone? Dice Man was asked to murder someone."

"That was a novel. And anyway, he wasn't *asked* to murder someone. He *chose* to, or, at least he chose to let his dice choose. He had *millions* of options—I only had *one*. To say yes."

Ian waved my explanation away and continued.

"The second thing, I hope that after nearly getting your face bashed in by a stranger in a club, you put an end to all this. Yes, so you had a lovely breakfast in Camden with Matt and the others. But I know you, Danny, and a lovely breakfast in Camden with Matt and the others will never be enough for you. You'll decide that it *meant* something."

"It did! It represents a whole new way of life!"

"Oh, God. Look, Danny, this has to do with Lizzie, isn't it?"

"It's got nothing to do with Lizzie!" I said.

"Before she left, she said, 'Come and visit me in Australia some-time,' and you said no."

"I didn't say no! I said, yes, definitely."

"But you *meant* no, didn't you? You had no intention of going!"

"It'd be punishing myself," I said, sulkily. "Why fall for someone who lives eighteen thousand miles away?"

"That's academic," said Ian, who had a habit of using words like "academic" in order to sound wise. "You already *had* fallen for her."

"Ian, this is about all manner of things. You know how I was living my life. And you know how I *should* live my life. *That's* what this is about. And that's why I've decided to continue with it."

"*Continue* with it? You can't! Fair enough; be a bit more open, say yes a bit more, but don't just do it blindly. Use some discretion!"

"I need to see where else it takes me, Ian. Just for a bit. Just for a week."

"A week? No! You've done it for a day! Don't do it for a week! I guarantee you, you *will* end up murdering someone. And nobody likes a murderer."

"One week is all I'm talking about."

"Starting when?"

"Starting now."

Ian stared at me. "Okay . . . so will you buy me a pint?"

I stood up and got my wallet out.

Ian smiled broadly. "Actually," he said, "I like this quite a lot."

The thing that Ian just didn't understand—could probably *never* understand—was just how good saying yes had made me feel. It was utterly liberating. My life was in the hands of everyone but me. Where would I be tomorrow? Where would I be the day after that? Who would I meet? What would we do? I had given up control.

I told Ian that we would meet in one week's time, back in the Yorkshire Grey, and I would prove to him I was taking this seriously. I would go back to my diary. I would make a note of everything I'd done. And I would present him with the evidence.

"Is a diary truly evidence?" he'd said.

"If it's admissible in court," I'd said, "it's admissible to *you*."

Ian thought about it and nodded, and said, "Fair enough."

I left the pub and began my week of Yes.

Now, conventional storytelling dictates that if I were doing this properly, I would now tell you everything that happened over the course of the next few days in the correct order and one at a time. I'd tell you what happened on Monday (which was great), and then on Tuesday (similarly great), and then I'd tell you what happened on Wednesday (which I really rather enjoyed).

But this *isn't* a conventional story. And if we were down at the pub, you and me, and you asked me to tell you what happened next, it would take all my concentration and willpower not to skip straight to this next bit, tell you it, then grab your shoulders, and shake you, and say, "So what d'you think of *that*?!" I know I shouldn't do it, but believe me, I've told the story to friends in pubs, and this is the way a story like this *should* be told. So I want to skip forward slightly. Only to the end of my week of Yes. To Friday. Because what happened on Friday was *incredible*.

It was Friday.

I'd been saying yes to everything for four whole days now, and it had been going well. Yes was proving to be an interesting companion, constantly urging me to enjoy myself a little bit more.

I woke around nine and wondered whether today would be the day I'd go into BBC Broadcasting House—the place where I am loosely employed as a freelance radio producer—and decided that no, it probably wasn't. Not while there were Yeses running free in the wild, begging to be captured.

I got up, made a cup of tea, and checked my e-mails, eager to see what this day could hold as the experiment eased to its conclusion.

I'd noticed that since I'd replied to the kind and generous offer from the Amazing Penis Patch people, the amount of spam I was receiving had increased somewhat. It was like my computer had started shouting at me. . . .

```
Discount drugs! No prescription needed! Click here!
Cheap softwares for you! All are original Genuine!
Viagra at $0.95 a dose! Excellent value! Click here!
```

It was funny. It seemed that just because I was the kind of person who would respond to the offer of an Amazing Penis Patch, the world had suddenly decided that I might also like weight-gain supplements, acne pills, books on how to succeed with girls, revolutionary hair transplants, and Viagra. I just couldn't work it out. What was it about a man who'd buy a penis patch that screamed "help"?

Nevertheless, seeing each missive as an instruction and understanding my duty to stick rigorously to the word "yes" until the week was out, I did as they asked, and clicked where they wanted me to, and studied the relevant Web sites. Incredibly only one led to an actual purchase, posing as it did a yesable question, and then following it up with an achievable instruction . . .

```
WANT TO BE A LEGALLY ORDAINED MINISTER?
```

Yes!

```
BUY OUR MINISTRY IN A BOX!
```

All right then!

Ten minutes later, and I'd filled in the on-line application and purchased my very own ministry in a box. I would now, apparently, be legally allowed to set up my own church, and then marry couples and baptise small children. Or large children. Hell, I could baptise anything I wanted, whatever its size! I was a bloody minister! And within twenty-eight days, I would have the small, plastic card which proved it—and all for a mere one hundred and nineteen dollars! And they say spam is bad.

I was excited. Who'd have thought, a week before, that I, Danny Wallace, would be one step closer to founding his own church?

As well as spam, I'd also started to get more e-mails from my friends. The first I found my way to was from Matt.

Danny,
    Up for a kickabout? I've got a new ball! We're meeting
in Hyde Park at twelve.

Was I up for a kickabout? Of *course* I was up for a kickabout! I
wrote back and said I'd be there, shorts 'n' all.

An hour or two later, freshly showered and wearing odd socks, I made
my way to the Tube. It was a sunny day; perfect for football and friends.
But as I got to the station a few minutes later, I noticed a man with a
white stick and a slightly concerned look on his face. He wasn't really
moving—just standing there—and I wondered for a second what the etiquette was in a situation like this. Should I be politically correct and
ignore a blind man as I would anyone else looking lost outside a Tube
station, or should I take the fact that he was blind into account? But then
I thought . . . what if this was an opportunity? What if we struck up a
conversation and became instant friends and ended up going on a wonderful adventure together like the kid and that bloke from *Scent of a
Woman*? It was unlikely, but surely it was an opportunity?

In the end I took a breath and took the plunge.

"Hi. Are you okay?"

The man seemed a little startled by my intrusion, and I instantly
regretted my decision.

"Yes. Yes, I'm fine. I'm just . . . waiting for someone."

Of course he was. I was an idiot. A patronising idiot. But then he
added a gracious "Thank you, though," and I felt less awkward. I
started to walk away, the promise of a marvellous adventure with the
man fading fast. But as I was nearly up the little steps, he said,
"Actually . . . could you help me?" and I walked back to him.

He had two fifty-pence pieces in his hand, and he held them up.

"Do you have a one-pound coin?"

He opened his other palm, ready for me to place a quid there.

"Oh, right . . . Sure . . . Hang on . . ."

I searched my pockets and gave a slightly unnecessary running
commentary as I did so. But I didn't have a pound coin. Just a fiver.

"Hang on . . . I'll go and get some change."

I jogged over to the little newspaper stall outside Bow Road station and bought the cheapest paper they had: the *Sun*.

I returned to the man moments later.

"Got one," I said.

"Great," said the man, and I popped the pound coin in his hand.

And then I waited for him to give me my two 50p pieces in exchange.

But he didn't.

He just said, "That's brilliant, thanks."

And I just stood there.

"That's okay," I said.

And I stood there some more.

"I was just a bit short," he said. But still there were no 50p's to be seen.

"Oh," I said.

And I waited another couple of seconds for him to give me my money. I didn't really know what to do. I mean, he'd shown me those 50p's. That was clearly part of the bargain. And yet the moment I'd given him my pound, they'd disappeared. But what could I do? He was a blind man! I couldn't demand that a blind man give me two 50p's! There was probably a law or something!

"Thanks, then," he said, clearly bored of my presence and willing me away.

"That's okay," I said rather pathetically, and drifted away, confused by my encounter and slightly dirtied by it, too.

I walked down the stairs and found my way to the train. Ah well. At least I had a newspaper to while away the journey. I suppose some good had come out of it.

I started to flick through it, determined to make full use of it, taking in the day's news and humming a happy tune. So engrossed was I that I didn't even look up when something fell out of the middle pages and onto my lap. It took me another two stops to realise that whatever had fallen out was, on first glance, some kind of advertisement. I very nearly went straight back to reading the paper, but then something about it caught my eye. It was a competition of some kind. A sheet of scratch cards. With an instruction.

An invitation.

An *opportunity*!

PLAY SCRATCH-A-MILLION!

Okay!

But hang on. What was Scratch-a-Million?

I immediately scanned the rules on the back of the sheet. Inside the newspaper, it said, were six numbers. All you had to do was check your free scratch card for those numbers, and then rub them off. If you got three matching amounts, that was the amount that you would win. Simple!

I set about finding the numbers and discovered, to my delight, that my scratch card had all six of that day's numbers. I felt a bit silly all of a sudden. I scanned left and right just to make sure no one was watching me. I, like you, am all-too-aware of what a rip-off the scratch cards that fall out of newspapers and magazines are. I used to fall for them all the time as a kid. "Well done!" they'd tell you. "You've won a star prize!" And then you'd run to the phone and dial the number and spend fourteen pounds of your parent's money in order to find out you hadn't won one of the star prizes, like a boat or one of only three brand-new widescreen TVs. No. You'd won one of six million hairclips.

But this was no time for embarrassment. Not anymore.

So I rubbed away the first panel.

TWENTY-FIVE THOUSAND.

Cor! A great start! Twenty-five thousand pounds!

I looked up, proud of my latest accomplishment, but no one was there to congratulate me, so I continued.

I rubbed away the next panel.

TWENTY-FIVE THOUSAND.

Brilliant! Another twenty-five thousand pounds! All I needed now was a third TWENTY-FIVE THOUSAND, and then a world of unthinkable riches would be mine. But as you and I both know, that's not how scratch cards work. They give you a thrill, a moment of escapism in which you're happily tricked into thinking you might have a chance of winning a new life, and then they dash your hope just as quickly as they got it up. Oh, yeah. I knew how it worked, all right. I knew what to expect. I was one step ahead of those scratch card boys, and one step ahead of the rest of the *Sun*-reading public, too, as I scratched off a third box and saw . . .

TWENTY-FIVE THOUSAND.

Hang about.

What were those numbers again?

Oh . . .

Oh. My. Lord.

TWENTY-FIVE THOUSAND. TWENTY-FIVE THOUSAND. TWENTY-FIVE THOUSAND.

I couldn't breathe.

I had just won twenty-five thousand pounds.

I told you it was incredible.

CHAPTER 4

In Which Daniel Makes an Unfortunate Error

I was happy. Maybe a little too happy. But winning twenty-five thousand pounds on a scratch card you never would've normally scratched can do that to a man. Evidently it was rather suspicious.

"Why are you smiling so much?" asked Hanne. We'd met up again, in a café not far from Holborn. She wanted me to apologise for my behaviour; I wanted to tell her all about my scratch card win.

"Danny? What's with the smile? Really?"

"I'm just really happy," I said, building up to my moment.

Hanne just looked at me.

"You're scaring me, Danny."

"I'm just happy, honestly. Happy for so many reasons. Happy to be here. With you. Hanne. My ex-girlfriend."

Hanne's eyes got a little wider.

"And I just wanted to say how fantastic—how really *fantastic*—it is that you've found this new man. I think it's fantastic. I think it's really fantastic."

I smiled broadly to show just how *fantastic* I really thought it was.

"Danny . . . are you . . . *high*?"

I considered the question and conceded.

"A little."

I was, in fact, and to quote our American friends, high on *life*.

"First of all," I said, "I *insist* on paying for your latte."

I held both my hands up to show that there would be no arguing with me on this one.

"Thanks," said Hanne brightly (although some might say a little too quickly). "Why are you in such a jolly mood?"

"A jolly mood? I suppose I *am* in a jolly mood. Wouldn't *you* be, after winning"—I paused for dramatic effect—"twenty-five thousand pounds?"

Hanne looked stunned. Absolutely *stunned*. I laughed.

"You won twenty-five thousand pounds?" she said. "You *really* won twenty-five thousand pounds? *How?*"

"Well . . ."

I thought about it. Do I tell Hanne exactly how? Do I tell her I owe it all to what she'd call a "stupid boy-project"? The very thing that had split us up? Maybe it would finally convince her that these are *good* things! But that would also confirm everything she thinks she knows about me . . .

"All I had to do was scratch . . ."

She looked impressed.

"You're good at that," she said. "You were *always* scratching when we went out. But my God, Danny! It's incredible! Twenty-five thousand pounds!"

"I know!"

"So . . . when do you get the money?"

Ah.

Now, that was the problem.

One hour later. The Yorkshire Grey with Ian.

"Ian, I am going to tell you something. Something *brilliant*."

"You've written a poem."

"No. Better. This . . ."

I pulled my diary out of my bag.

". . . is my diary. I want you to read it. It will tell you all the things I've said yes to over the past week and give you some idea of my dedication and commitment to the cause."

Ian started to flick through it, found a page, and stopped.

"'Bought some new printer cartridges.'"

"Ignore that," I said, taking it from him and finding the correct week. "Here . . ."

Monday
Passed the Scientology centre on Tottenham Court Road. A lady asked me if I wanted to undertake a free personality test. I said yes. It took forty minutes, and it turns out I am quite nice.

"Are you sure she did it properly?"

"Read on."

The mad preacher on Oxford Street, who walks around with a loudhaler telling people "Don't be a sinner! Be a winner!" shouted at me as I passed him today. He said "You! Are you ready to take the Jesus test?" I walked up to him and said that yes, I *was* ready to take the Jesus test and asked him what it was, and would Jesus be doing it himself. He didn't seem to know what to do next and ignored me and just carried on shouting about how we shouldn't be sinners but winners instead.

"Danny, what's all this leading . . ."

"You'll find out. Read on."

And I stood up to go to the bar.

When I came back, pint in hand, Ian had made good headway.

"So . . . you attended a golf sale, yes?"

"Yes."

"And you said yes to a waiter's recommendation of the fish, even though you don't eat fish, and you never have?"

"Yes. I was wrong about them. I always thought they were looking at me strangely—even the ones without heads. Turns out they were just being tasty."

Ian retraced with his finger what he'd already read.

"And you went to a gig. . . . You bought a new type of shower gel and a sandwich from Boots, 'thanks to clever phrasing on their in-store marketing' . . ."

"Yep."

"You took a leaflet for an English language school and did as it said by checking out the Web site. . . . You tried a new type of chocolate bar. . . . You sent off for a brochure about Turkey. . . ."

"Turkey: Land of Great Wonder."

"You said yes when someone asked if you'd mind lending them a tenner."

"I did."

"You bought some stamps off an old woman. You said yes to going out for a drink with a boring colleague. You made good use of a money-off voucher. And you attended the leaving do of a man you'd never met and consequently weren't all that sorry to see go."

"All that and more. Where are you up to?"

"Thursday."

Thursday

A heart-stopping moment on the Tube today. I saw an advertisement, which read CAN YOU REALLY AFFORD NOT TO BUY IN SPAIN?

For a second I knew one thing: I was going to have to invest in a villa.

And then I reread the ad and realised that, actually, yes, I really *could* afford not to buy in Spain.

Ian rolled his eyes, which I thought was a little unfair.

Said yes to giving a bloke some change. Said yes to a market researcher.

He started to speed-read.

Yes to meeting with Wag next week. Yes to applying for a new type of credit card. Yes to going for coffee with Hanne. Yes to man obsessed with saving the whales.

He got to Friday.

Friday
I bought a ministry in a box.

"What's a ministry in a box?"

"I can do weddings and stuff. Read on."

"What do you mean you can do weddings and stuff?"

"I'm a minister. I can do weddings and christenings and stuff. Read on."

"You're a *minister*?!"

"Read on!"

He did as I said but then stopped, dead. He didn't look up. He read, and reread the sentence in front of him. And then he said it out loud: "I won twenty-five thousand pounds."

He looked up at me, slowly.

"You're bloody kidding me."

I shook my head.

"You're bloody *kidding* me!"

I had prepared for this. I reached into my pocket and brought out my winning scratch card—the same scratch card that had stunned Hanne into silence just an hour earlier. I slid it across the table to him.

He picked it up and took in the numbers.

TWENTY-FIVE THOUSAND. TWENTY-FIVE THOUSAND. TWENTY-FIVE THOUSAND.

He shook his head, bewildered.

"How did . . ."

"I said yes to going to play football, right?"

He nodded.

"If I hadn't, I wouldn't have left the flat when I did. I bumped into a man, who I otherwise wouldn't have met, and he needed a pound. I said yes. But I had to get change. So I bought a newspaper, which I wouldn't have done if I hadn't said yes, and in the newspaper, which I wouldn't have bought if I hadn't needed change for a man I wouldn't have met if I hadn't said yes in the first place, was a scratch card. And it said I should play it, and I did. And I won."

Ian laughed. "Wow . . . , " he said.

"It was a chain reaction, Ian. Each yes took me closer to that twenty-five thousand pounds. Yes *wanted* me to win."

Ian slid the scratch card back across the table to me.

"God . . . so . . . When do you get the money?"

What I now had to tell Ian, and what I'd had to tell Hanne before, was a little difficult for me to go through.

It's something that, until *you've* won twenty-five thousand pounds while sitting on a Tube train dozens of miles underground and surrounded by complete and utter strangers, you may find a little difficult to relate to. But this is what happened, and there's not a part of me that wishes it hadn't.

Ten minutes after winning twenty-five thousand pounds . . .

. . . I lost twenty-five thousand pounds.

The very second I'd won the money I'd wanted to tell someone. Anyone. But phones don't work underground, and it wasn't as if I could just run up and down the carriage screaming and dancing, as this is London, and even sneezing in public is illegal if you make eye contact. So I just had to bite my lip and sit there and try somehow to suppress my giggles and smiles.

Twenty-five thousand pounds!

I'd get off at the next stop. I'd get out of the train, head for the streets, and then phone the claim line. And then I'd go to Rio or Cuba or wherever the travel agent recommended this time of year, and I'd smoke elaborate cigars offered to me by dusty street urchins, and I'd . . . I dunno . . . I'd buy a panda. Yes! I'd buy a panda! For my mum! And a top hat for my dad! A top hat of solid gold!

But as the train lurched and rocked its way through the tunnels, I suddenly started to feel a little paranoid. What if I'd done this wrong? What if I was mistaken? What if I *hadn't* won twenty-five thousand pounds after all?

I rechecked the numbers. My fears were unfounded. I'd *definitely* won. They were the same.

But what if it was an old card? From another day?

Nope. It was today. Absolutely.

I rescanned the rules. *"Scratch off the six numbers . . ."*

The six numbers? Well, I'd only scratched off *three*. So, quietly and secretly, I found the other three numbers and matched them too.

FIVE THOUSAND.

Next one . . .

FIVE THOUSAND.

Blimey! What if I got another five thousand?

I scratched the next one. . . .

TWO.

Gah! Nearly another five thousand there! How cool would that have been? To have landed the only multiwinning scratch card ever produced! And it made me wonder . . . What was under the other squares? If there was another five thousand, would that mean I could claim for *thirty thousand pounds*?

Quickly, I scratched away . . .

ONE.

One! Pah! I laugh in the face of one! I had twenty-five thousand of those now!

FIVE.

Gah. Not good enough.

But the next one . . .

FIVE THOUSAND.

Five thousand!

My God! That can't be right! What did *that* mean?

I struggled to maintain my composure but failed, and let an odd, slightly feminine yelp sneak out. Could they count? I know that only the first six really counted, but what if there was a loophole of some kind? What if I'd now won *thirty thousand pounds*?

I tore through the pages once more to find the rules. There was one box with big, bold letters telling you what to do and how to do it. And there was another box, which seemed to stretch out over half the page and had some of the smallest print known to mankind . . .

I squinted to read it.

"Minimum age" . . . fine . . . "claim line" . . . fine . . . "three like amounts" . . . fine . . . "late claims will not be accepted" . . . "cards containing printing errors will be void" . . . "limited prize pool" . . . fine, fine, fine . . .

But what about the extra bonus money? Was there anything about that?

"Numbers will be published all week" . . . I scanned on . . .

"Claims must be" . . . I kept scanning . . .

"Residents of" . . . I scanned on . . .

And then I saw it.

"Only scratch the silver panels which match your numbers . . ."

Hang about . . . *What* was that?

"Scratching silver panels which do not match your numbers will void your card."

I read it again.

I looked at my card.

I thought about what I'd done.

And then I said the word "shit" so loudly that the entire row of people opposite of me looked up.

I hadn't really known how Hanne would take it at the time. I suspected she might think it was, you know, "typical." She'd gone bright red for a moment or two, and I thought I might be in line for a lecture, so I'd said, "I'll still pay for your latte."

Ian's reaction had been more instant. He had taken it very badly. To begin with he too had gone bright red, and then he took a breath so deep, I was momentarily concerned he was going to get some balloons out and start crafting model animals.

And then he let rip.

"You . . . *stupid* . . . bloody . . . *idiot*!" he said, teeth gritted and eyes angry.

"What?" I said, slightly offended.

"You had twenty-five grand, Danny! Twenty-five *grand*! And you threw it away!"

He seemed unnecessarily vocal. Perhaps he thought I owed him twenty-five grand or something.

"I can't believe what you did! How do you lose twenty-five grand?"

"I didn't read the small print."

"You didn't read the small print," he said matter-of-factly with his hands in the air.

"Yes," I said. "The small print telling me to only scratch the numbers that I had."

He crossed his arms and shook his head.

"*Why* didn't you only scratch the numbers that you had? Why do you think they had numbers?"

"I don't know. There was another panel there, which said, 'Void if removed.' I figured that so long as I left that one untouched, I could scratch whatever I liked! I was just too tempted. I was sitting on a Tube train, and I couldn't get off or tell anyone I'd won, and I just did it!"

"But even though you scratched too many panels, you still had the winning numbers?"

"Yes, and I tried to explain that to the lady on the claim line, but she didn't want to know! She told me that the rules were there in black and white. I told her that the rules were also in the tiniest writing known to man and tucked away where I couldn't see them!"

"Oh my God, man . . . you *threw it away!*"

"I didn't throw it away; I just made a mistake. But look, that's not the point, because . . ."

"What do you mean that's not the point? What other point *is* there? You had twenty-five thousand pounds in your hands, and you threw it away! So much for saying yes to stuff. Well, I hope you've learnt your lesson. . . ."

But Ian was wrong. There *was* a lesson to be learnt, but not the one he thought. And it was a valuable one. I tried to explain it to him.

"The point is, mate, I *won* that money. I won twenty-five thousand pounds!"

He looked confused.

"No, you didn't."

"Yes, I did. I *won* it!"

"But you lost it again!"

"Forget that bit."

Ian looked like he was about to burst. "No! That's ludicrous! How am I supposed to forget that bit? You're saying all this like there's a lesson to be learned! There's no lesson here! There's just a tit called Danny Wallace!"

But I'd already rationalised the whole thing in my head. And I knew I was right.

"Listen to me—it doesn't *matter* that I lost the money, Ian. Not in the least! The point is if I hadn't said yes, I wouldn't have won it. It's what it *signifies* that matters! I said yes to playing football, right? If I hadn't, I wouldn't have met the bloke, bought the paper, sat on the train, and played the scratch card. I would still be sitting here in the pub with you, but we'd be talking about how this whole Yes thing had ended, rather than . . . how it *begins* . . ."

Ian looked more confused than ever.

"So it begins with you losing twenty-five thousand pounds?"

"No, it begins with me *winning* it . . . *That's* the point! Yes made me *win!*"

Perhaps, psychologically, it was a survival thing. But losing that twenty-five thousand pounds just as quickly as I'd won it really didn't bother me. If anything, it excited me *even more.*

I'd told myself that I'd got *on* that Tube train without the money, so I shouldn't be bothered if I got *off* it in the same way. Yes had won me that money. Saying yes had *made me rich.* Fair enough; being an utter *twat* had made me poor again—but that wasn't the fault of Yes. Yes *wanted* me to have that money. It *wanted* me to do well. And it surely couldn't be long before saying yes gave me another, similar opportunity, if only I gave it *time.*

"I've got something here," I said. "Something I want you to look after."

I opened my diary again, at the back this time, and pulled out a paper napkin.

"You want me to look after a *napkin?*"

"It's not a napkin. Not anymore. It's all I could find to write on. Read it. It's a manifesto. A *Yes Man*ifesto."

Ian sighed and read out loud, something he was getting better and better at today.

YES MANIFESTO

I, Danny Wallace, being of sound mind and body, do hereby write this manifesto for my life.

"Oh, you complete and utter—"

"Read it! It's important! This is about my life!"

I swear I will be more open to opportunity. I swear I will live my life, taking every available chance given to me. I swear I will

say yes to every favour, request, suggestion, and invitation—the
little things that come my way every day.

I SWEAR THAT HENCEFORTH, I WILL SAY YES
WHEN ONCE I WOULD HAVE SAID NO.

I will do whatever I can to achieve Yes. But people who know
I'm the Yes Man are not allowed to tell other people or take
advantage of my situation. That means you, Ian.

"I don't need to take advantage of your situation! You're doomed!"

I waved him on, determined for him to understand the significance
of the moment.

This will continue until New Year's Eve of this year.

P.S. This is *not* a Stupid Boy-Project. This is a Way Of Life.

"Oh, for God's sake," said Ian. "The end of the *year*?! That's
months away! You'll *die*!"

"I'll be *fine*!"

"What if you get asked to be in two places at once?" he said.

"Then I'll do my best to make it happen."

"People will notice! They'll notice all you ever say is yes!"

"I've refined the scheme. I won't say yes, Berlin is in Scotland, or
yes, I am a pregnant mother of two. I will essentially remove the element of dishonesty. But I *will* say yes to opportunities. To favours. To
requests. To suggestions. And to invitations. People will just think
I'm . . . happy."

"They'll think you're *simple*!" Ian was getting very agitated.
"And . . . oh my God! . . . What if you *do* get asked to kill a man?"

Ian's face flashed a look of fearful concern. I tried to calm him.

"That doesn't happen in real life, Ian."

"Him!" said Ian, pointing at an old man in the corner. "Kill that
fella there!"

"Ian, that doesn't count," I said, glancing at a now rather worried-
looking pensioner. "You know what I'm doing—you don't count—
you are automatically ruled out from giving me . . . 'opportunities.'
And you can tell no one. Okay? *No one.* I want this to be a learning

experience. A genuine human experiment in happiness and positivity."

"And what happens when you fail?"

"What do you mean *when* I fail? How can I fail? It's only saying yes to stuff! How can you fail at that?"

"It's saying yes to *everything*. How can you *not* fail?"

"Nonsense. I'll keep showing you my diary. I'll keep you updated on everything I do."

"But you'll never do it!"

"I will!"

"If ever there was a time for a drunken bet, it was now. . . ."

"No. No bets. This is more important than that."

"Fine. But if I find out you've been saying no, then . . ." He looked at me with steely determination.

"Then what?"

"Then I'll think of something. And you'll take your punishment like a man."

"Fine," I said.

"Fine," he said.

"Fine," I said.

We both sat back in our chairs. I thought about what a pity it was that we didn't have American accents, because that would all have been a lot more dramatic if we had. I think Ian was probably thinking the same.

And then he said, "Pint?"

And I said, "Yes."

CHAPTER 5

In Which Daniel Receives Word from the Sultanate of Oman

Let there be no doubt about this whatsoever.

By carefully crafting my Yes Manifesto, I knew I'd just made the most important decision of my young life.

This was big. Bigger than A-Levels. Bigger than university. There was no discernible target to speak of. What was I aiming for? What did I hope to achieve? There was no one else involved; no bet, no rival, no one to impress or beat but me. Yeah, so Ian had talked vaguely of a punishment—but that was just macho posturing. This was the ultimate in self-help. A key to getting out more. To random meetings with random people doing random things . . . I was no longer in control. I could no longer make things happen. I could only agree to them. I could *literally* only agree to them.

I awoke at about nine, a day into my life of Yes, and wondered whether today would be the day I'd pop into BBC Broadcasting House and try to get some work done. I decided it probably wouldn't. I still had too much to do. Too much to say yes to. Once the novelty had worn off, and I'd got into the swing of yes, *then* I'd pop into work. For now I'd claim to be "working from home." You can do that when you're a freelancer.

I flicked my computer on, made a cup of tea, and checked my e-mails. There was the now-usual array of spam messages, urging me to look at their Web site, or yelling at me about mortgage deals and low prices (thankfully, none of them had resorted to just *asking* me to buy their stuff). But then as I clicked onto the next one, I was startled and confused.

```
To: Danny
From: SULTAN QABOOS
Subject: URGENT BUSINESS TRANSACTION
THE PALACE-MUSCAT
P.O. BOX 632 MUSCAT PC 113 OMAN
ATTENTION PLEASE,
```

I TAKE THE PLEASURE TO GET ASSOCIATED WITH YOU AND DESIRE
TO INTRODUCE MYSELF, REQUESTING FOR YOUR EXPERT ADVISES AND
IMMEDIATE LINE OF ACTION.

I AM OMAR, SON OF THE MURDERED SULTAN, SULTAN OF THE SUL-
TANATE OF OMAN.

Jesus! I had just received an e-mail from the son of a sultan! I didn't
know whether to curtsy or to bow! What was the son of a sultan doing,
e-mailing me?

I CAME TO KNOW YOUR EXPERTISE AND PROFESSIONALLISM IN
BUSINESS FROM MY FATHER, AND AM THUS CONFIDENTLY WRITING,
THAT YOU WILL ACCEPT MY REQUEST TO PROVIDE YOUR EXPERTISE
PROFESSIONALLISM IN BUSINESS.

My professionallism in business? *What* professionallism in business? And is that really how you spell "professionalism"?

I ASK YOU TO KEEP THIS CONFIDENTIAL. I AM TO TRUST YOU
WITH MY LIFE, AS MY FATHER DID.

What?

MY FATHER WAS LAST NIGHT MURDERED BY HIS POLITICAL ENE
MIES.

What?!

NOW THOSE SAME ENEMIES ARE ATTEMPTING TO TAKE CONTROL OF
HIS FINANCES. I HAVE BEEN ABLE TO SECRETLY TAKE $40 MIL-
LION AND INTEND TO FLEE THE COUNTRY.

How do you *secretly* take forty million dollars? Do you nick a dollar a week for forty million weeks?

I WILL LIKE YOU TO USE YOUR EXPERTISE AND PROFESSIONAL-
LISM IN BUSINESS TO HELP ME ESCAPE MY MONEY AND INVEST FOR
ME.

What professionalism in business?!

ON YOUR CONFIRMING ACCEPTING MY REQUEST IN TOTALITY YOU
WILL RECEIVE 25% OF THE MONEY ($10 MILLION).

Okay, say no more; that's fine, when do we do it?

PLEASE KEEP THIS TOTALLY CONFIDENTIAL. PLEASE I HOPE YOU
WILL SAY YOU WILL HELP ME. PLEASE ACT SOON, WE MUST PRE-
PARE. IT IS GOD'S WILL.
OMAR

Good God!

The son of a murdered sultan was asking for my help. Me! And he
was offering me ten million dollars. Ten million dollars if I said yes!
That beats twenty-five thousand pounds any day! Already, Yes was
planning to make me rich again!

Now, usually, of course, I'd be a little skeptical. This kind of thing
rarely, if ever, happens to me. In fact now that I think about it, I can't
remember the last time I helped a sultan. Even a little. I'm not proud
about that. It's just that I'm not sure I'd even know how to do it or what
they'd need help with. I'm ashamed to say I know very little about magic
carpets as it is, and if you gave me a big curly sword, I'd probably give it
straight back to you. But here was a man in need, so I wrote back . . .

To: SULTAN QABOOS
From: Danny
Subject: Re: URGENT BUSINESS TRANSACTION
Dear Omar, son of the murdered sultan Qaboos,
Yes, of course I will help you!
Danny
P.S. Sorry about your dad

• • •

And that was that.

So right now, somewhere in the middle of cyberspace, my agreement and best wishes were winging their way to a troubled son of a sultan, a man probably cowering under a table in some ornate mansion somewhere with a chair forced up against the door and only a big bald genie for protection. Or maybe he was already on the run. Maybe he was sneaking from village to village, under the cover of darkness, dressed as a peasant woman and fearing for his life! How happy he would be when he read that I, Danny Wallace, a specky bloke with toothpaste round his mouth, would indeed lend him some of his professionalism in business!

I sat by my computer, eagerly clicking the Get Mail button, hoping each time that the next click would bring a response from Omar. But time after time, all I heard was the mocking dull thud that whoever designed my computer decided would represent the sound of "no mail." But I wasn't giving up on Omar. I made another cup of tea, found a biscuit at the back of my cupboard, and sat, staring intently at my screen, willing him to write back, willing him to know that it was all going to be okay, willing him to *just hang on*.

And then I got bored and got on with my day.

I was doing the washing-up when I heard a *bing-bong*. New mail! I ran to my computer, fearing Omar was in danger.

It was Hanne.

> Danny,
> Just checking you're not too depressed about losing that 25 grand.
> Hanne

I replied.

> Hanne,
> Not to worry. I just agreed to help the son of a murdered sultan, and he said he'd give me ten million dollars.
> Danny

I waited around for a bit, but Hanne didn't reply. She was probably busy.

Aside from Omar, there didn't seem to be too much happening
today. Not much to say yes to. So I decided that today *would* be the
day I'd go in to work, after all.

The first of Australia's Big Things, since you ask, was the Big Banana.

Erected in 1963 by an American immigrant named John Landi, it
was a personal and heartfelt tribute to the banana and was intended to
attract visitors from miles and miles around.

It worked.

From all over Australia, banana lovers flocked to the Big Banana to
celebrate the world of bananas and immerse themselves in the adjoin-
ing banana plantation. It became a symbol of all that was right with the
humble banana, somewhere for dedicated banana fans to centre their
energies and focus their banana-based efforts.

And it also meant that from 1963 onward, John Landi sold a *lot*
more bananas.

Perhaps for that reason the idea took off.

Almost immediately Australians of the north, south, east, and west
realised that they could draw major national attention to their farms,
their businesses, and even their hobbies just by building huge, colourful statues in honour of whatever was at the core of their obsession.
From Sydney to the Sunshine Coast, just like Lizzie had told me,
these Big Things began to line the highways and byways of Australia.
Naturally some garnered more praise and plaudits than others . . . the
Big Pineapple of 1972, experts agree, is probably the most successful
of all the Big Things, and in the seventies and early eighties really
brought pineapples and pineapple-related issues to the foreground.
But the Big Oyster, a towering testament to the vast oyster beds of the
Manning River region, is something that few Australians like to talk
about. It plays, they will tell you with their eyes fixed to the floor, a
sad second fiddle to the Big Prawn, only a few miles to the north.

I was beginning to really love Big Things. And right now, sitting in
an office at the BBC, I was clicking my way around the Web, finding
out all about them. I was fascinated. And I was slowly finding my

favourites, too. The Big Rock, for example (imagine that!), or the Big Avocado, to be found at Duranbah's popular theme park, Tropical Fruit World (formerly known as Avocado Adventureland, an experience which sounds only marginally more appealing than an afternoon at my very own Shelf Adventure).

"Dan, can I have a word?"

It was my boss's voice, and I spun round in my chair, deftly quitting the Internet as I did so in order to hide the words *Tropical Fruit World* from my screen. Sadly all it did was bring up the game of Minesweeper I'd been playing earlier, but my boss politely ignored it.

"Listen, say no if you don't want to, but there's a meeting over at TV Centre later this week—some kind of development thing—and they want someone from radio to attend. Everyone I've asked seems very busy all of a sudden. Funny how everyone gets busy when there's something they don't want to say yes to. So how about you? Can you make it?"

"Yes!" I said, proud that I was bucking the trend. "Definitely. What kind of meeting is it again?"

"Development. The usual thing. People sitting around coming up with ideas. But you're up for it?"

"Yes."

"Okay. Great. I'll tell them. Thanks, Dan. And enjoy Tropical Fruit World."

He closed the door, and I decided I'd better get on and do some work.

Working from home is a great thing, but so is working from BBC Broadcasting House—home to a thousand scruffy, cardiganed radio producers. Part of my freelance contract demanded that I spend a couple of days a week sitting in one of the offices here, working up ideas, and that was just dandy by me.

I'd worked for the BBC ever since leaving university, when I'd somehow talked my way into a six-month traineeship in the Light Entertainment department, and now here I was, a bona-fide Light Entertainment producer, a few years shy of thirty and my first-ever cardigan. What qualifies as Light Entertainment I've never been sure, though you and I both now know that cardigans are involved, and I'm fairly sure it also has something to do with Nicholas Parsons.

But Broadcasting House is a fantastic place to work, steeped as it is in glorious radio history—from Churchill's wartime addresses to the comedy of The Goons—and it was always with a sense of genuine pride that I walked through the huge, brass doors with my special BBC pass clipped to my jeans. Fair enough, it's not as if I was the man charged with making the type of quality journalism that the world has come to rely on as the most trustworthy and respected on the planet. It's not as if I was one of those who were bringing down governments or exposing corruption or staying up all night poring through secret dossiers and turning them into the next day's global headlines. But I *was* one of the ones making silly and obscure little programmes that might pass the time on the commute home or be heard by a lonely shepherd tuning in to the World Service somewhere on the Savannah Plains or confuse a prisoner in some jail somewhere with a topical joke they blatantly wouldn't understand, because they'd been inside on arson charges since 1987.

So anyway, I was trying to get some work done. I really was. But there were a couple of things against me. The first was the growing realisation and excitement that my life was in the hands of just about everyone else in the world, but not me, and that just one well-placed yes to one well-placed opportunity could change or improve, or if Ian was to be believed, destroy my life forever. And the second thing that was against me getting any work done today was that there was very little work to be done. I was between projects. Sure I could start a new one. But that would just be making work for myself. Who does that?

"Hi, Danny," said a voice to my left, all of a sudden.

"Hello!" I boomed, still imagining myself to be quite important.

"How are you?"

It was Robert, a technician I'd worked with on a rather intense weeklong edit. An edit which had actually seemed like it was closer to a month, mainly because Robert was cramming for a pub-quiz final and kept stopping every five minutes to tell me a little-known fact about the animal kingdom.

"I'm fine, thanks, Robert."

"I'm going to have a little party next week, Danny. Nothing fancy, just a few friends from 'the industry.'"

He used his hands to signify the quotation marks, and then laughed and shook his head as he enjoyed what he'd done.

"I was wondering whether you might like to come along?"

Ordinarily this would have been a tricky one to answer. It's not because Robert is a boring man—he's not, and I'll always defend him on that—it's just that he's terribly dull.

"Of course I would, Robert," I said, pleased at least that I'd have another thing to pop in the diary. "I'd be delighted, in fact."

"Oh, cool. Ace. You're the only one from the BBC who can make it! Everyone else is really busy at the moment."

"I've been hearing that, yes."

It was still sunny as I walked down Regent Street, and I was smiling. Since my scratch card win, I'd started to wonder something: What if, potentially, every single moment I was awake could lead to somewhere wonderful? What if all I had to do was keep my eyes wide open and welcoming? After all, the man on the bus had made me realise that sometimes the little negatives of daily life don't have to be negatives at all. The crush of the Tube, or the bus that doesn't stop for you, or the nightclub that won't let you in . . . Before I'd thought of those as self-contained little moments. I'd never really considered that they might be beginnings, that they might lead somewhere, that they might be for the best.

Once again the Tube was at a standstill. I joined the back of the queue and looked around me. Perhaps a hundred people were here, with more on the other side of the street, all of them waiting for the station to reopen, all of them cursing their luck or shouting into their phones or kicking their heels in the sun. It was a tired, frustrated mob, and for a moment I was nearly one of them . . . until I remembered that the last time this kind of thing had happened to me was the night I'd met the man on the bus. And then I realised. This was *perfect*. This was another opportunity to see what life would throw at me! Did I want to stand here by a busy road with its dust and honking horns and smoke, or did I want to treat this as a *chance*? What if I just walked past the Tube and just took life as it came? What would happen?

So I walked.

• • •

That night I walked to wherever the wind seemed to take me. Down Oxford Street into Soho, toward Picadilly Circus, and then Leicester Square. I was walking slowly, willing opportunities to come my way, but gradually noticing things I'd never noticed about London before. Just little things. Like the statue of Charlie Chaplin in the centre of Leicester Square. Or the telephone boxes in Chinatown that have been crafted to look like pagodas. Or the tiny dance put on by the little wooden peasants hidden inside the clock at the Swiss Centre, which they perform faithfully once an hour, on the hour, to the delight of tourists and tourists alone. I was starting to discover that for someone who lived in this city, I really didn't know it very well.

I walked toward Holborn, exploring Fleet Street and stopping to study a plaque in honour of someone called Wallace. I walked through Chancery Lane and sat on a bench in the city of London, while I watched a man in a suit silently fit an entire bagel into his mouth. I sauntered and I meandered and I ambled along . . . and before too long I realised I was most of the way home. It was strange. Before, I'd always rushed my way around my city. London was just the collective term for lots of different places I'd had to get to, quickly. But tonight . . . I'd *walked* home. Slowly. And taken everything in. And enjoyed it. I had gradually rediscovered, and then quickly fallen back in love with, my own city.

I arrived back at my flat late but relaxed and happy. I shoved a curry into the microwave, flicked on the kettle, and sat down at my computer to check my e-mails.

Hi! I'm Sandi! Would you like to see me get hot and wild with my college roommates?

Now, I didn't know who Sandi was, but she seemed friendly enough, and it was a lovely offer, but it could wait.

Another e-mail came from Robert the technician with full details of his party. "Bring a fact!" it read. "Stump a stranger and break the ice!"

And that was about it.

I got out my diary, added the date of Robert's party, and added all the other things I'd said yes to today. But I was disappointed. My walk around London had enthused me. Surely I could find *something* else to say yes to?

I sat on the sofa with my cup of tea and started to idly flick through the *Tower Hamlets Recorder*—a newspaper I tend to hide when being visited by my mum, seeing as how every other story tends to heavily feature one or more of the words "stabbing," "robbed," or "police believe the muggers are targeting the bespectacled"—trying to find something of interest.

There was the usual array of crime. A fete. An article about a historic bench.

But there on the opposite page, tucked away next to a birthday advert and a picture of a very old cat, was the following important announcement:

The Starburst Group Would like to invite anyone and everyone to our third local meet-up! Come along if you are nterested in aliens, telepathy—any*think*! Blind Beggar, Whitechapel, Wednesday, 6 p.m. Ask for Brian.

An invitation! To anyone and everyone! Including me!

Granted it looked a bit strange. Usually I'd go to great lengths to avoid hanging around with *anyone* who says "anythink" instead of "anything," but not this time.

I smiled. Wednesday was tomorrow. I made a note of the address, I switched the computer off, and I went to bed.

Well, no, hang on.

I smiled, I made a note of the address, I clicked on a link and looked at a colourful picture of Sandi getting hot and wild with her college roommates, I smiled again, I switched the computer off, and *then* I went to bed.

The Blind Beggar pub, not too far from my own home, is a piece of East End legend.

It was there that Ronnie Kray, one of London's celebrated gangster twins, the Krays, shot and killed a burly ex-con named George Cornwell. Every cab driver in London will tell you that they were there the night it happened, and it's best to just keep quiet when they say this. According to police reports, the only two other people who *were* there that night were a couple of rent boys, and I can tell you from experience that cab drivers don't like it if you ask them what it was like to be a 1960s male prostitute.

The Krays, of course, did *something* almost *everywhere* in East London. Grab a pensioner in the East End and point at whatever you like.

"Yes," they'll say. "That is the very wall that the Kray Twins probably once saw on their way somewhere. Are you a tourist? Can I have five pounds?"

Of course some landmarks are more famous than others. There's Pellicci's Café, in which the Krays used to do their business and drink their tea. There's Turnmills Nightclub, where Mad Frankie Fraser got shot in the head and lived to tell the tale. There's the house on Evering Road in Stoke Newington, where Reggie Kray stabbed Jack "the Hat" McVitie. Who, before you ask, was a man and not a hat, and will doubtless remain that way until *The Animated Adventures of the Kray Twins* finally gets the green light.

The Blind Beggar, though, is the true East London Krays experience, and a bit of an odd choice for the Starburst Group to hold one of their meetings in.

"Of course," said James, one of the people I'd correctly identified as a Starburster, "I know someone who was here the night it happened. Saw the whole thing."

The others—Laura, Bob, and Brian himself—all looked fairly impressed.

"Is he a cab driver?" I asked.

James looked at me, shocked. "Why, do you know him?" he said.

I decided it would be better for me not to introduce myself to the group with lighthearted tales of male prostitution, so I shook my head and said, "No."

The Starburst Group, it turns out, meets once a month in various pubs around London and is essentially made up of these four people, the odd guest, and one other regular, who was currently on holiday in Malaga.

"There are others, though," said Brian. "Plenty of others. Many in the States, a couple in France, and of course there are hundreds on the mailing list whom we've never met. Though I doubt we'll ever truly meet *them*. . . ."

Brian looked knowingly at the others, and they chuckled.

"How come?" I asked.

"Let's just say they know a little more about us than we do about *them*," said Brian, and Laura, I *think*, mouthed the word "government."

I was excited to be here. Saying yes had introduced me to my first bunch of strangers. Strangers with some rather strange ideas.

"So," said Brian, "Bob's got some things to run past us on his pyramid theories. Bob's our resident Egyptologist, Danny."

"Right!" I said, enthusiastically. "Brilliant!"

"Do you know much about the pyramids, Danny?" asked Bob, who was bald with a silver-grey-haired goatee and a waistcoat with little moons on it.

"Er, well, I know that they're in Egypt."

"That's right, very good," he said, sincerely. "But who built them?"

I thought it over. "Egyptians?" I tried.

Bob smiled. "That would certainly conform to popular opinion," he said. "While it may be true that some Egyptians *were* involved in the process, I think they may have had a little help."

At this point Laura, who was still wearing a hat even though she was indoors and there was central heating, made a little mm-hmm sound as if to confirm what Bob was saying.

"Who do you reckon helped them?" I asked.

Everyone looked at me, ready to gauge my reaction.

"Aliens," said Bob.

My reaction was to blink a couple of times and then say, "Aliens?"

"Think about it," said Bob.

I thought about it. It didn't help.

"Are you completely sure about this?" I said.

"Actually, Danny, it's not all that far-fetched," said Laura. "Studies

of ancient hieroglyphics show that the Egyptians often talked of
beings from the sky who would impart great wisdom and bestow won-
derous new technologies upon them."

James nodded and looked enigmatic. Brian sipped at his lemonade.
Bob continued.

"Moreover the Pyramids at Giza are built in the exact layout of the
stars in Orion's Belt. And when you divide the circumference of the
Great Pyramid by twice its height, you get the figure 3.141."

"Pi," said Brian with a wink.

"But . . . do aliens *have* pi?" I said. "Why couldn't it just have been
some Egyptians who, you know, were good at building?"

"A possibility! Certainly a possibility!" said Bob. "But there is
absolutely no record of who built them. And the Egyptians recorded
everything. Wars, kings, pharoah worship, everything that went on. But
not the building of the pyramids. Odd, eh?"

Brian let out a sudden and short burst of totally inexplicable laughter.

I tried to work out how simply not knowing who built the pyramids meant that aliens did it. I mean, I don't know who nicked my
bike from outside Loughborough Leisure Centre when I was nine,
but it seems unfair to lay the blame at the feet of our extraterrestrial
cousins. If they have feet.

"But anyway, to the new stuff," said Bob, and James and Laura
leaned in slightly. "An American Starburster put this to me this week
over MSN Messenger, and I promised I'd share it with the group."

I was a *Starburster*! Brilliant!

"Now, I hadn't heard this before, but the Cydonia site on Mars
provides us with better evidence than ever that the pyramids were
indeed built by aliens. Early pictures of Mars—and I have checked
this out on the Internet—do show what appears to be a face and some
pyramidical monuments located side by side."

James got a pad out and urgently made a note of something.

"Closer inspection of the face shows it to be humanoid in struc-
ture . . ."

This was the first time I had ever heard the word "humanoid"
used by any humanoid, ever, and I enjoyed it greatly. I nodded along,
fascinated.

"And in many ways very similar in form to that of the sphinx."

Everyone just sort of looked at one another, and then at me. I looked back at them and stuck my bottom lip out, nodded, and raised my eyebrows as if to give the impression that I had been won over by the weight of their evidence, which was only polite.

"Fascinating," said Laura. "That is fascinating. You have to wonder how pyramids got up there on Mars."

James looked up at the ceiling, probably for clues.

"Maybe it was some Egyptians," I tried, and immediately regretted it.

But then Bob laughed. And James laughed. And everyone laughed. And then Bob spoiled it by saying, "No. It was *definitely* aliens."

"So, what made you decide to come to one of our meetings?" asked Brian half an hour later.

"You invited me," I said. "Well, you invited *everyone*. I saw your ad."

We were standing by the bar, away from Bob, Laura, and James.

"I was a little annoyed by that advert, I'll be honest," Brian confessed.

"Why?"

"Well, I phoned it in, and they put a little border of stars around it, for a start, which I did *not* ask for, and which just makes us look *mad*. And then they played with what I'd written. I said, 'Come along if you are interested in aliens, telepathy—anything at all.' And they changed it to 'Come along if you are nterested in aliens, telepathy—any*think*!' Still, I suppose it worked. You came. You just thought, 'I'll go to that,' did you?"

"I . . . um . . . I don't know," I started. "I guess it just felt right. I just thought I'd be open to it and say yes."

"Well, that's good. The closed mind is a disease. You need to have an open mind; otherwise life will just pass you by."

"I'm trying to say yes more in general," I said. "As a person, I mean." You'll notice I glossed over the part about "in general" meaning "all the time, to everything, ever."

"Are you? That's a good idea. Be open to experience. Why did you decide to do that?"

"Something someone said to me. A bloke on a bus. I'd ended up chatting to him after our Tube home got cancelled, and there we were on this bus, when he came out with it. 'Say yes more,' he said. Out of virtually nowhere. So that's what I'm doing."

Brian pulled an overly intrigued face.

"Wow," he said. "And you're taking him seriously?"

"Well, yes," I said.

"Who was he?"

"I dunno. He was an Asian guy—a teacher, he said. From around here, actually. Aldgate."

Brian stuck his bottom lip out and raised his eyebrows.

"A teacher," he said. "Makes sense. So he struck a chord, did he? When he said that?"

"Could be my traya!" Laura said suddenly, and Brian laughed at her.

"Your what?" I said.

"No, no . . . *Maitreya*," said Brian. "The world teacher."

"What's a world teacher?" I said.

"I wouldn't worry," said Brian. "He doesn't exist."

"He *could* exist," said Laura, coming to our side of the bar. "We just don't *know* he exists. Same goes for most deities or enlightened beings."

I was intrigued. This sounded interesting. I mean, not as interesting as aliens building the pyramids, but fairly interesting all the same.

"Enlightened beings?"

"Beings who walk among us and help us with our daily lives. You could say Maitreya is in charge of them. He's supposed to live around here," Laura explained.

I looked toward Brian, but he had wandered over to Bob and James at the bar, and although I made a mental note to ask more about Maitreya, the God of the East End, the conversation soon moved on.

Despite the slightly strange undertones, I'd enjoyed hanging out with the Starburst Group. Brian (chosen subject: "Them," what "They" are up to, and how "They" achieve it) had a mysterious past and was the most intense of the four. Laura (chosen subject: angels, the afterlife, and "hidden helpers") was a former social worker and had a quick and quiet laugh. James (chosen subject: conspiracies, conspirators, and the conspired-against) liked motorbikes and had chosen tonight's venue because it was "biker friendly." And Bob (chosen subject: aliens, Egyptology, and the TV series *Stargate:*

SG = 1) used to teach woodwork but saw a UFO while driving through the Lake District in 1982 and decided woodwork seemed a bit pointless in comparison.

"We're having another meeting in six weeks or so, in Willesden Green," said Laura. "It's near my house. Will you be coming to that one?"

"Yes," I said, reaching into my pocket for my diary. "Yes, I'll be there. Definitely."

I caught Brian's eye. He smiled at me.

"We haven't decided what we'll be talking about yet," Laura said.

"Perhaps we could talk about Maitreya," joked Brian. "Seeing as you've met him."

I laughed. But Laura was insistent.

"We could if you like," she said. "Or if you've any other unusual interests?"

It was clear what she was getting at. She wanted to know if I liked angels. Or UFOs. Or if I had a poster of Spock on my wall.

"I'm pretty . . . open-minded," I said. "There are lots of things that interest me."

"Like . . . ?"

Well, what was I going to say? I couldn't exactly say "badminton," could I?

"Ghostbusters."

Clearly I had failed to impress them.

"Hey—my friend Wag reckons that men can have babies. . . . They just haven't worked out how yet. What do you think of that?"

"Oh," said Laura. "I have actually heard that before."

Of course she had.

"A man named Linton—I *think* that was his name—proposed an interesting theory of fatherhood. He had worked out that the man needs to be around forty and sexually active. The man and the lady lie side by side and use their forefingers only, and I won't say too much more if that's all right, and anyway, if they are successful, then around a year later the man will find he is able to have a baby."

"Oh!" said James. "On his own?"

"No," said Laura. "By another man. But the interesting thing about all this is that men can actually nurse babies, using their breast, but after birth they will have to cork their birth canal."

I saw Brian shift slightly uncomfortably at the thought of corking his birth canal.

"Some people say that this was the way man got life before woman was created," said Laura. "Though, obviously, I have my own theories about that."

Obviously.

As I trudged toward the Mile End road, I smiled. That had been a good, solid Yes. I'd had a fine time with the Starburst Group—against all the odds, in a way. Or, at least, against my preconceptions. I liked the fact that those four key members had found one another. I liked the fact that while their beliefs were slightly off-kilter, they'd created their own club in which anything could be discussed, considered, thrown about, and shared. And that they were so welcoming.

When I got home, I was pleased to see I had received a reply from Omar, my endangered Sultan friend.

> To: Danny
> From: SULTAN QABOOS
> Subject: RE. RE.: URGENT BUSINESS TRANSACTION
> DEAR danny
> MAY GOD BLESS YOU danny FOR TAKING MY OPPORTUNITY. MAY ALL YOU DO AND MEET BE SUCCESS. I MUST HAVE YOUR COMPLETE FAITH AND TRUST danny. I FEEL I CAN TRUST YOU 100%.
> MY FATHER'S ENEMIES ARE MOVING QUICKLY AND SOON WE WILL HAVE NO TIME. I MUST ESCAPE THE $40 MILLION URGENTLY.
> I REQUEST YOU TO KINDLY TAKE THE MONEY INTO A BANK ACCOUNT IN AN APPROPRIATE BANK, WHERE THE MONEY IS SAFE.
> AFTER THE SUCCESSFUL COMPLETION OF THIS VENTURE I WILL INVITE YOU TO MY SULTANATE SO AS TO TO KNOW YOU ON A PER-SONAL LEVEL.
> LOOKING FORWARD TO YOUR IMMEDIATE RESPONSE. ARE YOU STILL WILLING TO HELP. SEND ME YOU BANK ACCOUNT DETAIL AND PHONE NUMBER danny.
> OMAR

Thank God Omar was all right. He'd had me a little worried there, but I suppose you get busy when you're trying to sneak out of the country with forty million dollars.

Tonight had taught me it was important to grab my Yeses, wherever they come from. So I thought about what to write back to Omar. It was lovely of him to make this personal; to invite me to his sultanate after we'd done our business. Clearly he thought of me as a friend now. Just look at the gentle way he was writing my name. He wasn't writing in that scary, shouty, all-capitals way when he said my name. No. I wasn't "DANNY." I was "danny."

My reply was swift and, I would hope, helpful.

> Dear Omar,
> How exciting! I would love to come and visit you in your sultanate so you can know me on a personal level. And hey maybe you can come and stay in my flat in Bow afterward. I can only offer you a futon, but it's KING SIZE. Is a king bigger than a sultan? I suppose if he was a fat king, like Henry the Eighth, then yes, but there are probably loads of fat sultans too.
> I am sorry if that is offensive.
> Moving on, yes, I am still willing to help you. I will look into opening a bank account asap.
> Cheers!
> Danny

I updated my diary, and I went to bed, happy.

This was all working out beautifully.

SELECTED EXTRACTS FROM THE DIARY OF A YES MAN

June 22

What a lovely day!

Not only is it sunny and bright, but I am pleased to announce I have been contacted by the people at Capital One. I have been "specially selected" to be invited to apply for "a new type of credit card"! I sent off my application immediately, enclosing a friendly note of thanks.

June 23

Saw an advert in the *Sun*. It said DO YOU LOOK LIKE SOMEONE FAMOUS? DO YOU WANT TO MAKE SOME MONEY? FILL IN OUR ON-LINE APPLICATION, SEND US A PHOTO, AND EARN YOURSELF SOME SERIOUS CASH!

I decided that the answers to their questions were yes and yes. And then I tried to work out who I looked like. I decided I could probably either pass myself off as Harry Potter's older brother, or as one of the Proclaimers. They were one of my favourite bands when I was a little boy, and I suppose it's just blind luck I ended up looking like one of them. Or looking like *both* of them, in fact, seeing as how they're twins and everything.

I sent my photo off with the heading: "Meet Britain's only one-man Proclaimers tribute act!" I don't see how they can turn me down. Two twins for the price of one!

June 24

Joy!

I accepted an invitation from American Express to apply for a "new type of credit card." How many new types can there be? Maybe I can start to classify them, like some kind of plastic-obsessed Darwin. "Look, that's a Wallace credit card," people of the future will say. "How do you know?" other people will ask. "You can tell by the markings," the first group will say. "And also by the fact that there's no money left on it."

June 26

A woman sitting opposite me on the Tube had her newspaper folded in an odd way this morning. Virtually screaming out at me on one side were "Want to get clean?" and "Clean your whole house—experience the magnificent power of steam cleaning!" on the other. Next to a picture of the new Light 'n'

Easy Steam Cleaner was a picture of a smiling Su Pollard, who was hailing it as "brilliantly simple, simply brilliant!" She must really *love* it. The manufacturers were proud to be able to offer it to me at the new low price of just £24.95. I have ordered one. I am going to experience the magnificent power of steam cleaning. I will let you know how I get on once it arrives. Hopefully it will be both brilliantly simple and simply brilliant.

June 28

Today I accepted an invitation from Morgan Stanley to apply for "a new type of credit card." I also received my new type of credit card from the Capital One people. It's shiny.

I also bought two copies of the *Big Issue*.

July 1

Worked all day, then had a pint with Wag. Turned into many pints. He has a remarkable knack of saying, "D'ya fancy another?" I invited him to both the parties I was invited to tonight. Sadly one was deep in West London, so we could only stay for twenty minutes, because we had to go to one in the far reaches of East London, which was just finishing as we arrived. Wag wasn't very pleased.

July 2

While walking through Hackney a few days ago, I noticed a piece of yellow paper stuck to a lamppost reading WANT TO GET RICH QUICK? I decided that yes, I did, and I read further. All I had to do was send off a cheque for twelve pounds, and I would receive a book, free, in the post. It arrived today. It is called *501 Ways to Make Easy Money When You're Skint*. It is brilliant. Among its suggestions for simple moneymaking schemes are goatherding, glamour photography, and inventing a game, "such as Monopoly, or the Rubik's Cube."

It also read, "A small piece of land is all you need to start a go-kart centre!"

It would seem they've forgotten that it's quite important to have go-karts too. And qualified instructors. And insurance. And protective headgear. And a license.

Nevertheless I have decided that if they're offering me the opportunity to earn lots of money, I cannot turn it down. I have chosen to try and earn some money by having a letter published in a newspaper.

July 4

I have experienced the magnificent power of steam cleaning. It was both brilliantly simple *and* simply brilliant, though, due to a slippery step, I did at one point very nearly scorch my gentleman's agreements.

July 5

In my efforts to "get rich quick" by writing to newspapers and magazines, I noticed that the *Sun* says on its Letters page that it pays twenty pounds for letters, as well as handy hints or tips it publishes. I sent this one in today:

A handy hint or tip for quick moneymaking is to send a letter to the *Sun*. According to its Letters page, they pay £20 for letters, as well as handy hints or tips, they publish!
D. Wallace, London

I await my twenty pounds. But just on the off chance the *Sun* didn't like it, I also sent this one in:

A small piece of land is all you need to start a go-kart centre!

Easy money.

July 6

I have had word from the lookalike people. They have decided "upon careful consideration" that I do not look like *either* of the Proclaimers. *Either* of them! I am a little upset at how frankly they put this. Couldn't they have had a little sensitivity?

If I ever start a lookalike agency for people who think they look like one or more twins, it will definitely be one that *cares*.

CHAPTER 6

In Which Daniel Breaks the Law

I awoke in the morning to find a most exciting surprise in the post.

A letter from the Patent & Trademark Institute of America! Finally the Do You Have an Invention? people had written back to me.

How important I felt! Strangely, though, the Patent & Trademark Institute of America seemed not to be based in Los Angeles or New York or San Francisco. No. It was based in Blackpool, England. On a very normal-sounding street.

Encouragingly, however, they appeared to be taking me very seriously. They even started their letter to me with "Dear Inventor." Immediately I knew I was in safe hands. These people knew what they were doing. They had clearly recognised the ability in me to create life-changing and practical inventions and had decided, after careful consideration, to offer me a "free new product analysis."

"There is no cost for this initial analysis," they wrote. "Why not invest a few minutes today to properly document an idea, and our expertise will be available within a week."

Good God! I had the ear of the Patent & Trademark Institute of America!

I was excited. I wish I could say I come from a long family line of inventors, but I don't. Unless you consider the fact that I was born and bred in Scotland—the country responsible for anesthetics, golf, quinine, marmalade, the steam engine, the adhesive postage stamp, the microwave oven, the fridge and, yes, hollow-pipe drainage. And which of us hasn't got a few stories about what hollow-pipe drainage means to us?

I had my own inventions, of course, mostly based around the game Twister. There was Travel Twister, for starters, but later I'd taken this one step further and invented the Twister bedspread. I was sure that this would be a surefire hit with male students, at last giving them a valid excuse to invite girls back to their rooms. But I was heartbroken when, a year later, I discovered in a Sunday supplement that someone else had had the exact same idea but had actually gone to the trouble of patenting and marketing it. Damn the organised and resourceful! Well, I wasn't going to get caught out like that again. Not since I now had the ear of the Patent & Trademark Institute of America.

But I did still have one little trick left up my sleeve: *the electric toilet-seat lifter!* Never again would men have to stoop down to lift up the toilet seat. Never again would men have to ask themselves that universal and age-old question: Why *do* women always leave the toilet seat down?

Now, thanks to me, couples all across the country would have one less thing to argue about.

I threw some cereal into a bowl and began to devour the information pack sent to me by my new friends at the institute, looking for more hints and tips on what they were after, just in case my fallback idea somehow wasn't right. But that was the thing—there were no hints on what they *were* after. Just what they *weren't*:

RESTRICTED IDEAS *NOT* TO BE SUBMITTED
Perpetual motion devices
Military weapons

Bollocks. My first two obvious ports-of-call, ripped from my hands by the invention fascists. I *love* inventing perpetual motion devices.

Pornographic devices

A pornographic *device*? How many pornographic devices were they getting? And what *is* a pornographic device, anyway?

Untested or unproved chemical formulas or cures for illnesses.

Well, that wasn't fair. Now I couldn't send them untested or unproved cures for illnesses. I had *loads* of them!

Products based on unrealistic levels of technology

Bang goes the time machine. This was getting harder by the minute.

Literary or musical works

Right. So I couldn't invent a poem or a new musical note. Which, if you've ever heard me sing, is all I seem to do.

Toilet-seat lifters

What?!

But mine's *electric*!

Well, that was fine, I suppose. This would obviously just take a little more work on my part. I sat down to think about what I should invent.

I looked around the flat for inspiration.

The mug. Invented.

The chair. Invented.

Shoes. Done.

Blimey. How do you go about inventing things?

The door. Invented.

Stairs. Invented.

The telly. Invented.

It was all very frustrating. Why was everything in my flat already invented? I had to admit that maybe development just wasn't my thing.

I put on my jacket and grumpily prepared myself for the development meeting at the BBC.

I walked into BBC Television Centre to be met by a man named Tom.

"So you've worked in television before, haven't you, Danny?"

"Well, yes," I said. "But not very much. I prefer radio."

"Ah, why's that? Because the pictures are better on the radio? Because there are less people involved, and your vision can become a reality?"

"Um, yes. And also the radio department is a lot closer to my flat."

We walked through the vast, shiny corridors of power toward the lifts that would take us to our meeting. Television Centre is rather different from Broadcasting House. On the whole the latter is rather tatty with musty carpets and lightbulbs that have needed changing since the Second World War. Television Centre, on the other hand, is a vision of the future with huge, glassed-in newsrooms, and reception areas that look like they've been hit by some kind of pastel bomb, and even areas for producer relaxation that have been dubbed "ThinkPods." I'd love to work somewhere that had a ThinkPod. I'd probably get a lot more thinking done. And I've *always* liked pods.

We arrived at the development meeting, and I took a seat.

"Okay, everyone, this is Danny. He's joining us today from the radio department in order to give us a different perspective on things."

I smiled eagerly and waved to my TV colleagues. One of them waved back.

"Danny, do you want to just tell us a couple of the things that you're working on right now?"

Hmm. Tricky. Should I mention the inventions?

"I'm working on some new radio show ideas," I said, before adding by way of taking up a bit more time, "which I am working on."

This seemed enough for everyone, and we cracked on with the meeting.

"Right then," said Tom cheerily. "The first thing we need to do is decide whether or not to continue developing this chat-show format."

"No," said a man opposite me, dismissively. He was wearing designer spectacles and a T-shirt with an ironic saying on it, so he certainly looked like he knew what he was doing.

"I agree," said the girl next to him. "Kill it. It's going nowhere."

"Danny? What do you think?"

"Well, I don't really know anything about it," I said.

And so they filled me in.

And to be honest it didn't sound like a bad show. I'm not allowed to tell you much about it, but it involved a pretty big concept, a host like Johnny Vaughan and a guest like Delia Smith. I didn't know that much about development work, but I was sure they could probably get *something* out of it.

"So bin it or keep it?" said Tom, and there were a few murmurs of "bin it."

"Danny? Would you watch that show if it was on?"

I thought about it. Was that an invitation? A suggestion?

"Yes, probably," I said. "I suppose it depends upon the trailer."

"Hmm," someone said quite loudly.

"Really?" said the man in the T-shirt, smirking. "The trailer?"

"Well, yes," I said, standing my ground. "I mean, you know, if it looked . . . inviting."

"I see what you're saying, Danny," said Tom. "It's crucial that this show feels inclusive."

Phew.

"That is definitely what I was saying just then," I said.

"Good," said Tom. "I think it's got potential, too."

Hey!

The man in the T-shirt was quick to backtrack.

"Yes, well, obviously, with a bit of development and the right kind of—"

"So," said Tom, cutting him off, "who wants to take the idea on? Do a bit more work on it?"

No one said anything.

"Danny? How about you?"

"Me?"

"Well, I mean, there's no pressure. Just to see how you get on?"

"I'll do it," the T-shirt man said immediately.

Tom ignored him.

"Danny?"

"Yes. Sure."

"Good."

No, not good. Bad. What the hell was I doing? I knew nothing about this idea except that it had Delia Smith in it. And now here I was taking responsibility for it! What was I supposed to do with it? And now Tom was moving his way through the agenda, and everyone was saying no, we should drop this idea, or no, that idea is going nowhere, and here I am saying yes, I'll do a little work on that idea, or yes, I don't mind doing a bit of development on this one. I watched in horror as more and more documents and show outlines and pieces of paper were put in front of me. I was actively volunteering for all this work!

"Arse," said Tom. "Look at the time. I'm late. Right, so . . . who's doing what for the next meeting?"

Everyone looked at me.

"I think Danny's doing, well, *everything*," said Sam.

"Oh. Right. Well. Danny," said Tom, "do you want to come to the next meeting on Friday and let us know how you got on? I'll clear it with your radio people."

"Yes," I said, slightly heavily. "That would be excellent."

"And in the meantime, I'd like everyone to come up with three new ideas for Saturday night entertainment shows. Okay? Good. See you Friday."

"This is terrible, Ian," I said, walking away from Television Centre, mobile in hand. "I'm in over my head. I just kept saying yes every time they asked me to do something."

"Oh, come on! You're a producer! You can produce!"

"No . . . I'm a *radio* producer. In Light Entertainment. We are unique. We are a different breed. We were born to get to work a bit late and spend the morning eating bananas and surfing the Internet, and then head for the pub in the afternoon. We are not like television producers. Television producers are hungry for success, and they get up early, and they eat cocaine, and they dress like people out of magazines, and they know people like David Beckham and Ant 'n' Dec.

"Well, so what? You've said yes to the work, so do it, and then just forget about it. I've a feeling that once they see what you're capable of, you won't have to worry about being asked back."

"But they're expecting success! And Tom wants another three ideas on his desk by Friday."

"What kind of ideas?"

"Just . . . ideas. Ideas for entertainment shows."

"Oh . . . ," said Ian.

"What?"

"Nothing. It's just that, well . . ."

"What?"

"*I've* got some ideas."

"Meet me in the pub in half an hour."

"No, Ian."

"Why not? It's a perfectly good idea."

"*How to Get Fat* is not a perfectly good idea. Who's going to want to watch a show that tells them how to get fat?"

"Skinny people."

"No."

"This one, then," he said, sliding another piece of paper across the pub table.

"*What Do Moles Mean?*"

"You know . . . What does it mean if you've got a mole on your cheek? Is it different from having one on your ear?"

"No."

"How do you know?"

"I *don't* know. I'm saying no to the idea. It's rubbish."

"There is no such thing as a bad idea, Dan!"

"What?"

"I saw a lady on telly saying that. 'There's no such thing as a bad idea,' she said. 'And even a bad idea can lead to a good one.'"

"But I thought that *no* idea was a bad idea," I said, confused.

"Exactly. No idea is a bad idea. Exactly."

"But if there are no bad ideas, how can we get from a bad idea to a good one?"

"Exactly, my friend. No idea is a bad idea. There are only . . . ideas. How about *A Toddler's Guide to War*?"

"That's a bad idea."

"Yes, true enough. *My Philosophies and Beliefs*?"

"What's that?"

"It's just a show about my philosophies and beliefs. Each week Ian Collins takes a sideways glance at—"

"No."

Ian looked at me, coldly.

"You say no a lot these days. . . ."

I left the pub, and with a slightly grumpy face, headed off to do my homework.

Once home I flicked on my computer and prepared to come up with some Saturday night entertainment brilliance.

How to Get Fat.

Maybe there was something to it.

I typed the title onto an otherwise blank document and stared at it for a little while.

But then there was a *bing-bong*. An e-mail had arrived.

From Omar.

> DEAR BROTHER danny
> THANK YOU FOR YOUR LAST NOTE YOU SENT ME. BUT WE MUST
> MOVE QUICKLY. I MUST HAVE YOUR BANK DETAILS RIGHT NOW. SEND
> THEM TO ME.
> ARE YOU ALSO FREE TO TRAVEL TO HOLLAND, NETHERLAND. YOU
> NEED TO BRING CASH GIFTS TO ASSOCIATES OF MY FATHER, WHO
> HELP US MOVE THE MILLIONS OF DOLLAR.

Eh?! He'd never mentioned that I'd have to travel to Holland before! And what was all this about bringing cash gifts?

> I KNOW IT IS MUCH TO ASK, I AM TAKING A BIG RISK IN CON-
> TACTING YOU.
> PLEASE SIR WE MUST MOVE NOW. IT IS GOD'S WILL. SEND ME
> YOU DETAILS.
> OMAR

I'll be honest: In the two days since I'd last heard from Omar, my feelings toward him had cooled slightly. And paranoia had set in. What if he wasn't *really* the son of a murdered sultan? What if he was just after my bank account details? Neither did I like this fresh talk of international travel and gifts for mysterious strangers. It felt like next he'd be telling me I had pretty hair, and could I please look into marriage visas.

Dear Omar,

Is it really necessary for me to travel to Holland with cash gifts for your father's associates? I mean, I'm essentially saying yes, but could you perhaps loan me a million or so for the time being and take it out of my final cut? I'll pay for the flight and stuff and keep the receipts in a special envelope.

Cheers!

Danny

I pressed Send and hoped that my e-mail would at least find Omar well. He was probably just excited, poor chap. After all, he'd be moving house soon, and that's quite an exciting thing. I suppose if worse came to worse, I could stump up for the cash gifts. I had a few grand I'd managed to save up due to basically never leaving the house, and I could always use that. So long as it didn't turn out to be one of those Nigerian e-mail scams you hear so much about.

Nah. I was just being cynical. And Yes was about not being that way.

The following morning there was no word from Omar. I decided not to worry about it. I had a few chores to do in town and so set off for the shops.

Now, you'd think that this would be quite a risky business, when you've decided to say yes to invitations, offers, and suggestions, but I'm pleased to tell you that the modern-day advertiser has missed a vital trick. It seems the more "sophisticated" they think they've gotten, the less direct questions they ask, and the fewer direct suggestions they make. In the old days, of course, I'd have been utterly surrounded by easy-to-follow instructions, such as "Drink milk" or "Buy bread," and would have spent my days both drinking milk and buying bread. But nowadays, with their aspirational photo shoots and subliminal messages, they were missing out on the simpleton market—the people like me, who'd do as they say, if only they said it.

Ha. They'd never get me now, I thought as I walked out of the Virgin Megastore with my BUY 2 GET 1 FREE bag of DVDs, and started to cross the road toward Picadilly Circus.

I fancied another walk around London today, seeing where the wind took me and letting life lead the way. I crossed the road as a stiff wind cleaned the streets and battered the tourists, and noticed that up ahead of me there appeared to be a small group of leafletters. I suddenly felt a little wary; I'd already adopted two grannies. I didn't need any more—unless I was thinking of starting up some kind of pensioner-crèche facility. But nevertheless I continued to walk toward them, and, once I noted a total absence of green bibs or clipboards, took a leaflet from a girl in a summery dress and auburn hair.

SAY YES TO PEACE

I read it again. It still read, SAY YES TO PEACE. It seemed oddly appropriate. Like it was a sign of some kind. A sign that saying yes was the way ahead.

Come together *now*! Greet someone new today—smile, say hello, shake their hand, and let the peace begin. . . .

Well, that was nice. And so I did what it said. I walked straight up to the person who had given it to me, I smiled, I said hello, I shook their hand, and I waited for the peace to begin.

"I'm Katherine," she said.

"Danny," I said.

And then I let life lead the way.

Katherine, Josh, and Mike are three people who share a love of peace.

"It's all about making connections with people," said Katherine. "If you can make people understand peace, you are quite literally giving them the world."

Katherine is also someone who says "quite literally" a lot.

"It quite literally gets up my nose that people just walk around, when they could be making a difference."

If they were quite literally getting up her nose when they were walking around, then I would suggest she's probably standing a little too close to them.

"We believe in something called 'social acupuncture,'" said Mike, the tallest of the three, and the man who'd printed out the leaflets. "You can make a difference with a single conversation."

"It's all about spreading a message," added Josh, who was wearing quite a smart baseball cap and a Nike top and didn't really look like he belonged there. "You can give people hope, if they know you can create peace."

Katherine nodded. I got the sense that she was the driving force behind the team. We were standing near the Eros statue in the middle of Picadilly Circus, and I didn't really know where things were heading. But I liked the three of them. They seemed genuinely committed to spreading peace through the considerate use of leaflets.

"What do you think of the war in Iraq?" said Josh, clearly testing me.

"Well . . . war is bad," I said, and he and Mike nodded.

"Sometimes a simple message like that can be the most powerful," said Katherine.

"Feel free to use it," I said, hoping perhaps that "War Is Bad" might be the next "in" slogan.

"Thanks," said Josh, and I realised that maybe it could.

"Would you be interested in helping us spread that message?"

It had all happened rather quickly, but now here I was standing in the middle of Picadilly Circus with a Virgin Megastore bag in one hand and my very own bunch of SAY YES TO PEACE leaflets in the other. Bloody hell! I had left the house a normal man. I would return as a *peace activist*!

Katherine, Josh, and Mike were very pleased and were enthusiastically showing me how it was done.

"Do you like peace, sir?" said Katherine, to one middle-aged man who simply strode past her, putting one hand up to bat away her leaflet.

"Say yes to peace," said Josh to a lady holding a phone in one hand and a shopping bag in the other, and who didn't really look like she wanted to stop and chat about bringing about world peace. I imagine that kind of attitude quite literally wound Katherine right up.

I managed to give a man a leaflet. I was quite pleased with myself and watched him walk away reading it, but then he stopped and turned around.

"What does this bit mean?" he said. He pointed it out to me, and I read it.

War is a state of the flickering human mind—fear breeding fear breeding fear, feeding back over and over throughout time, reinforcing myths of self-justification.

I hmmed. The man looked at me. I read it again.

"To be honest I'm not really sure *what* that means," I said. "I think it essentially means that . . . war is bad."

He handed the leaflet back to me.

"Deep," he said with more than a hint of sarcasm in his voice, and I felt terrible for letting Katherine and the others down. My slogan was obviously rubbish. So I looked at the leaflet, and said, "Be the change that you want to see in this world!" and smiled. I wasn't sure if I was doing this social acupuncture thing very well. Judging by the look on the back of the man's head, he wasn't either.

"We're going to chalk for peace in a bit," said Katherine after ten minutes or so. "Up for it?"

"Yes!" I said. "What's chalking for peace?"

"We get some chalk and write antiwar slogans all over the place," said Josh.

"Like where?"

"Pavements, mainly," said Katherine.

"Does it work?" I asked.

"Yes," Katherine said matter-of-factly. "Of course it does."

"Got the chalk," said Mike, striding purposefully into the group. "Here you go . . ."

He handed out three pieces of chalk each. I got a red one, a white one, and a blue one. Perfect, I thought. The colours of the Union Jack *and* the Stars and Stripes. Now I could *really* let those governments know how I felt.

But what to write?

Katherine, Mike, and Josh were already hunched over or squatting or sitting down, letting the world have it.

"Katherine, what should I write?" I said, genuinely lost for inspiration.

"Write what you said earlier."

"'War Is Bad'? I think it might be a bit *too* simple," I said.

"Well . . . I like writing 'Our New World Order Is Love.'"

"Yes, that's nice," I said and then looked to see what the others were writing.

Mike was writing "Anti Breeds Anti," which sounded a bit too close to incest for my liking, and Josh was writing "We Are All Responsible."

"Just write what you feel," said Katherine. "Look at the leaflet or something. We get a lot of our stuff from the Web site. We share our consciousness."

"That's quite good," I said. "'Share Your Consciousness!'"

Katherine didn't look too sure.

I thought about it some more. Write what you feel? What did I *feel*?

I decided to write MAKE TEA, NOT WAR.

It'd been *hours* since my last cup.

Katherine crept up behind me.

"That's good," she said. "'Make Tea, Not War.' Tea is a conduit to conversation. It is a peaceful action. When we make tea, we make conversation and through conversation, we can stop war. Guys! Look what Danny's written!"

Mike and Josh jogged over.

"'Make Tea, Not War,'" said Mike.

"Tea . . . ," said Josh. "War." And then he smiled and nodded. "It's a bit like 'Make Love, Not War,' but with tea."

"Yes," I said. "It's a more British version. A little less rude."

"What made you think of that?" asked Mike.

"I . . . like making tea." I shrugged. "And I don't like . . . making war."

I don't think I'd been quite meaningful enough for them, so I tried harder.

"And also, tea is a conduit to conversation. And conversation . . . can stop wars."

"Tea *is* a conduit to conversation," said Josh. "Hence the tea ceremonies of ancient Japan or the tea gardens of seventeenth-century Holland."

I nodded and pointed at him, like that was *exactly* what I'd meant.

Mike clapped his hands together a couple of times and said, "Brilliant," and went straight off to write MAKE TEA, NOT WAR on the side of a wall. Katherine looked at me proudly. I suddenly felt like I was doing my bit.

"'Make Tea, Not War,'" said Katherine. "You're good."

"I'm quite good with social campaigning," I admitted. "I intend to one day write a song entitled 'Stop the Mugging, Start the Hugging.'"

"That's really *nice*," said Katherine, who I think may have been falling in love with me slightly. "Could I take your details?"

Yep. She *definitely* was.

"Because my girlfriend and I run regular songwriting workshops."

Oh.

Katherine had been very thorough when she'd taken my details. She'd wanted to know my home address, home telephone number, e-mail address, mobile number, and whether or not I had access to a fax machine. I told her what she wanted to know. I trusted her and Mike and Josh. They seemed good sorts. Out to change the world, but doing it quietly and with chalk. And anyway, it wasn't as if she was likely to try and use my details to burgle me. She'd be more likely to break in and replace all my vegetables with organic ones.

"Thank you for your help today, Danny," said Katherine.

"That's okay. I enjoyed it."

"You took to it very well. I suppose you're always helping with things, are you?"

"Not really," I said, shrugging. "But you asked, and so I thought I would. Oh . . . hang on, though. There's another man I'm helping at the moment. A sultan. Well, the son of a sultan."

The others looked impressed, and they were right to be.

"He wrote to me to ask for my help. He needs to get forty million dollars out of Oman before he is murdered by his late father's political enemies."

"Oh," said Katherine, slowly.

"Internet scam, is it?" said Josh, and Mike elbowed him in the ribs.

"You're always so bloody negative," said Mike.

"It's not an Internet scam, actually," I said. "It is a cry for help."

Mike put his hand on my shoulder and nodded sincerely.

We were now in a pub called the Goose, a moment away from the Brixton Tube station, having taken the "Say Yes to Peace" campaign as far as it could go in Picadilly. Both Katherine and Josh (who, as it turned out, were flatmates) lived not far from here, and Mike, who'd only met them a couple of months before in this very pub, was thinking of relocating.

"It's too easy to say that the people in charge are morons," Mike said, directing the conversation at me. "Too easy to say get out of government. Instead we say yes. To peace."

Mike got a packet of fags out and offered them around. Both Katherine and Josh took one.

"It's just the best way to do things," said Katherine, topping off our glasses with a bottle of rather rough red wine. "Changing the world one person at a time."

Mike offered me a cigarette. Instantly my hand went up to indicate I was fine. It was force of habit. But then I remembered who I was and what I was doing, and I said thanks and took one.

"And positivity is the stronger message. It works. It's the only way to fight a battle, if you . . ."

She paused while Mike lit her cigarette, then Josh's, and then mine.

I sucked hard at it. I'd seen enough smokers to know the drill.

"Anyway," said Josh, cutting her off. "No is the most negative word you can say."

"Literally," said Katherine, happy for him to take over.

"And yes is the most *positive* word you can say. So we go from the double-negative 'No to War' to the double-positive 'Yes to Peace,' and you can see how much better that sounds."

I was trying to, but my throat was burning. I had, up until this point in my life, avoided cigarettes. I coughed and passed it off as an energetic nod.

"Yes, no . . . yes, no . . . I know which one *I* prefer," said Josh.

I pressed on with my cigarette, although I now wasn't really inhaling the smoke. I was just sucking it in, holding it in my mouth, and blowing it straight out again. Straight *at* people. As such I was creating an oddly smoky atmosphere. But I'll tell you what—I felt strangely cool and grown-up. I probably looked a bit like James Dean, only with glasses and watery, weeping eyes.

"But it's so hard to interest the media," said Katherine. "It's a *positive* message, you'd think they'd be up for that."

"I put in a call to BBC Bristol the other night," said Josh. "They said if we can assemble a large group there and chalk for peace, they'd probably cover it."

"That's good," said Mike.

"Have you ever thought that maybe . . . you just need to simplify your message?" I said, and the attention of the group was mine. "I mean . . . I know 'War Is Bad' is too simple, but I think maybe saying things like, you know, 'War Is the State of the Flickering Human Mind' might put a few people off."

"We got that leaflet from the Infinite Possibility Web site," said Katherine. "I actually think that's a great message."

"It is, it is," I said. "It's just that I don't really understand it."

"Well . . . ," said Josh. "Can you come up with something better?"

I now had my challenge for the evening.

Mike had bought another bottle of rough red wine and was now off playing the trivia machine. Katherine and Josh had been debating the ethics of the U.S. using oil as a wedge to gain political control over other countries, a debate I had tried to join in on until I realised that they'd both done some background reading while I'd only seen an episode of *Dead Ringers*.

I'd been doing my best to come up with a punchy new media campaign to help this brave group of peace campaigners to victory. But inspiration just wasn't coming.

"Have a go?" said Mike, back from the machine and holding out what looked like a rubbish cigarette. It was a joint.

"In *here*?" I said, looking around the pub.

"Outside," he said. "Not in here."

My God. This was a watershed moment. Could I really allow Yes to make me break the law?

Yes.

"Right," I said. "I've got it. I've absolutely got it this time. This is brilliant."

I assembled my notes, which came in the form of a beermat and, as such, didn't really require much assembling.

"Okay . . . what are we aiming for?"

"Peace," said Katherine.

"Yes, peace," I said. "But what else beforehand?"

"Media coverage," said Josh.

"Precisely. I have devised a new and original media campaign which will lead directly to the governments of this world laying down their weapons and picking up . . . I dunno . . . chalk, instead."

I had been outside the Goose, breaking the law with Mike, when it had happened. I'd looked up, seen a beautiful painting hanging from the front of the pub, and been transfixed. Utterly transfixed. The smoke had framed the painting for a moment, and it was then that the idea had struck me.

"That's it!" I'd said. "That's the message!"

"So what is it?" said Katherine.

"This has to be catchy, yes? And it has to communicate a real, social message?"

"Yes."

"Well, how about we use . . ."

I looked from person to person, anticipating their reaction.

"Geese."

I didn't get quite the reaction I'd hoped for.

"Geese?" said Josh.

"Geese," I confirmed. "'Geese for Peace.'"

I let the words hang in the air. No one said much.

"Oh, come on. 'Geese for Peace'—it's brilliant!"

Still no one said anything. I decided this might require further explanation. And despite the room appearing to spin slightly, I gave it a go.

"What we do, right," I began, "is we make tiny little signs saying, 'Geese for Peace.' And then we stick them outside geese farms and near geese in general. We then tip the media off that the geese are getting agitated about this whole war business and have started, against all the odds, to stage their own animal peace protests."

Katherine and Josh just nodded at me, openmouthed—clearly they were impressed. This was going well.

"We get some photographers down there. We secretly tell people up and down the country to make their own 'Geese for Peace' signs, and quietly stick them in the ground in farms and zoos. The media will have a field day. People *literally* won't believe it, Katherine! It will be like Mother Nature herself is rising up and saying *no* to *war*!"

Katherine put her hand up to correct me.

"*Yes* to *peace*."

"Sorry. But it will be like the geese themselves are making a stand. Imagine it! Geese, the world over, saying yes to peace!"

"I like it," said Mike, who was clearly on my level although I couldn't help but suspect he was a little stoned. Lucky *I* wasn't, or we wouldn't have "Geese for Peace."

"But why geese?" said Josh.

"It rhymes with 'peace'!" Mike and I said, in near unison.

"Ohh," said Katherine, obviously finally realising the brilliance of my scheme.

And then—quite out of the blue—I had *another* excellent idea.

"Hey, Mike," I said. "Imagine this . . . What if there was a shop called Pizza Hat . . . and all it sold were *hats* shaped like *pizzas*?!"

And then Mike started to giggle, and then so did I, and then we couldn't stop ourselves, and we laughed like mentals, and I hit my hand down on the table and nearly knocked over the wine, and Mike laughed even more, and we both started to virtually cry with laughter at the thought of hats shaped like pizzas.

"Pizza *Hat*!" Mike exclaimed. "Hit the Hat!"

Yep. He was definitely stoned.

And then we talked about my brilliant "Geese for Peace" idea a bit more.

An hour or so later as I stumbled home, I realised that maybe the effects of the little disco cigarette I'd had with Mike had affected me in more ways than I'd previously thought. Once home I decided that a nice cup of tea was what I needed most in this world. So I started to make one. It took a lot longer than it usually did, and I found the plume of steam that rose from the kettle so fascinating and beautiful that I must've watched it boil three times before even trying to find a tea bag.

When eventually I did, I got the milk out the fridge and found a spoon, which I promptly dropped. It clattered on the floor.

As I stooped to pick it up, I suddenly realised this was it. *This* was my invention.

A spoon you couldn't drop!

A spoon . . . that hovers!

That'd be amazing! But how would I make it hover?

Tiny fans, maybe?

Yes, that's it! Dozens of tiny fans attached to the underside of a spoon.

I ran to my desk and started to make some rudimentary sketches. I was buzzing. I had just invented the hover spoon! Oh, how the offices of the Patent & Trademark Institute of America would stop and applaud when news of the hover spoon spread! And best of all we could do spin-off spoons . . . teaspoons, table spoons . . . even a huge, hovering ladle!

I phoned Ian.

"Hello?"

"Ian, it's Danny!"

"How's it going?"

"Not bad—listen. What would you say if I told you you could have a spoon"—I paused to allow him time to picture a spoon—"that could *hover*!"

Ian didn't say anything. Well, clearly, he had some pretty big thinking to do. Ian always thought he knew where he was with spoons, but
I'd just messed with his preconceptions. The boundaries of cutlery
had been given a severe kick into the future, and I think Ian knew
that. I was a revolutionary, passing on my insight and vision to, well,
a *normal* person. I mean, *you're* a normal person. What would *you* do
if a visionary like me phoned you up and told you he'd invented the
hover spoon?

And then I realised Ian had hung up.

I decided that my so-called equal, Ian, was just too caught up in
convention. He was still living with a very 1990s view of spoons (and
cutlery in general to be honest), and if you ever meet him, I'd like you
to promise me that you'll point that out to him.

Moodily I switched my computer on and checked my e-mails.

Omar had written to me again. And he sounded antsy.

```
DEAR danny
   BUT WHAT IS THE ACCOUNT DETAILS. I MUST HAVE THE DETAIL
SO I CAN GIVE YOU THE MONEY. WHAT ARE THE ACCOUNT DETAILS.
GIVE THEM TO ME.
   IT IS GOD'S WILL!
   OMAR
```

I made a "harumph" sound, I drank my tea, I ate an inexplicably
large amount of toast, and then I went to bed.

"You're going to do *what*?" said Ian, slamming his pint down on the
table.

It was the next day, and I was seeking his advice.

"I'm going to give Omar my bank account details."

"You're going to give him your details! Oh, brilliant! First the
hover spoon, now this. Two of the worst ideas in the world in just
twenty-four short hours . . ."

I thought it best not to mention the peace geese, which, for some
odd reason, had lost some of its power overnight.

"Well, what if I don't give him my savings account details? What if

I started a brand-new account into which he can deposit his many millions of dollars? I have to help him."

"But *why*?"

"He seems very insistent. The poor lad is about to be murdered by his late father's political enemies, Ian!"

"It's a scam, Dan!"

"Oh, not *you* as well," I said wisely and with some degree of pity in my voice. "I have experience of scammers, my friend. And if this is a scam, then it's a bloody clever one."

"Danny, of *course* it's a scam! I've seen stuff like this on *Watchdog*! They send out thousands of e-mails, and if you respond, they know the e-mail address is real, and then you get loads more of them. All they need is one person like you—a person who says yes when they should blatantly say no! They're going to try and rip you off!"

"Listen here, Mr. Cynical. I was like you once. Not so long ago I would have *definitely* thought it was a scam too. But this whole Yes Man thing has started to teach me the benefits of thinking positively. I should trust my fellow man. Approach things with optimism. Treat people like they're already friends. And is it *really* too far-fetched to suggest that the murdered sultan of Oman, whom I never met, used to speak of me with such affection that his son, facing a possible murder plot by the same men who killed his father, might want to get in touch with me, Danny Wallace, in order to secure the safety of forty million dollars?"

"Of *course* it's too far-fetched, you fucking idiot!"

Sometimes I pity the cynical.

"He's invited me to his house, Ian. I hardly think he'd invite me to his house if he were planning on scamming me before I even got there. It'd make dinnertime a little awkward, don't you think? He just wants a little of my professionalism in business."

"*What* professionalism in business? You can't even use a stapler properly! This was all done by e-mail, wasn't it?"

"Of course. Omar is lying low at the moment. He had to set up a free e-mail account so that he was in no way traceable. You know. By his enemies, and others."

"And he's asked you for your bank account details?"

"Yes. And to travel to Holland with cash gifts for his late father's business associates."

"Anything else?"

"My phone number."

"And I suppose you gave that to him as well, did you?"

"Ian, it is God's will! And anyway, this is incredibly liberating. I feel like I don't have to make any choices anymore. Everything's done for me."

"Look . . . I forbid you from giving this man your bank account details. Okay?"

"You can't forbid me from stuff! What are you going to do? Tell my mum and dad?"

"If I have to."

"*Please* don't tell my mum and dad."

"This Yes thing is a little dangerous, Dan. I thought all you'd be saying yes to would be nights down at the pub and perhaps lending me a tenner now and then. I didn't realise you'd be doing things like this. This is dangerous. And it could get out of hand—these e-mail things often do. You're lucky Omar is the only one who's asked for your details. . . ."

I didn't say anything.

It dawned on Ian.

"Other people have asked you, haven't they? Oh, Danny, no . . . who else has asked you for your bank account details?"

The fact of the matter was *loads* of people had suddenly asked me for my bank account details. And word of my willingness to help Omar, son of the murdered sultan of Oman, must have spread in some pretty royal circles.

In the days that had followed our initial exchange, I was contacted by people like His Highness Shaik Isa Bin Sulman al Khalifa, Emir of the State of Bahrain, who had apparently heard some pretty good things about me and wanted me to be his property manager abroad in return for a share of one hundred and twenty million dollars.

And let's not forget King Asiam Okofonachi of the Aziam village deep down in the Accra native clans and the great-great-grandson of the mighty warrior legend Okofonachi. King Asiam had just been told

he had one month left to live and while he was dealing with that just
fine, he was nevertheless determined not to leave his huge gold fortune
to his two sons, because "they are involved with drug sniffings and harlot doings." He was happy, however, for a random stranger like me to
have his money—provided I promised not to spend it on drug sniffings
and harlot doings. Oh, and P.S.: Could I please pop over to Ghana and
bring lots of money for, you know, setup costs and that.

Actually, hang on. These were *definitely* scams, weren't they.

No. Wait. *Trust in Yes.*

"Right. Okay," said Ian, rubbing the bridge of his nose in the way
that slightly weary teachers who wear glasses often do, just to show
you that they care, and they're a lot more intelligent than you. "And
you didn't find it suspicious at all that kings and emirs and bloody
Dukes of Hazzard were all suddenly e-mailing you out-of-the-blue
and claiming you're their saviour and then asking for your bank
account details?"

"I thought it was unusual, yes, but optimism is . . ."

"*Unusual?* Danny, they're all claiming to be billionaires, and
yet they write their own bloody e-mails, and they use bloody
Hotmail!"

I made a grumpy face. What was it about me that Ian thought sultans, emirs, and kings wouldn't want a part of?

"Listen," I said. "When Omar, son of the murdered sultan, comes
good and hands me my share of forty million dollars—"

"Who have you sent your details to?"

"No one yet—I'm thinking of doing a mass mailing . . ."

"You're not!"

"I am! But Omar was first. He should—"

"Dan. Just tell me. What's this Omar's e-mail address?"

He was looking at me, sternly. I found it a bit frightening.

"If you're saying you can't get out of this, Dan, then maybe I
should do it for you—before you get beaten up by a couple of sultans
in a Dutch hotel room . . ."

I nodded, silently.

"So . . . what's the address?"

• • •

To: Omar

From: Ian

Subject: Bad News

Dear Omar,

I take the pleasure to get associated with you and desire to introduce myself, requesting for your expert advises and immediate line of action.

I am Ian, friend of Danny.

This morning Danny was arrested for a crime he did not commit and is now in a big jail. Before they took him away, he talked of you with great affection and trust.

He has entrusted me with his affairs, and I have noticed that he has over £1,000 in his bank account. It is my opinion that his mum will try and take this off him as she has access to his bank account details too.

I wish to flee the country and move to somewhere like Oman, where I could live with you in your Sultanate.

If you help me move this £1,000 into a safe foreign bank account then for your troubles I am prepared to give you 25% (£250).

It may be necessary for you to travel to Holland to present gifts to some of Danny's mates. They're not fussy; buy them a Toblerone at the airport or something. It is God's will, etc.

Please my brother we must move quickly. His mum is closing in.

Send me your bank details. I trust you 100%.

Ian

P.S. This is not an e-mail scam.

And that, my friends, is how Ian bloody Collins lost me ten million dollars.

And not just ten million dollars. But the share of one hundred and twenty million dollars that the shaik had offered me. And the eighty-seven million dollars worth of gold that the king had waved my way. And nearly two hundred million dollars more from other assorted dignitaries in apparent need of a little of the Wallace magic.

Ian had come around that night and, after e-mailing Omar (who I hope wasn't too annoyed and was indeed fibbing about the whole murder plot thing) set me up with a powerful junk-mail filter. Now, he said, I wouldn't have to worry about spam anymore. I could concentrate on the *proper* Yes opportunities, he said. Like going to the pub and lending him tenners.

Omar never wrote back. But I was grateful to Ian.

"Look at these," he said, clicking from Web site to Web site. "These show you the stories behind the scams. Some of them are lucky and just lose a few grand after paying ridiculous 'set-up' costs that don't exist. Some of them end up heading off to Holland where they're told they'll be able to pick up their money. They're met by a representative of the king or the emir or the bloody sultan, fleeced for all their money, and in some cases beaten to a pulp."

"But I thought Holland was so laid back!" I said. "Why are they beating people to a pulp? It doesn't seem right, somehow."

"It's the European capital of scams, Dan. And of big men who beat you up."

"But who are they?"

"Thugs, mainly. I mean, many of them are harmless. But some are gangs. Drug gangs, linked to organised crime."

I shuddered.

"That could have happened to me! Omar asked me if going to Holland would have been possible! I would've gone! I would've been beaten up by a burly drug gang!"

"That's why I'm saying, Dan . . . Look, maybe this Yes thing has gone far enough already. What are you learning here? What have you done so far of worth?"

I was confused. But I shook my head.

"No, Ian. That Yes happened for a reason. And you were there to ward it off. You saved me. And anyway, it won't happen again, will it?"

"It shouldn't. The junk-mail filter is on maximum. Just avoid the bloody Internet, Danny. You'll get stuck in a rut. You'll be falling for scams and buying penis patches and saying yes to any old nut job who can find your address. Avoid your bloody e-mails."

I nodded.

"Fine."

"And remember—one no is all I need to unleash the full and ter-rifying power of . . . the Punishment!"

I looked him in the eye.

"You haven't thought of a punishment yet, have you?"

He shook his head.

"No."

Ian was right. I had to avoid my computer. It was nothing but a world of risky Yeses in a neat little box. That wasn't what I wanted. I wanted safety. Security. Comfort. A world without risk or challenge.

So I drank my tea, and I stayed in the kitchen, and I vowed to not look at my computer once.

And then I walked into the living room, switched it on, and checked my e-mails. There were two: one from Tom at the BBC, reminding me of the next day's development meeting, for which I should bring plenty of ideas and energy. And the other from Brian the Starburster:

> Danny,
>
> I have some interesting information for you. . . . Are you free to meet me at the New Clifton Bengali Restaurant on Whitechapel Road tomorrow night at 6 p.m.? Just next to Aldgate Tube. Do say yes . . .
>
> Brian

Oh, bollocks. Ian had been right. Now I'd have to spend another entire evening talking about aliens and pyramids again. Maybe all this *was* pointless.

I thought about what to write back. But then I noticed that Brian hadn't quite finished his e-mail.

I scrolled down.

And I was intrigued.

> P.S. It concerns your man on the bus.

CHAPTER 7

In Which Daniel Proposes a Theory, Attends a Party, and Vexes a Rival

I didn't know precisely what Brian wanted to tell me about the man on the bus. It seemed strange to me that he had anything to tell at all. The man on the bus was, after all, just a man on a bus. But I'd written back to Brian almost immediately, and told him that, yes, I would meet him at the curryhouse in order to hear his very important information. It was an odd Yes to be saying, but that was fine by me. Odd Yeses still counted—they all did, whatever their level.

Because yes, Yeses come on levels. There are, in fact, several levels of Yes. The Yes levels (yevels) are everywhere (yeverywhere), and they do their best to help us along in our everyday lives.

The Five Levels of Yes
Level One
The easy level. This is saying yes to questions such as "Would you like some free money?," "How about one for the road?," "Would you like to see a picture of a pony?," and "Why don't you take the rest of the day off?"

Level Two
The still-quite-easy level. Level two is only slightly trickier. It's saying yes to doing that hilarious impression you do. Saying yeah, okay, I'll tape that thing on BBC2 tonight for you. It's saying yes, of course I'll make you a cup of coffee, and what's more, I don't necessarily expect a coffee back one day, either.

Level Three
The making-an-effort level. It's level three, and things are getting harder. But not so hard that you'd want to make a fuss about them—that's the

beauty of level three. It's saying yes to the party you don't really want to go to—and then actually going to it. It's saying yes to going for a drink after work, when really, what you want to do is watch *The Weakest Link* and eat a samosa. It's saying yes to anything that requires a journey of more than forty minutes, and/or more than one change of bus. It's agreeing to accompany an elderly aunt to the toilet and not running off when she shouts, "I'm finished!"

Level Four
The too-much-effort level. Ah, level four. Our old enemy. This is saying yes to attending a Christening—*any* Christening. Yes to anything that involves modern dance or having to make and bring your own canapés. It's saying yes to something you know will feel awkward doing; it's saying yes when what you really want to say is absolutely not.

Level Five
The forget-it level. Most of us never attain level five status. This is saying yes to attending a wedding. In Mozambique. It's saying yes to going to a terrible dinner party on the other side of town that you know you're not welcome at because the last time you were there you insulted someone's wife and were sick in the hostess's shoes. And it's fancy dress. And Claire Sweeney will be there. It's anything involving planes. Anything involving pains. Anything that you totally, utterly, wholeheartedly can't, won't, or mustn't say yes to. *That*, my friend, is level five.

I reasoned that so far, in my adventure, I'd been hovering pretty much around level three . . . and that was fine by me. Like I'd said to Ian, this was still early days. December 31 was still months away. But things were chugging along quite nicely. I was making an effort. Getting back out there. Saying yes to things I usually just couldn't be arsed to do. It was all pretty much level three stuff, but level three was where I was happiest. It just felt right, and I felt better. Other people, too, were remarking upon the sudden change they'd seen in me.

Wag was delighted that I was out and about more now. He'd begun to realise that all he'd have to do was pick up the phone, and I'd be there, in a flash and a jiffy, unless, of course, I'd said yes to being somewhere else . . . but rules are rules: a little bit of effort, and I'd usually be able to swing both. Wag was touched, and I wasn't going to disillusion him. I'd also been able to catch up with friends I hadn't seen in ages—just because I was now usually in town on an evening and could get pretty much anywhere, quickly. And so I caught up with Carl and Stefan and Nerys and Nathan and Dara and Nina and Noel and more.

It was 4 p.m., and I was walking out of BBC Television Centre with a spring in my step. My second development meeting had gone incredibly well. I mean, *ridiculously* well.

Fair enough; most of my ideas had been poo-poohed before I'd even finished saying the titles, and after a couple of them I'd sensed a few people in the room actually struggling not to boo, but as far as I was concerned, I'd managed to say yes to almost everything I was asked about, and as such, I deemed the meeting an outright success. Plus quite a few mediocre ideas and at least three awful ones had been saved from the dustbin thanks to a little bit of blind positivity.

I'm paraphrasing, but after the meeting Tom had told me he liked me. I was fresh, he said. And not cynical and jaundiced like most of the people who came to these things. I wasn't dismissive. In fact—and I'm still paraphrasing here—I was the opposite! I was a *nurturer* of ideas. I was *positive*.

"You *understand*," he said. "That no idea is a bad idea. And even bad ones can lead to a good one. That's what development is all about."

I was smiling rather widely. All I'd done was approach things in an incredibly positive manner and look what was happening: I was being lavished with praise!

"Just out of curiosity," said Tom, "what kind of contract have you got with the radio department?"

"A couple of days a week at the moment . . . just while I'm looking for new projects, so . . ."

"And what do you do the rest of the week?"

I drink tea, Tom, and I write to sultans.

"Oh, you know . . . this and that."

"Have you ever thought about working over here for a while?"

"Sorry?"

"We've got a space on one of our teams. We need someone like you, I think. Someone who can come in and bring a sense of positive energy to the room."

Wow! Positive energy!

"Can you send me your résumé?"

"Yes," I said.

"Good. You've proved you're a natural developer. You can take an idea and run with it. I mean, okay, you ran in a pretty weird direction with that *How to Get Fat* idea, and what you got out of it wasn't brilliant, but . . ."

"Hey," I said, raising my finger. "There's no such thing as a bad idea!"

"Precisely, Danny. Apart maybe from that one case. But all I'm saying is consider coming on board."

"Okay," I said. "I will."

"So where are you off to now?" said Tom.

"I'm off to meet a man about a bus," I said.

The New Clifton Bengali Restaurant is on Whitechapel Road, just a stone's throw from the Blind Beggar pub—the place I'd last met Brian and learned all about how aliens had built the pyramids.

Brian was already there when I arrived.

"Hello!" I said, happily taking a seat.

"Danny, hello," he said, "thanks for coming. I assume it's because you're still saying yes more?"

"No, no," I said, because I didn't want to be rude and make him think that was the only reason I'd shown up. "Well . . . yes."

"That's fine. Because it would appear you are doing the right thing."

"Am I?"

He nodded.

There was a brief silence. I wasn't sure whose turn it was to speak next. But Brian didn't say anything, so I decided it was probably mine.

"So . . . what's up? Shall we order something?"

Brian caught the eye of a waiter, and we ordered some curry.

When the waiter disappeared, Brian tapped his fingers on the table and then, slightly coy I thought, said: "Danny, over the weekend I did a little research . . . just a few Internet sites and so on, but I thought it was worth sharing the information with you."

"What kind of research?" I said, knowing all too well that when grown men use the words "research" and "Internet" in the same sentence, a court case usually follows soon after.

"I was reminded of something, that was all. When you told me— us—about the man you met on the bus that night, Laura made reference to the Maitreya. . . ."

"Yeah, but that's not real, though . . . I mean, you said it yourself . . ."

"Yes, but I also said it is good to keep an open mind on things. So . . . could you just run what happened by me again?"

This was all a bit odd. What I'd told them about the man on the bus seemed pretty clear. A man on a bus said something to me. And that was it. But nevertheless, I obliged . . .

"Um . . . well, I was sitting on a bus, next to this man, and . . . ."

"What did he look like?"

"He was an Asian guy. And he had a beard."

Brian turned over a small piece of paper that had been facedown on the table and held it up to me.

"Is this him?"

I couldn't really tell. The picture had been printed from the Internet and was black-and-white and rather blurry. It was of an Asian-looking man with a beard, wearing a white robe, and standing in a large crowd of people. It was subtitled "Kenya, 1988." I was amazed. Brian had brought props!

"I'm not sure . . . ," I said, and I could see faint disappointment in Brian's face, so I took another look, keen to be as helpful as possible. "I suppose the *beard* looks quite similar."

Brian closed his eyes and signalled for me to continue.

"Anyway . . . we were talking about this and that and about what we'd done with our weeks, and I mentioned how I was basically staying in all the time and turning things down, and he said, 'So say yes more.'"

Brian frowned.

"And that was that? You just started saying yes more after that?"

"Yes."

"And is it working? What's happened?"

"Well . . . I've been having fun. I've been out a lot more, and I've met new people, and I'm off to a party later, and I nearly won twenty-five thousand pounds. I bought a steam cleaner, and my career seems to be benefiting too, so . . . yes."

Brian folded his arms and leaned forward in his chair.

"This may sound a little outlandish to you, Danny, but what if I were to tell you that there is a school of thought which suggests that Jesus himself is alive and well and living not five minutes from here in Brick Lane?"

"Er . . . I don't know *what* I'd say to that," I said. "I suppose I'd say: Is he?"

Brian sat back in his chair.

"Jesus. The Christ. Boddhisvata. The Iman Madhi. Krishna. Maitreya. Call him what you will. But yes, he is. According to some, anyway."

"And . . . what's this got to do with me?" I said as politely as I could, because it suddenly appeared you never knew *where* Jesus might be sitting.

"Maitreya, as we shall call him, has been living among the Pakistani-Indian community of Brick Lane since the 19 of July 1977, according to my research. He is what they call a master of wisdom, come here to oversee and to teach. He is a spokesman for justice and sharing."

I considered what Brian was telling me.

"He's been quite quiet," I said. "For a spokesman, I mean."

"No, Danny, he hasn't. Apparently, he has been actively working among us these twenty-five years and lives in the world today along with several other masters of wisdom. And those masters are training people, and touching their lives, and changing the world."

"And . . . how do they do that?"

"I'll get to that. But according to those in the know, around eighteen and a half million years ago, a group of beings from planets like Venus were brought to Earth to help us get started . . ."

"Can I just stop you there for a moment," I said, but as it turned out I couldn't.

"I'm not saying I believe this, Danny, I'm just saying this is what is believed. They have lived among us for a millennium in some of the most remote areas of the world—the Himalayas, the Rocky Mountains, the Gobi Desert, the Andes, for example—and they have taken care of us from afar. But now, masters like Maitreya are said to live among us. There's a master in New York, one in Geneva, one in Darjeeling, and another in Tokyo. Along with Maitreya in London, of course."

"Right," I said although I wasn't really sure that it was. "And you're saying that I've met him?"

"No," he said. "I am saying some would say it is possible you met him."

"But why me?"

Brian shrugged.

"Why not? Now, again: I'm not saying I believe all this. But to show you how seriously he is taken, in 1984 it was promised that Maitreya would show himself to the world's media. Reporters from all over the world turned up to hear what the great one had to say. The *Telegraph*, the *Observer*, the *Sun*, they were all there."

"Where?"

Brian raised his eyebrows and opened his arms.

"The New Clifton Bengali Restaurant."

Huh?

"Here?" I said, utterly amazed. "It was *here*?"

"Well, no. The New Clifton Bengali Restaurant used to be on Wentworth Street."

"Oh."

"But it's here now."

It wasn't quite the same.

"Why did he choose to reveal himself in a Bengali restaurant in the East End of London?" I asked.

"I don't know," said Brian, slightly testily, batting my question away like it was the first thing people *always* asked. "Anyway, the journalists were assured that Maitreya would make his entrance, and then announce his message to the world."

"And what was his message?"

"Well . . . he never showed up, so no one knows."

I was starting to wonder why Brian had insisted we meet at the New Clifton Bengali Restaurant—a restaurant that wasn't even the same New Clifton Bengali Restaurant as the one that a man *hadn't* shown up in twenty years earlier. I mean, there were *millions* of places that weren't even the same place as the one that a man hadn't shown up in twenty years earlier. There was my flat, for example, or Bristol.

"Anyway, it was announced later that despite not appearing at the New Clifton Bengali Restaurant because the time wasn't right, he would be continuing his work here on Earth of overseeing the evolution of"—he pointed at me— "lesser people."

I didn't know whether to be grateful or annoyed. On the one hand it's quite nice to think that if he does indeed exist, Maitreya chose *me* to oversee that night. But on the other I can't help but feel a little peeved that out of all the people living in London today, *I'm* the one he decided was that little bit less evolved than all the others. But I was finding it all a little hard to believe. I decided to call Brian's bluff.

"Well . . . if Maitreya lives on Brick Lane, why don't we pop around? We could go there now and say hello, and I could see if it *was* the same bloke after all."

"I don't know where his flat is," said Brian, shrugging and ripping a piece of naan in two. "I know it's above a shop, and I know it's near a temple, but that's all I know. To be honest, I'm no great expert. But . . . I'd like you to meet someone who *is* . . ."

At this point it would have been *brilliant* if Brian had pointed at the door behind me, a jaunty tune had started up, and Maitreya himself had walked in waving, like we were all on some kind of very spiritual chat show. But he didn't, and I felt a little bit like how I imagine those journalists must have felt in 1984.

Instead Brian just said, "Pete."

"Pete?"

"Pete. He's a sometime-Starburster and an expert on this kind of thing. What I know about Maitreya I learnt from Pete."

"I suppose you think I should meet with Pete, then," I said.

"Yes," said Brian.

I left the restaurant that night rather confused. I wasn't entirely convinced that the man I'd met on the bus that night *had* been Maitreya. Fair enough, he'd had a beard just like Maitreya. And fair enough, he was a teacher just like Maitreya was the "World Teacher" (which seems rather ambitious—the marking alone must be a job in itself).

Still, I'd given Brian the go-ahead to give my details to Pete, and I was told to expect a call within the next week or so, once Pete had "checked me out."

I arrived at Robert the technician's party at eight on the dot.

Amazingly it was already in full swing. There were people in the kitchen, people on the landing, people already leaving. This just wasn't right. Whenever I've organised a party and told people to turn up at eight, the first ninety minutes have usually consisted of me and a bowl of nuts. But no. Here we all were. In quite a swanky apartment.

"Nice place, Robert," I said, impressed. I'd always imagined Robert living on the set of *Robot Wars*. But no. He had taste. And style.

"It's my brother's pad."

Ah.

Robert and I walked into the living room, and now there were more people, sitting on dining-room chairs in a near perfect circle.

"Everyone, this is Danny."

"Hello, everyone," I said.

"Hello," said everyone back.

Robert sat down and so did I.

"Right," he said. "Facts."

Oh, bollocks. I'd forgotten to bring my fact with me. What did I know? What did I know that no one else knew? How was I supposed to stump a stranger? I hadn't realised this was going to be so . . . *formal*.

"Here's mine!" said a girl called Rosie. "The call of the Howler Monkey can be heard at a distance of up to ten miles."

She looked very pleased with herself, and the group made appreciative noises. Cripes. Mine was going to have to be good to compete with that one.

"Okay, my turn," said the man to her right.

Shit. What was I going to say? What did I know? I've got loads of great facts . . . facts about lions, facts about helicopters . . . but what *were* they?

"The national flag of Italy was designed by Napoléon Bonaparte."

A couple of people said, "Really?" and the man nodded enthusiastically as if he'd discovered it through a detailed research expedition of his own.

"Who's next?" said Robert.

Why did we have to break the ice at the *start* of the party? Why couldn't we all just ignore one another until midnight or so, and then drunkenly make friends just as the taxis were arriving?

"I'll go . . . ," said a girl in a pink top. "Right . . . If a statue of a person on a horse has its front legs in the air, then the person died in battle. If the horse has one front leg in the air, the person died as a result of wounds *received* in battle. Finally if the horse has all four legs on the ground, then the person on top of it died of *natural* causes."

This bloody *stormed* it. The girl was suddenly the most popular person in the room. And all through knowing a bit of otherwise useless trivia.

"Danny?" said Robert. "What's your fact?"

Right. Quick. Come up with something. But my mind went blank.

"Danny?"

Think!

"Since, er, since the first McDonald's restaurant opened . . . in, er, 1969 . . . in a diner just off . . . California Beach . . . ," I said, adding extraneous invented details in the hope that it would give an air of confidence to wherever this was going. "The, er . . . McDonald's corporation has sold . . . *in excess* of"—I pointed my finger in the air to add a feeling of gravitas—"one *million* hamburgers."

The group looked at me in stunned silence.

And then a couple of them wrinkled their noses, and someone said, "oh" with a hint of disappointment in her voice.

"A million hamburgers?" said the girl in the pink top. "Doesn't sound like very much."

"In *excess* of," I said. "Which means more than."

There was an awkward pause. The girl in the pink top looked at me like I'd really let her down.

And then my saviour came.

"The first ready-to-eat breakfast cereal was Shredded Wheat in 1893, beating Kellogg's Corn Flakes by a full five years."

The heat was off. The group was impressed again.

The man gave me a wink.

The man who had saved me went by the name of Gareth.

"Thanks so much for that," I said. "To be honest I made that McDonald's fact up. I mean, it's *probably* true, so I wasn't *technically* lying. . . ."

"Yes," said Gareth. "I imagine the fact that they've sold more than one million hamburgers probably *is* true."

"It's a lot, isn't it?" I said, still trying to make it seem more impressive than it was.

"Yes," Gareth said, slowly. "Anyway, how's it going? Where have you come from tonight?"

"Bow," I said. "You?"

"Forest Hill. Just moved in with my girlfriend."

Gareth worked in TV as someone big in forward-planning for *Richard & Judy* on Channel 4.

"Oh!" I said. "That's a *great* show! I was *on* that once!"

And I had been. When I'd started my own cult—the cult that Hanne hadn't taken too kindly to—I'd been invited on to the *Richard & Judy* show to explain what had happened. I'd had a brilliant time, and it was one of the highlights of a very odd year.

"Yes! I saw that one!" said Gareth, which was only to be expected, seeing as he worked on it. "I thought I recognised you. Yes . . . I remember Richard saying afterward, that was such an . . . *odd* edition of the show."

Let's just say that quote won't be making it onto my résumé.

And then someone new had arrived at the party and informed the room with great gusto that in Hartford, Connecticut, you can receive a five-dollar fine if you transport a dead body using a taxi. He received a round of applause and an admiring glance from the girl in the pink top.

Gareth and I looked at each other, and I mouthed the word "bastard."

My new friend and I talked about all manner of things, and I was finding out that since I'd started my Yes experiment, I'd become a fascinating human being with new experiences to talk about and opinions on all manner of things. I told him in great detail about how men actually *can* have babies and about how I'd hung out with peace activists and come up with both the War Is Bad slogan *and* the Geese for Peace campaign that he'd probably heard about by now and about how aliens built the pyramids and how earlier that evening I'd had curry just down the road from where Jesus lives.

And he nodded and took it all in and seemed to be thinking something over in his head.

"Danny, do you have a number where I can contact you?"

And I said I did and gave it to him.

And then he said he had to be up early, but would give me a call soon about something, and he left. Maybe I wasn't as fascinating as I thought.

I decided I would never again try to tell a stranger how to cork his birth canal.

It was an hour later, and I was having a great time.

Already I'd talked to a Spanish girl who'd seen a ghost when she was four and a bloke who once owned a windmill. I had also attracted the attention of a girl who was very impressed that my friend Wag was, the very next morning, to set off for Germany with Busted.

Next up was Thom, a bloke who worked in the city but had the look of a traveller about him. And that was exactly what he was about to do. An unusual move, for a man who worked with stocks and shares.

"Of course, it's good money, but sometimes . . . you know . . . you just have to take a risk. Turn your back on the easy way. Which is what I'm doing. So I'm moving to New Zealand to do something else. Something new."

"What kind of thing?"

"I don't know yet. I've just always had a thing for New Zealand. I've got enough money to see me through the first few months to get me set up and so on . . . but I just kind of want to see what happens."

I admired Thom for this. He was someone who had it all, but had decided that he didn't need most of it.

"Wow," I said. "How long have you been planning it?"

"I've thought about it for years. But I never thought it would come to anything. And then me and my girlfriend split up, and that changed things because it was only my job tying me down after that, and I thought, sod it. I'm going to do what I want. Which means moving somewhere where the quality of life is far greater than in London."

"That's brilliant, Thom," I said. "Really brilliant. And quite . . . *inspiring.*"

And it *was* inspiring. Plus, it was a Yes. A Yes to himself. Although God knows what moving to New Zealand was in terms of yevels. Thom looked really pleased. Like a man on the verge of something. He was excited.

"So I'm basically all packed up. I've got one more week in London and then that's it. I'm off."

"Well. I wish you the best of luck with it."

"Thanks, Danny. If you're ever in New Zealand, look me up."

We clinked beer cans, and he started to walk away. What a nice bloke.

"Oh, hang on," he said and turned back toward me. "I've asked everyone else, so I may as well ask you . . . I don't suppose you'd be interested in buying a car, would you?"

Twenty-four hours later, and I had worked out that, yes, I probably could just about afford to buy a car. It would wipe out most of my

savings in one fell swoop, but with the guarantee of an overdraft (and
the promise of another contract at the BBC) it was possible.
Especially if I engaged in some hard-nosed haggling with Thom.
The problem was I didn't really know *how* to haggle. Not where cars
were concerned, anyway; I knew nothing about them. I hadn't even
asked Thom what model it was. I'd stopped when he told me it was
a Nissan. I knew my limits.

I'd been in town, working out my money situation and dropping in
at work, and was nearly at the bottom of Oxford Street, when a
bored-looking man holding a placard in one hand and a leaflet in the
other said in an accent I think was probably Spanish, "You want?"

I mouthed a "yeah, okay," and took a leaflet and strode on, glancing down to see it was for an English course at University College
London. I folded the leaflet and was about to stick it in my pocket,
when it became all too apparent that someone else had seen me take
that leaflet.

"Learn English?" said the man, holding his leaflet out at arm's length.
He'd made a special effort to stop me and said, again, "Learn English?"

I half-smiled, took the leaflet, and kept on walking, slightly
alarmed by the look in the man's eyes. I've walked down Oxford
Street plenty of times and very rarely accepted a leaflet. Mainly
because no one else ever does. I'd noticed a real hunger in that man's
eyes, replaced by instant relief when I'd taken one of his leaflets. I
kept my head down and my speed up, but moments later another
leaflet was in front of my eyes. It was for English as a foreign language
at Premier College London. I took it and then, suddenly and forcefully, there was another one from another angle. English at Academy
College. Another one came at me from over my shoulder. English at
No. 1 College. Where were all these leaflets coming from? Where
were all these dodgy colleges? Why did everyone think I needed to
learn English? I glanced up as I moved off, but I was instantly
blocked. Two men were standing in front of me, like zombies, holding out leaflets and saying the word "English." I was becoming over-
whelmed by this neverending group of well-meaning foreigners
making their minimum wage on the streets of London, so I snatched
a couple more fliers, and tried to make a dash for it, toward the Tube,

toward home, toward a world free from student zombies . . .

"Thinking of learning English, are you?" said a voice to my right.

I looked up. It was Hanne. Smiling. She'd just stepped out of Tottenham Court Road Tube.

"Hey. Shit. Hanne. Hi," I said.

"How's it going?" she said.

"Good. Yeah. Good."

I glanced down at my fistful of leaflets.

"Would you like one?" I said.

"Ah . . . no."

"I'll keep them, then," I said, stuffing them into my pockets.

"Hey . . . er . . . this may be slightly awkward, but . . . there's someone you should probably, you know, meet."

She beckoned to someone standing by the lamppost.

"Danny, this is Seb."

I looked at Seb. I looked at Hanne. What were Hanne and this man called Seb doing together? And who was Seb, anyway? It was seven o'clock. Hanne should be at home by now. She should have had her tea and be settling down to watch the news with a yoghurt.

"Oh," I said. "Hello, Seb."

"Hello, Danny," he said, and we shook hands, limply. "I've heard a lot about you."

"Oh," I said. I didn't like Seb. There was something about him. Ah, yes. It was that his right hand was resting gently on Hanne's back. But hang on. This was my ex-girlfriend. My *ex*-girlfriend. What did I care where some bloke's hand was? And then I realised I was staring quite a lot at where Seb's hand was. He slowly moved his hand away. Shit. Now they thought I wasn't cool with it.

"You had your hand on Hanne's back!" I said with a big smile.

"Sorry, I . . ."

"No! It's good!" I said.

"Danny," said Hanne. "Let's not cause a scene, okay . . ."

"No! Hang on—I think it's *good*! I think Seb should put *both* hands on your back!"

Hanne made the face she used to make when she thought I was being sarcastic.

"I'm not even being sarcastic! I think it's fantastic! Put *both* your hands on her back, Seb!"

This was terrible. The less sarcastic I tried to sound, the more sarcastic I sounded.

Seb's mobile went off.

"Okay, I'm going to get this . . ."

He walked a few feet away and started a conversation. He sounded like he was quite important. Hanne and I just stood there, awkwardly. I tried to change the subject.

"He seems nice."

"Let's just forget it . . . ," said Hanne.

"You're on a date, then," I said.

"Yes, well . . . ," said Hanne, looking to the ground.

"Cool."

"Cool," she said. "I was going to tell you, over that coffee, you know, about . . . tonight, but you distracted me by losing twenty-five thousand pounds. You said you're okay with things, though, yeah?"

"Yes," I said, "Absolutely I am. Of course."

Hanne looked over at Seb. She was keen to go, but he was still on the phone. And I didn't feel I could leave without clearing things up with Seb. Eventually he hung up the phone and rejoined us.

Seb smiled at me, so I smiled back at him. Hanne smiled at me. Then Hanne and Seb smiled at each other, and then they both looked at me and smiled, in that way that couples do. Gah. Couples! Seb and Hanne! Hanne and Seb! All of a sudden it sounded annoyingly . . . *right*!

I coughed.

"So, I'll be going . . . ," I said, which was the right thing to say, seeing as I now wanted to be literally anywhere else on Earth.

"Right," said Hanne.

"Right," I said, and I started to move off.

"Unless . . . ," said Seb, and I stopped in my tracks. "Unless you'd like to join us?"

My stomach turned over.

That was an invitation. *An invitation.*

My stomach flipped again, and my cheeks started to burn with embarrassment.

Seb was obviously just being polite. *Obviously.* He really didn't want me there. And neither did Hanne. And the only person who wanted me there less than *them* was *me.* Shit. This was *so* level four.

How could I get out of this? Was there any way in the world?

Hanne smiled at me gently, then closed her eyes and did a little nod . . . giving me permission to make my excuses and leave. She knew full well that the proper—the *only*—course of action would be for me to say something along the lines of "oh, thanks, but I have to be somewhere else" and then leave. Seb was just being a gentleman; showing Hanne he showed no ill will and harboured no petty jealousies toward her ex-boyfriend. Bastard. Even *I* was starting to fancy him.

"Well . . . ," I started. And then I had an idea. I could get out of this! All I'd have to say was that . . .

"Because you'd be welcome to join us, Danny," he said.

Bollocks! This was becoming a cast-iron invite!

He smiled at Hanne. Hanne smiled at him.

I looked at Hanne with some degree of panic in my eyes. She smiled sympathetically as if to say she knew what I'd have to say next.

Seb took my silence to be a no.

"Hey, sure, sure . . . ," said Seb, nodding and holding his hand out for me to shake. "Well, I guess we'll—"

"I'd love to," I said, quickly and with instant regret.

Seb's hand remained outstretched. He looked confused. Hanne's eyes widened.

"*What?*" she said sharply.

"If you're sure. I mean, if you're actually inviting me along, Seb, then yes. Yes, I'd love to."

I had gone bright red. And so had Hanne. But not for the same reasons. Seb, though, ever the gentlemen, regained his composure, took his phone back out, and said "Right . . . well . . . let me just call the restaurant and tell them it's a table for *three* . . ."

It was *horrible.*

The three of us were sitting in near-silence in a rather posh restaurant called Circus. Seb and Hanne were sitting opposite each other, and there was I, perched in the middle, sitting on a hastily added chair at a table quite clearly meant for two.

I mean, it was *really horrible*.

We'd been sitting there for ten minutes. The candlelight was doing nothing to melt the ice in the air.

It became all-too-apparent that this was Hanne's very first date with Seb—and here I was, gatecrashing. But still, this was how it was to be. All I could try to do was jolly things along . . .

"So . . . how did you guys meet?" I said in as friendly a way as I could muster.

"Danny, do we have to . . . ," started Hanne before Seb chipped in.

"Through a friend," he said. "I work with Cecilia."

"Oh, Cecilia, yes," I said.

"Yep," said Seb, picking up his menu.

"Cecilia," I said again, for some reason in an amusing northern accent this time.

Seb didn't respond. Hanne just stared at me.

"Cecilia," I said normally, to prove that I could.

Seb continued to study his menu.

"It's like that song, isn't it?"

"What song?" said Hanne, sternly.

"Cecilia," I said. "By Simon and Garfunkel."

"Yes," said Hanne. "It is."

"Have I told you my mum's Simon and Garfunkel story?"

"Yes," said Hanne. Seb didn't look at all interested in hearing my mum's Simon and Garfunkel story. Even though it is excellent.

At a table somewhere else in the restaurant, someone coughed.

"Yeah," I said, taking a deep breath. "Cecilia."

I bit into a breadstick. "How does that song go again?"

"*Jesus,*" I heard Hanne say under her breath before picking up her menu.

So I looked at my menu as well, and the three of us sat there in silence, pretending to be deep in thought.

A waiter arrived.

"Would you like to order some wine?"

I don't think he'd ever heard three people say yes with such conviction before.

I'd love to leave that particular evening there. Really, I would. But I can't. Because it didn't stop there. Plus *I* had to suffer, and now so will you.

Twenty minutes had passed, and we'd all ordered.

The waiter had recommended the fish, and though even as a child I never really ate fish, I had gone for it. Hanne had raised her eyebrows at me when I did this. Seb hadn't really said anything in about ten minutes, and so it had fallen to me to make conversation. But how?

I thought about the joke I had made three nights earlier.

"I was thinking," I said, smiling, and Seb looked up for the first time in ages. Oh, this was it. If I could give them the gift of laughter, the most precious gift of all, surely then all this embarassment would simply evaporate?

I chuckled to myself in anticipation.

"I was walking past Pizza Hut the other day, and for a second I was sure the sign said 'Pizza *Hat*.' And then I thought, wouldn't it be funny if there was a shop called 'Pizza Hat' that sold hats shaped like pizzas?"

I chuckled and waited, eyebrows raised, for the rest of the laughter to start. Seb looked back down at his menu. I turned my head to see Hanne glaring at me.

"You know . . . ," I tried weakly. "Because it sounds like 'Pizza Hut,' only it's . . ."

I looked to Seb.

". . . a hat shop."

Nothing.

I couldn't work it out. That joke had been an absolute *stormer* when I'd been off my tits on drugs. I guess sometimes people just don't *want* to enjoy themselves.

"Hey, I nearly got ten million dollars the other day," I said, but I was interrupted almost immediately.

"Look, Danny," said Seb. "Why don't you just eat your fish and fuck off?"

Hanne's eyes hit the floor. Seb's remained locked on me.

And so I quietly ate my fish and off I fucked.

I walked out of the Tube a deeply embarrassed man. I decided, quite rightly under the circumstances, that I needed a drink.

I texted Ian as I headed for the pub.

IF YOU WANT A PINT, I AM IN THE ROYAL INN.

He texted back instantly.

WHAT?

I checked what I'd written. Thanks to a distracted mind and predictive text messaging, I hadn't quite got my message across.

HE YOU WANT A RIOT I AN GO THE ROYAL INN.

I phoned him. "Pint?"

"Yes," he said. "Or we *could* start a riot."

In the pub Ian laughed in my stupid, bespectacled face.

"You said *yes*?! Why the hell did you say *yes*?"

"Have you forgotten about this whole saying yes thing, Ian? It does involve rather a lot of saying yes to things."

"I know, mate, but what's wrong with you? You've got to have limits!"

"*Limits?* Be consistent! You're the one who threatened to punish me if I so much as *dreamed* a no!"

"Oh, I'm not being consistent, am I?"

"No! You were the one with all the threats at the beginning. 'Oh, I'll have to punish you if you don't do it properly.'"

"I don't need to punish you! You're punishing yourself!"

"Jesus, Ian, I looked like a tit. I'm *happy* for Hanne; it's great that she's found someone new. I don't want her thinking I'm not cool with it."

"Yeah, it does kind of look that way. What with you forbidding her from seeing a new man one week, and then gatecrashing their date the next. Maybe you should tell her about the Yes thing. Stop it from happening again."

"I would rather Hanne thought I was having a mental breakdown than indulging myself in another stupid boy-project. Which this is not, by the way."

"Sounds like one."

"You're not being much help, Ian."

"Not much help? Now I'm inconsistent *and* not much help! All I do is help! Without me, you'd have been beaten up by Omar in Amsterdam!"

"Or I would have got ten million dollars."

Ian laughed.

"Yeah, right," he said. "Prick stick."

Suddenly I took great and brutal offence. It had suddenly become quite an emotional evening, and I wasn't going to sit here in my own local pub, being called a prick stick just because I dared to have a little faith in my fellow man.

"Prick stick?! I'm *not* a prick stick!"

I was probably overreacting.

"I'm just saying, Ian . . . maybe Omar really *was* in danger! You can't totally discount that!"

"We talked about this! I proved it to you! The man was a scammer! You're being stupid! This whole thing is pointless and stupid!"

"It's not pointless! I'll find the point! And I'm not being stupid, either! Are you really telling me, despite all the recorded evidence, that there was absolutely no chance whatsoever—*whatsoever*—that Omar wasn't really a scammer at all? That he *wasn't* the son of a murdered sultan? I'm being human, Ian!"

Ian simply looked at me. "I had a *brilliant* idea for a punishment for you. But now I'm going to scrap it. I'm going to find something a hundred times worse."

"Fine."

"Fine."

"Fine."

I walked out of the pub that night, my mood not exactly enhanced by two pints with Ian and a bottle of wine with Hanne, Seb, and humiliation. I'd been hungry, so I had stopped at a shop on Roman Road and ordered myself a packet of chips and a can of Fanta. The chips were drenched in vinegar, ketchup, and chilli sauce—the three options the man had given me, the three I'd agreed to—and I didn't even make it halfway to my flat before furiously throwing them in a bin.

When I got home, I flicked the computer on and started to make myself a sandwich.

Sure, I thought. The argument with Ian aside, Yes had dealt me a pretty major negative tonight. But it had also dealt me a few positives. And who knew? Maybe this would eventually make me and Hanne closer friends.

My phone beeped.

A message from Hanne.

TWAT.

I decided she'd probably misused her predictive text too, and she'd meant to write "Twav," which was probably Norwegian for something nice, like flowers, or a tiny waving baby.

I sighed. Remember: positives. Yes had dealt me positives.

And it was about to deal me another. Another positive which would shut Ian up once and for all. Oh, this was great. This was brilliant. *This* would show him. This would teach him to have a little faith in a project! This would force him to admit that I wasn't a prick stick.

Only one e-mail sat in my in box, hopeful and alone.

It was from a Dr. Molly Van Brain.

She was writing to tell me I had just won twenty million dollars in the Spanish lottery.

I was amazed. I hadn't even *entered* the Spanish lottery.

And now Dr. Molly Van Brain wanted to invite me to come and collect my winnings from her personally.

All I'd have to do was get on a plane.

To Holland.

CHAPTER 8

In Which Daniel Lands Himself in a Spot of Bother

The fact that this was a leap straight into level five both excited and scared me.

Clearly this was something I simply shouldn't be doing. I can admit that now. Ian had already proved to me that 99 percent of these unsolicited junk e-mails were scams designed to delight and entice hapless, gullible people. But surely that still left 1 percent. And one in a hundred aren't bad odds . . . think of how the odds were stacked against my *Sun* scratch card win, after all the one thing I still clung to as proof that Yes could work . . .

But I knew what Ian would say to thinking like this. He'd say that I was stupid. That Dr. Molly Van Brain probably wasn't a doctor. Or a Molly. Or even a Van Brain.

But c'mon . . . this was worth a shot. Worth a further look. Worth a *yes.*

It was like the world had shifted slightly. Now I was dealing with a whole new and fascinating universe. A universe of what-its . . .

Like . . . What if the Spanish lottery really had somehow picked me out as a winner? And . . . What if right now, somewhere in a room in Amsterdam, a lady doctor really *was* counting and recounting my twenty million dollars out in front of her and saying, "Well, I hope *this* one turns up, because everyone else seems to just *ignore* my e-mails. . . ."

It was unlikely, sure. But it was *attractive.*

As the train made its way into the city, I looked once more at her e-mail.

My name, it read, had been chosen by a computer ballot system "drawn from 91,000 names from around the world!" But I had to keep completely quiet about my win. "Due to a mix-up of some names and addresses, it is imperative you keep this award completely personal until your claim has been processed. Do not tell anyone at all." This was part of their efforts, it read, "to avoid unwarranted taking advantages of the situations by other participants or improper impersonators."

Very sensible! And of *course* I'd keep it quiet—the last thing I needed was Ian or Wag popping on a pair of glasses and impersonating me. But it was the next bit that was the best.

```
You have therefore been approved for a payment in cash
credited to file reference number: LIP/63474-444/RT6. This
forms a total cash prize of $20,756,820.00 (Twenty Million
Seven Hundred and Fifty-six Thousand Eight Hundred and
Twenty Dollars).
```

And there, underneath it, the name that had brought joy to my heart. Dr. Molly Van Brain. There was another name too—someone called Albert Heijn from the Legal department. I was to deal with him after processing my details with Molly, who'd told me all I had to do was come to Holland as quickly as possible or, more conveniently and desirably, contact Albert, and he would deal with all the paperwork and legal aspects for a one off-processing fee (seven thousand euros, which they would require before presenting me with my cheque). It would only take about fifty pounds and forty-five minutes to fly to Amsterdam, where I could take care of business myself. Besides, seven thousand euros seems a lot of money for a bit of processing.

So I'd written back to her, saying, "Tell Albert not to worry! I will come to Amsterdam and meet with you directly! I have my ticket and will be there tomorrow!" If that didn't excite the socks off Dr. Molly Van Brain, then nothing would.

I stepped off the train as we rolled into the city centre and strolled into the Internet café.

Here we go. Bring on the riches. I logged on and went straight to my e-mails, but was a little surprised to see I had no mail. Molly hadn't replied. Not even a friendly "hello" or a "looking forward to seeing you!"

No matter. Maybe she was just busy getting my money ready and buying pastries and balloons for the official handover. It was a little disappointing, that's all. You'd have thought at the very least Albert could have made the effort to write. With no processing to do, the man suddenly had loads of spare time on his hands!

So I wrote another e-mail to Molly.

```
Dear Molly,
     It is I, Danny Wallace, winner of the SkyLow Lottery
International! I have spectacular news! I have done as you
suggested and come to Holland! I hope Albert isn't annoyed
that he won't get to do the processing, but I thought I'd
save myself seven thousand euros!
     Anyway. I am just sitting around near the Magna Plaza,
waiting to meet up. Please e-mail me or call me on 0044
7802 *** ***  to let me know what I should do next.
     Danny
```

My main worry was that it was already getting close to four o'clock. I wanted to get in touch with these guys before business hours were over. I was only booked into Amsterdam for one night—after all, Amsterdam's not the kind of place you want to be when you've got twenty million dollars burning a hole in your pocket—and I had an early flight home in the morning.

The one thing I found really strange about Molly's e-mail—aside from its very nature—was that it contained no phone numbers whatsoever. And the only address on it was for the offices of Albert the legal expert.

I wandered away from the Internet café and toward the Magna Plaza, but before I'd walked even a few feet I looked up to see a man, tanned and in his thirties, slowly moving down the street, holding in his hand a small leash. He was smiling and making an odd clicking noise. And on the end of that leash was a small, fat, brown cat. I had to do a quick double take. Yes. It was a man. Walking his cat. In the middle of the day. I stood and watched.

Amsterdam is, I suppose, a city of Yeses, and one of the most liberal in the world. It is a city of freedom and acceptance, a place where new ideas are embraced, not dismissed out of hand. In the sixties, Amsterdam's youth threw themselves into hippiedom with gusto and glee, and it's from that basic mindset that a place of outright social progressiveness grew. Most notably, of course, when it comes to drugs and prostitution. Gay marriages were legalised in 2001, and the city is one of the most gay-friendly in the world. A city which, just as it should, accepts everyone equally. Street crime is rare, and friendly faces abound. It was all quite warming to the heart. I thought about that and watched as my cat-walking friend ambled down the street, pausing every so often to allow his little friend to sniff a bollard or lick a street corner, and I thought, *Good for you, sir. Go—walk your cat and hold your head up high. For you are in Amsterdam, city of acceptance. There is no shame—even for men who walk their cats in public.*

I wandered past a gift shop and wondered whether I should buy a souvenir. Did one night in a foreign city warrant a souvenir? In the end I opted for a tiny windmill on a stick and decided to write Lizzie a postcard. It had been a while, and I missed her. Plus I feel postcards are important. They give the impression that you are a worldly and well-travelled person with culture at their fingertips and the lifestyle of a jet-setter. I flicked through the postcards and found one with a big clog on it. Yes. That was *precisely* the image I wanted to portray.

Dear Lizzie,
I'm in Amsterdam! No reason why, really. Sometimes you've just got to do these things and live a little.
Hey—they walk cats here. It's brilliant.
Love,
Danny

I found a postbox, popped the postcard in, and went for a walk around the huge Nieuwe Kerk, where I took in the Gothic pinnacles and soaring lines, and a couple of Neptunes blowing on conches. But who was I kidding? On a normal day, of course, I'd have spent more time there, tried my hardest to see everything, had my photo taken with a trumpet-playing cherub. But today? Today I wanted to be in an Internet café. . . .

I dashed back inside the café, logged on, and to my delight found an e-mail waiting.

But it wasn't from Molly. It was from something called the Standard Trust Agency of Amsterdam.

I clicked it open and read:

> Hello Mister Danny,
> Thank you for your e-mail to SkyLow Lottery International. We are their agents, and we will be handling your claim. Please, we need a few things as soon as possible, as we are running out of time on your claim.
>
> 1. Full name and address and *all* telephone and fax numbers
> 2. Bank account information
> 3. Passport number and nationality
> 4. Two thousand euros to pay for an indemnity document, which will be used in filing process. Please, it is your responsibility to cover this cost.
>
> We will also require a one off-payment of 2,650 euros for tax purposes within 24 hours to ensure the claim can be made in time.
> Immediately the process is started, you will receive all the necessary documents to receive your money.
> Robison Shaw

Hang on a second! Who was this bloke? Where was Molly? Where was Albert? And what was all this about time limits?

I wrote back.

> Dear Robison,
> But I am already in Amsterdam at the request of Dr. Molly Van Brain! How can I collect my winnings from her? What are

```
these documents I need? I thought Albert Heijn was in
charge of this stuff? Where is Dr. Molly Van Brain?
    Danny
```

Something about this was deeply wrong. It was now 5 p.m., and I wanted to get this sorted out as quickly as possible. But I was at the mercy of Robison Shaw, who'd suddenly decided to take over from the much more friendly sounding Dr. Molly Van Brain. He'd given me no address, but there *was* a phone number. . . .

I got my mobile out and dialled the number. If there really was a time limit on my claim, surely this was the best way of handling things? The phone number worked . . . but there was no answer. I waited and waited, hoping it would click into answerphone, but it didn't. It just rang.

I tried the number again, but still the same happened. I had a bad feeling about this. I didn't like the cut of Robison Shaw's gib, either. He, unlike Molly, seemed a bit money-obsessed. I needed to straighten this out, but I had no way of getting in touch with her other than by e-mail.

Or did I?

I took the printout of Molly's e-mail out of my pocket, and there it was again: Albert Heijn, Westerstraat, Amsterdam. Sure, Albert was a bit out of the loop now that I'd decided to do the processing myself, but surely he wouldn't begrudge me a little visit? If I could find Albert, then I could almost certainly find out whether I really *had* won twenty million dollars.

I needed a map. And I needed confirmation that Albert Heijn really was where he said he was. Surely if it was a scam, they'd have made an address up?

I stopped a passerby.

"Excuse me," I said. "What number do I dial to find out other numbers?"

The lady looked at me blankly. "You mean like a database?" she said.

"Yes! Like, directory enquiries. Someone who knows the phone book."

"Ah!" she said, and gave me the number, which was full of 0s and 8s. I dialled.

"*Naam?*"

"Hello? Do you speak English?"

"Yes."

"I need the address for Albert Heijn, Westerstraat, Amsterdam."

"Of course."

Moments later I had it. Albert was real! A real man, with a real address! I could bypass Robison Shaw and deal with the people who'd been with me since the beginning. Now all I had to do was get round there. It was 5:30 now. I still had half an hour before most business would be shutting down for the day. And surely I could get there in less than . . .

My heart stopped.

The time difference.

Yeah, it was 5:30 by *my* watch, but *my* watch was on *British* time. The Dutch watches would all read 6:30.

I needed to get to Albert quickly. I ran to a main road and waited, sweaty, wild, and desperate for a cab to pass. A minute or two later I found one.

"Westerstraat," I said. "As quickly as you can manage!"

The taxi roared into action, and I got my phone out. I had to call Albert and tell him not to leave work yet. I had to convince him I was on my way and needed to talk to him about SkyLow, Dr. Molly Van Brain, and Robison Shaw . . . but would he want to talk to me? I'd robbed him of seven thousand euros' worth of work! I'd arrogantly thought I could do this myself!

The phone rang and rang, but no one answered. Had he gone home already? Or was this part of the scam? Was he sitting with Robison, laughing his tits off? Or was it real? Was he sitting with Molly, counting out my money and looking at his watch? I needed to get to him today. . . . I needed to sort this out today. . . .

"Here is Westerstraat," said the driver, pulling up. "Which number do you need?"

"I'm not sure," I said. "There was no number. Just this . . ."

I showed him my piece of paper.

"Ah! Albert Heijn," he said, and pulled out, back into the street.

"You *know* Albert Heijn?" I said startled.

The driver laughed. "Sure," he said. "Everybody knows Albert Heijn. He is an important man!"

I was thrilled. This alone would prove to Ian that the way of Yes was the true and right way! We drove a hundred metres or so, then slowed to a halt. The driver turned to me and pointed out the window.

"Here he is."

I looked to where the driver was pointing.

And there in big, blue letters he was.

ALBERT HEIJN

It was the name of a supermarket.

I was distraught. And I felt stupid. So, so stupid. Of *course* it was a scam. And the worst thing was I'd known it all along. It *had* to be. I'd never entered the Spanish lottery. Just as I'd never met Omar's dad, the murdered sultan so impressed by my professionalism in business.

The moment I'd seen the supermarket, I knew it: Ian had so obviously been right all along. The scammers had used a real name and address in the hope that anyone tempted to check out SkyLow would see that their "lawyer" existed. It would be like you or I claiming we were represented in court by a Bobby Van Walmart or the Taco Bell Twins. They just hadn't reckoned anyone would travel to Amsterdam to find out. I could see their point; Yes had been wrong to bring me here. Yes had clouded my judgment, brought optimism when it should have armed me with cynicism. I'd been suspending any disbelief in the vague hope that everything would come out well. I was excited by the trip, by the possibilities, no matter *how* ludicrous. Maybe I was just looking for another hit—another injection of excitement and surprise. The kind I'd had the day I won twenty-five grand but lost it again all too soon. I'd tasted glory that day, and I wanted more. Maybe Yes was addictive; maybe you lived in the hope that if you just believed, it would bring you good fortune.

I found a bench and tried to find the spin I could put on today's events. How could I make it okay again? What good could I find in this?

Well, I was on a bench in Amsterdam for one thing. I had an evening to waste in Holland that I otherwise wouldn't have had. And that, surely, beats just another night in front of the telly in London. At the very least I had that. And that, after all, is what this was all about.

I decided not to tell Ian about how I'd ended up in Amsterdam. And if I ever did, I'd lie and tell him I had actually won that twenty million dollars after all. I reckoned I could get away with that, even if it did mean I'd have to buy every round in the pub for the rest of my life.

So that was it: I'd decided not to be beaten. I would find fun tonight. Of course I would! I was the Yes Man!

The National Cheese Museum of Holland features more than three fascinating audiovisual displays on the history of cheese, taking in famous cheesemakers as well as the huge array of forward-thinking cheesemaking equipment offered to the modern cheesemaker today. Visitors to the museum in Alkmaar are able to sample more than six different cheeses, from Gouda to Edam and back again, and the whole, thrilling, cheese-based experience was kept from me only because the museum had closed two hours earlier.

I had with me a small pamphlet I'd picked up on the train into town that afternoon, full of useful suggestions and handy hints as to how I should spend my time. The problem was nearly everything it suggested was closed, shutdown, or finished. I'd even missed the "Holland Experience," on Jodenbreestraat, which promised 3-D glasses, a moving floor, and smell-o-vision. That was the last straw. You know a day's gone wrong when you've missed out on smell-o-vision.

My tummy rumbled, and at first I assumed it was a deep-seated rage borne out of a lack of 3-D windmills before realising that as I hadn't eaten all day, it was probably hunger. I was near the Leidseplein, the heart of touristy Amsterdam, with its bright and blinking neon signs and constant flow of people and traffic and people. I wandered away from the main square, still cursing Dr. Molly Van Brain under my breath (not only was I twenty million dollars down, but thanks to all the faffing around, I knew virtually nothing about cheese, either), and found my way to Leidsekruisstraat and a little restaurant called De Blonde Hollander.

The staff was friendly but the restaurant busy; so much so that they told me I may have to share a table, if many more people arrived. I shrugged and said that'd be fine, and then ordered a pancake and a beer.

All around me were happy people from all over planet Earth. I wondered how many people ended up here as a result of Dr. Molly Van Brain and her evil team of scammers. Surely it couldn't be just me? When I'd first thought about her, she was a kindly figure; an elderly lady scientist who most likely worked for free on cures for diseases during her spare time. Now, the name Dr. Molly Van Brain conjured up images of an evil lady torturer, who wore a long white coat and was probably really good at cackling. My beer arrived, and I tried to put her out of my mind. But then something else arrived too. Two men. Two men who had nowhere else to sit and had been shepherded, apologetically, to my table.

"Thank you, please," said the waiter, pulling out their chairs. They sat down.

"Hello," said the first man, and then the second.

"Hello," I said back.

Now, I know the drill when it comes to things like this. The person on their own is supposed to act like they don't even notice the other people are there, and they in turn will act like the first person isn't there, either. Then those two people will gossip loudly and mercilessly, and the person on his own will pretend he's gone deaf and isn't eavesdropping. I call it the "Wagamama Effect." But there was to be none of this. Because the first man extended his hand and confidently said, "I'm Jahn."

"Oh," I said. "Danny."

"This is Sergei," he said, and I shook Sergei's hand too.

And from there the conversation flowed.

Jahn and Sergei were backpackers. Or were they? They were certainly backpackers when they'd arrived, but they'd been in Amsterdam for nearly six months or so. Jahn—tall, thin, and blond— had arrived after travelling through Europe from South Africa, and Sergei—shorter, squatter, and bearded—was from Poland. The two had met in a hostel round the corner and been firm friends ever since.

"Amsterdam is the finest place I have visited," said Sergei. "Absolutely. When I am here, I feel at home. It's the way that things should be."

"We both tend to go where the wind takes us," said Jahn. "If I want to see somewhere, then I go. But sometimes I just sit back and see what happens. Get a casual job, stay in a hostel, see what comes up. My dad used to say, 'The only time you have no opportunities is when you decide to stop taking them.' I feel that way too."

We talked for another hour or so about whatever came up. About London, about Poland, about South Africa. Both Sergei and Jahn had wanted to know what I was doing in Amsterdam. I told them I was visiting my friend, Albert. They asked me where Albert was tonight, and I cracked under the weight of my deception, quickly explaining the whole thing. They laughed and told me not to worry. For twenty million dollars, they thought, it was worth a fifty-quid flight.

Sergei had to leave soon after to start work, but Jahn made me an offer I couldn't refuse. Mainly because there were very few offers I *could* refuse these days.

"If you're doing nothing this evening, I will show you around," he said. "You can experience my Amsterdam."

"Okay," I said. "That'd be great!"

This was actually really cool. I mean, it was only thanks to a precise but random chain of Yeses that I'd met Jahn in the first place. We should, by rights, never have crossed paths. But now that we had, what was the harm in allowing a stranger to dictate my evening? Particularly as we were in his city. If it'd been down to me, after all, I'd probably still be in the bloody cheese museum.

"Okay . . . First we must go to Warmoestraat . . . ," said Jahn as we left the restaurant.

"Right. What's there?"

"Argos."

I nodded.

Hang on.

"*Argos?*"

"It's a bar," said Jahn matter-of-factly. Clearly he'd had that conversation with Brits before. "A guy there owes me some money. We'll pop in, get the cash, and head off again. Cool?"

"Cool," I said.

We stepped out of the cab and straight into Argos. It certainly was unlike any Argos *I'd* ever been in before. Jahn was immediately cheered by a couple of guys on a nearby table.

"Some friends," he said.

I smiled as he moved off, and took a look about the bar. There was something . . . *different* about this bar. Something . . . missing. I couldn't quite put my finger on it. It had chairs. And lights. And drinks. And men. Black men. White men. Tall men. Short men. Lots of . . . men. And then I realised: girls. Girls were what were missing from this bar. And also . . . Oh! . . . Normal clothes. Normal, manly clothes, like corduroy and denim . . . There was a lot less corduroy and denim than I was used to in this bar. And a lot more, well, there was a lot more *leather* than was normal for me.

Oh my lord.

I was in a *leather bar.*

"Argos is Europe's oldest leather bar," said Jahn by my side again.

"Excellent!" I said, hoping enthusiasm would translate as some kind of urbane cool. "The oldest leather bar in Europe. That is bloody brilliant!"

"There are these two bars, and then there is the cellar."

"A cellar. Wicked. What's the cellar for?"

Jahn shot me a look. I knew at that moment it was probably best if I didn't know what the cellar was for.

Jahn went back to talk to his friends and get his money while an unnerving truth gradually dawned on me—a virtual stranger had taken me to a gay leather bar in the heart of Amsterdam. Now, don't get the wrong idea about me. I've been to plenty of gay bars in my time, and each one has been a stylish and plush night out. And I've nothing against leather—I own a real leather jacket, two leather belts, and when I was at primary school, it was the only material I'd even *consider* carrying a satchel made from. But I had never been to a gay bar—much less a gay *leather* bar—as *the Yes Man.*

I realised with some degree of terror that I was a man full of Yeses in a bar full of opportunities! What if someone had a suggestion to make? Or an *invitation*? Or—good God—a *favour* to ask? I'm not claiming to be a particularly attractive man who would have gay fellas flocking to him—I'm just saying that from what I've seen in gay bars in the UK, sometimes they're not all that picky.

"Hi!" said a voice to my right. "Are you a friend of Jahn's?"

The man was clean shaven, neatly turned-out, and very friendly. There was no leather to be seen, though his trousers did look a bit tight. Suddenly paranoia gripped me. Maybe he was after me! Hey— he *was* after me!

Now, I find homophobia to be a vile and despicable human trait. It is an uneducated and unevolved way of thinking, clumsily cultivated by that section of society who think singing "Wonderwall" by Oasis at pub closing time is high culture. But at the same time I had a moral obligation to say *yes* to this man. Whoever he was. Whatever he *wanted*!

I would have to think quick. I would have to dominate the conversation. I would have to steer it into safe waters. And I would have to say something soon, because he asked me that question about fifteen seconds ago, and I've still not answered him.

"Yes," I said suddenly. "Yes, I am a friend of Jahn's."

I scanned and rescanned the sentence in my head. Was there anything in there that could be seen as a come-on? Shit! I shouldn't have said yes. And I said it *twice*! That was like *flirting*!

"Jahn's cool," said the guy. "Where you from? England?"

What could I say to that? What wouldn't give him the wrong idea? "Yup."

"London?"

I nodded.

"And is he showing you around Amsterdam?"

I nodded again. "Yup."

"I'm going to the bar—would you like a drink?"

He shook his empty glass. Which is neither a euphemism *nor* rhyming slang.

But bloody hell! This was going terribly! All I was saying was yes!

And now I'd just nodded and smiled and accepted a drink! This man had me right where he wanted me! I think it only fair to point out that I would have been equally uncomfortable if this had been a bar in the city's notorious red-light district, and the guy had been a scantily clad girl. Well, *almost* as uncomfortable.

Suddenly Jahn was back.

"Hey . . . I got my money, shall we go?"

"Yes!" I said. "Let us do that."

The guy smiled and said, "Nice to meet you."

"Hello, Dieter," said Jahn, and Dieter raised his hand and did a little wave. "Dieter is one of the friendliest guys you can meet."

I suddenly felt a little ashamed. I had allowed my own paranoia and preconceptions to rule me. Dieter was just a really friendly guy.

"But you have to watch him," said Jahn. "Because he *will* try to sleep with you."

Dieter faked a look of shock.

"In fact, he'll sleep with *anything*."

Dieter laughed, called Jahn a bitch, and went to get another beer. I laughed too until I realised that in Jahn's eyes, I pretty much constituted "anything."

"So," said Jahn, "there's this cool bar in the red light that I should show you . . ."

Silently and to no one in particular I mouthed the word "help."

Before we braved the potential horrors of the red-light district, though, Jahn insisted on taking me somewhere just down the road from Argos. It would be a surprise, he said. A true Amsterdam experience. So long as it didn't involve leather chaps, I said, I'd be happy to take a look.

Moments later we were there, standing outside a place called, rather suspiciously, Conscious Dreams.

"What is this? A coffeeshop?" I said, knowing full well that the last thing people visiting coffeeshops in this town wanted was coffee.

"No, not really. . . . It's called a 'smart shop.' Do you smoke weed, Danny?"

"I find it best not to," I said. "The last time I did I became obsessed with geese."

Jahn looked like he understood.

"Well, come in . . ."

We walked in, and there again I noticed the words "smart shop."

"What *is* a smart shop?" I asked.

"It's where you buy drugs that are good for you."

"Like a chemist?"

"No . . . ," said Jahn, taking a seat. "Drugs that make your memory better or help you concentrate or bring you energy, you know? It's all natural alternatives to the chemicals. Why take LSD when you can have something from nature? Natural LSD. Much lower health risks."

"But LSD is illegal here, isn't it?"

"Sure. But all *this* stuff is *legal*. Good alternatives to speed, ecstasy, whatever you like. And really, since you're in Amsterdam, you should try a little of what goes on here. . . ."

He was smiling, now. I got the distinct sense that this was the kind of thing Jahn loved doing to people not as familiar with Amsterdam as he is.

"You could do magic mushrooms. Psychotropic. Totally legal when fresh."

"But they're bad for you," I said, a little offended at the suggestion. "When I was at school, we had a whole assembly on them, because Jonathan Davies ate some in a field and then spent the whole after noon chasing trees."

"But they are natural, and what comes from nature can't be too bad, surely?"

I thought about it.

"Earthquakes?" I tried.

Jahn shook his head.

"Hitler, then," I said.

Now he just looked blank.

"Well, maybe I'll buy a couple of mushrooms, yes," I said. "I'll take them with me tonight, when I leave. There's no need to dive straight in, you know."

"You can't take them home with you. And you can't let them dry out. If you do, they are illegal. There was a big fuss a few years ago when this place started selling magic mushrooms, but they got away with it, when they rebranded themselves as a greengrocers."

I looked around me.

"So, essentially, tonight you've brought me to a greengrocers?"

Jahn smiled.

"Come on. Are you willing to give a new experience a go?"

And there it was. The sentence which would push me over the edge. I felt like Marty McFly from *Back to the Future*, when someone dared to call him chicken.

"I have to say . . . I'm a little uncomfortable about this," I said. And I was. I had never, ever done anything even remotely approaching Class A drugs before. I'd struggle if you asked me to even name them all. It's just not something that my circle of friends has ever really considered. That comical cigarette in Brixton with the peace protestors was as far as I'd ever gone. And yet now here I was, feeling for all the world like the Amsterdam tourist cliché, sitting with a South African who deemed the whole thing perfectly normal and decent and fine, and about to take it to the next level.

"Only do it if you want to," he said. "I mean, you wanted to see how I live. And *I'm* going to have something. . . ."

He stood up and wandered over to the bar, while I sat there, wrestling with my conscience. I couldn't do this, could I? But I was in Amsterdam—the city of Yes. If I didn't say yes here, where *would* I say yes? Swansea? Suddenly I felt invigorated. I felt that I was approaching a watershed moment. If I did this—something that in everyday London life would have never even crossed my mind—then surely that would mark a certain level of commitment? That would mean I was *up* for this.

And hey—like Jahn said, it wasn't even illegal. Not technically, anyway.

He was back at the table a moment later. He lit a spliff he'd bought and sat back. And then he put a small pill on the table and slid it across to me.

"Try this," he said. "It'll blow your head off."

As a recommendation, that one was lacking something.

I looked at the pill.

"Jahn . . . when you say it'll blow my head off, well, I was more thinking I could have something a bit nicer and more gentle. Have you got anything that might stop short of actually blowing my head off, and maybe just give me a lovely headache instead? This sounds a bit . . . *bigger* than I was thinking."

Jahn tried to wave my worries away but failed. But I thought about what he'd said earlier. *The only time you have no opportunities is when you decide to stop taking them.* Well . . . this was an opportunity, of sorts. A chance to try something new. Something that, without a precise chain of Yeses, I never would've. A proper level five.

Suddenly I remembered something.

"Hey . . . are you . . . y'know . . . stoned yet?"

"A little."

I leaned forward and looked him in the eye.

"Imagine if there was a shop called Pizza Hat and all it sold was hats shaped like pizzas."

Jahn frowned, and then shook his head.

I couldn't believe it. That joke was actually getting *worse*.

"So, anyway," he said. "Are you going to try this?"

The answer was already yes.

"What's it called?"

"Well, the translation would be something like . . . mind . . . bomb."

"*Mindbomb?*" I said.

"More or less."

"But what *is* it? I can't eat a mindbomb unless I know what it is!"

"You don't eat them. And it's a bit like LSD. But more like a double-dipped tab."

"I have no idea what you just said."

"It's powerful but safe. I'm going to do one too. You'll be fine."

Jahn smiled. His confidence was reassuring, but I was still nervous. I can't stress enough how unusual a thing this was for me to be doing. I've never thought I would make a particularly good drug user. When I was a kid, I remember thinking I'd had an out-of-body experience after an out-of-date Junior Dispirin. How on God's green Earth would I cope with a psychotropic *mindbomb*?

Nevertheless, in perfect unison with Jahn, I picked up the mind-bomb, and slowly, carefully, placed it in my mouth.

• • •

The following morning at 7 a.m. precisely I sat bolt upright in a bed in the Novotel Amsterdam, confused, alone, dry mouthed, and wide-eyed.

I knew that things had happened in the last nine hours, but I didn't know what things, and I didn't know how they happened. I was still feeling woozy and boozy, and I appeared to have a sticker with a clog on it stuck to my face. Gradually a few images eeked their way back into my brain. A man. A flashing light. I looked down to the floor and noticed my jeans and one trainer, and next to them a small, black disposable camera. I stretched down to pick it up. The film was all used up. On the floor, under the cheap coffee table, there was something else. A scroll of some sort. Oh God. Please don't say I'd got married or something. Please don't say I'd gone back to the leather bar and got married.

I climbed out of bed, my head thumping, and leaned down to pick up the scroll. It felt strangely heavy, but then so did my whole body.

I unravelled the paper and saw . . . my God . . . what *was* this?

It was an unexpected and hugely confusing image.

It was an expertly crafted charcoal portrait of me and a tiny dog.

Suddenly the memory shot back to me: A street artist we stumbled past on the Leidseplein had asked me if I wanted my picture done. And I had giggled and shouted yes! But only—and I remember being very specific about this—if he would draw my dog as well. What dog? he'd said. Why, the little dog on my shoulder, I'd said.

And now here it was, the physical evidence of a barely remembered drug trip, which involved me wandering around Amsterdam with a tiny, happy dog on my shoulder. I think in my head it could even talk.

And not only that—but lord, it gets worse—I had photos too! Photos! Twenty-four of them! Either Jahn or myself must have bought the camera as we moved from bar to bar and landmark to landmark, happy and laughing thanks to the explosive effects of the Amsterdam mindbomb and some heavy duty lager!

I looked again at the portrait in the cold, blue light of morning. What the hell was I supposed to do with this? I'd paid good money for it—I wasn't throwing it away. But I couldn't exactly take it home and give it to my mum as a lovely gift, could I? How was I supposed to explain the dog? Did I just say that I hadn't noticed it was there? Should I say it just snuck in at the last minute? It is somewhat ironic that a portrait that came about just because I said yes, should so effectively illustrate the sentiment "Just Say No."

Much more of the night I can't tell you. I wish I could, but I can't. I have not seen or heard from Jahn since that evening, and I still do not condone the use of mind-altering illegal substances in any way (even if they're, you know, legal). I'm just telling you what happened, in the hope that maybe some young kid out there will read this and never have to have his portrait done with a miniature imaginary dog.

So here's my public-service announcement: If *you're* thinking of getting into drugs, and you want help, I have two photographs in particular I can show you. One is of me in downtown Amsterdam, pointing at a bus that I am sure has big, pretty eyes. And the other is of me lying on my back in the middle of the road with my arms outstretched as I tried to *tickle the moon*.

I refrain from publishing those photographs here only because no mother deserves to see that she has raised a moon-tickler.

I returned home to London, satisfied that—thanks to my dealings with Albert Heijn and the world of the mindbomb—saying yes had at least taught me two vital lessons.

Three, if you count the fact that no man should ever walk a cat.

SELECTED EXTRACTS FROM THE DIARY OF A YES MAN

July 18

There was a most incredible question in the back of a Metro I found on the Tube. In a little, boxed-out advert, were the words, ARE YOU BRITAIN'S MOST GERMAN-LOOKING MAN? An advertising agency was casting for Britain's most German-looking man and asking whether if you were, you'd like to be on TV. I thought about it for a few minutes as I rode the Tube. Was I Britain's most German-looking man? I tried to remember what I looked like and decided that, yes, I could probably pass for a German. My glasses could easily sit on the face of a more European man than myself. Maybe I was exactly what they were looking for. Maybe when I walked into their production offices, they would say, "I'm terribly sorry, sir, but you appear to be an *actual* German. I think you have misunderstood our advert. We are looking for British people who only *look* like they're German," and then I would smile, knowingly, and gradually it would dawn on them, and they'd say, "Really? Could it . . . are you . . . Gentlemen! Call off the search! We have *found* Britain's most German-looking man!" Imagine if I got the job! What would the people at the BBC think of this? What would they think when I walked into the office, threw my keys to the floor, and said, "Keep 'em! I'm off to be Britain's most German-looking man!" I imagine some of the girls would probably swoon. God, it'd be brilliant, being Britain's most German-looking man. I have left a message and look forward to hearing back.

July 19

I was reading the *East London Advertiser*, when I noticed a colourful article, posing the following question: "Are You Animal Crackers?"

I read on. "If you are," it read, "then your pet's mug shot could win you one hundred pounds and the coveted title of Advertiser Pet Personality of the Year!"

There were already some strong contenders, such as Bobbles of Mile End Road, and Pippy of Stebondale Street. Neither seemed to have much personality. One was just a dog someone had put some sunglasses on, and the other was just an overweight cat (I suppose they thought it was bubbly).

Well, I instantly knew one thing. Yes, I was animal crackers. Definitely. But I didn't have any pets to think of. I would have to get one, if I was going to ensure neither Bobbles nor Pippy robbed me of the title.

July 20

Today I saved eight pounds on a pair of "great fit practical elasticated denim jeans." The ad said they were only £7.99 with free delivery. They have a drawcord-style elasticated waist—the kind that grannies or the clinically obese use—and they are machine washable.

I will never, ever wear them.

July 21

Someone has put a sign outside my block reading, INTERESTED IN SQUASH? I NEED A SQUASH PARTNER—COULD IT BE YOU? Despite never having played squash in my life before, I buy a squash raquet, and then phone the man, whose name is Bjorn. We agree to play squash this weekend in Bethnal Green.

July 22

I read in the *Standard* that the UK Trichological Association in London are giving free hair examinations to all men. I decide to have my hair examined. I arrive at the clinic, and a man behind a big desk tells me what they do there, and it soon becomes clear that he is eyeing me up for a hair transplant. I'm not sure where he wants to transplant my hair, but he keeps looking at my head. He asks if he can just quickly examine me, and I let him. He stands over me with a big magnifying glass and prods about a bit before saying, "Yes, you are definitely in the early stages of male pattern baldness." He gives me such a fright that I can actually feel my hairline recede another millimetre. I am going bald! He made that happen! It is all part of his clever trick! He gives me some leaflets, and I go home and stand in front of the mirror for an hour with a comb and a ruler. The bastard was right. It *is* receding a bit. Wish I hadn't said yes. Then maybe this would never have happened, and I would have had the hair of a child forever.

On the way home I was stopped by another charity worker from Help the Aged. I think they have begun to target me.

July 23

Haven't been able to find a pet yet. Thought about buying a fish and sending in a picture, but this is a personality competition. I'm not sure how much personality it's possible to garner from a photo of a fish. It's not like anyone's ever looked at a goldfish and thought, "Now *there's* a crazy character!"

So in the end I took a photo of my neighbour's cat and sent that in.

Squash with Bjorn didn't go too well. I was hoping to rely on some kind of latent, natural squash talent, but it wasn't there. I don't think I'm his ideal partner. He has said he'll call me.

July 25

My spam e-mail offers me more drugs. I am offered Propecia (for hair loss) and Prozac (for depression). I feel you can't really take the first without the second. I order them both.

July 26

I have just realised that if I win the Advertiser Pet Personality of the Year competition, and my neighbours find out, I will have quite a hard time explaining the fact that I decided to enter their cat into a beauty pageant. Particularly as I don't know them. It would be an odd way of meeting. "Hello. I live next door. By the way, I have entered your cat in a competition."

So I sent another photo that I found on the Internet. It is also of a cat, but this one is wearing a tiny hat and a wig and will definitely beat next door's cat.

I have named this new cat Stuart, because hardly anyone ever names cats Stuart, and that must really upset a lot of people called Stuart.

July 28

The Propecia arrives. The Prozac arrives with it. I read the Prozac's list of possible side effects. Extreme fatigue. Listlessness. Constipation. Nervousness. Joint pain. Excessive sweating. Lack of concentration. Memory loss. Poor sexual performance.

I imagine you would have to be quite depressed for any of this to be an appealing alternative.

I try one pill. I feel a bit floaty for about ten minutes, but that might be because I haven't eaten. My knee joint hurts a bit now, but I don't think it's the Prozac.

August 1

I have invented something new! I was in the video shop, trying to find a Jet Li film, when I noticed a sign asking people to rewind their tapes before bringing them back. I realised that was a Yes moment I'd have to remember for later, but worried that I would forget. And that was when it came to me—the Incredible Automatic

Self-Rewinding Video Box! It works simply and effectively. Once the box is closed, a small magnet triggers the engine, and the tape rewinds as you walk home. It is foolproof and excellent. I sent it off to the patents and trademarks people today.

I wonder if Su Pollard is available for the ad campaign.

August 2

I have begun to feel very guilty for entering a stranger's cat into a competition. No matter. The hundred-pound cash prize will make it all worthwhile, although I will probably have to spend it on buying a cat to stop any tricky questions.

Also today I have begun the long and rocky road toward fulfilling an ambition I have never actually had—to be a nurse!

The University of Rochville in America is looking for new recruits for its on-line nursing degree. Apparently I will not need to study or learn anything about nursing. The degree is based on my life experience—from previous Ph.D.s or doctorates (of which I have none) to experience of home nursing (of which I have none) right the way down to "viewing habits." I have set the VCR for tonight's episode of *Holby City*. I can't believe I am going to be a nurse! I entered my details onto the Web site and paid the four hundred dollars in full, using one of my new "types" of credit card. I am nearly a doctor! Brilliant!

August 3

Bjorn the squash man still hasn't called. He *definitely* said he would call. Why are men such bastards?

CHAPTER 9

In Which Daniel Upsets a Stranger

Now, people often talk, almost embarrassingly loudly, about the power of positive thinking.

Take me: I'm usually quite a positive thinker. I tend to think things will generally work out okay. If I was stranded on a desert island, and I saw a boat on the horizon, but the boat didn't see me, I wouldn't get all in a fluster and a huff about it. "It'll probably be fine," I'd say. "I bet they'll probably be back in a bit." At least then, I'd die happy.

There are others who take a more rigorous approach to positive thinking and dedicate their entire lives to the practice. I once read an article about a lady called Jessica who'd read a self-help book about positivity and found it to be so inspiring that she bought a caravan in Cumbria and moved there immediately. She'd be free to spend her days wandering around, thinking positive thoughts and spreading happy vibes. According to Jessica, just thinking positively could cure your illnesses, revive your love life, and get you a better job. Which is great, if you like taking career advice from a woman who lives in a caravan.

"I'll give you an example," she said. "If we keep repeating something good over and over, then eventually it will *become* the truth. If you just keep on insisting to yourself that you are a wonderful person, and that your marriage is amazing, it *will* be true."

A handy tip for battered wives everywhere, there.

For me I had discovered that it's not necessarily positive *thinking* that changes your life, but positive *doing*. Now, to be honest, my trip to Amsterdam hadn't been quite as successful as I'd hoped. But that didn't mean it was a failure (note the positive thinking, there). It was just another example of letting go, of going with the flow, of letting life lead the way. Sure, it had led me into a bit of a cul-de-sac, but I'd had fun. Fun I would otherwise have missed out on.

Yeah, so I'd wanted to prove Ian wrong. And no, I hadn't returned home with twenty million dollars, despite endless positive thinking, but instead with a sore body and a portrait of me and a dog. Ian, of course, would say that this meant the whole endeavour was doomed to failure. Me, being both a positive thinker *and* a positive doer, would not. I was sure it was all for the best. And I was sure that one day I'd find out how. One day I might even meet supermarket magnate Albert Heijn, and we'd have a good laugh about it all.

My phone rang. It was Brian of the Starburst Group. He said that his friend Pete, who knew a lot more about Maitreya than he did, had agreed to meet with me, and when would be convenient? I told him to suggest a time.

"Danny?"

"You must be Pete."

"Come in."

I did as Pete asked and stepped into his flat.

We were in Chancery Lane, and I'd reasoned that as I was here for such an odd purpose, it would probably be less awkward to cut straight to the chase.

"Basically, Pete . . . I'm here because Brian told me that Jesus was living on Brick Lane."

Pete rolled his eyes and let out quite a piercing laugh.

"Hah!" he said, "Well, that's *utter* bollocks, for a start."

I smiled and tried a piercing laugh of my own, but it wasn't as good.

"So it's not true?" I said.

"No," he said, shaking his head. "No, Jesus does not live on Brick Lane."

"Good."

"No. Jesus lives in *Rome*."

"Oh."

"*Maitreya* lives on Brick Lane."

This seemed to be getting complicated.

"Brian said that as well. But he said Maitreya *was* Jesus."

"No. Some call him Jesus, but he is not Jesus. Jesus lives in Rome. Maitreya used to be Jesus, two thousand years ago in Palestine, but now Jesus is a master as well. Maitreya works closely with Him, but Maitreya is Maitreya, and Maitreya lives in London. So . . . why don't you tell me why you think you met him?"

"What you have to realise, Danny," said Pete as we sat in his living room, sipping at our Tetley, "is that we can never be sure where Maitreya will show up next. Or to whom. He can be anywhere, instantaneously, and can show up to people of any faith, because, you see, he is *all* faiths. He showed up last year in Paraguay in front of two hundred Christians. He appeared in front of two hundred Muslims in Morocco the year before. He's turned up just about everywhere else. But *never before* on a *bus* to *one man*."

I saw what he was saying.

"Fair enough. So it couldn't have been him. I agree. It was just some bloke. I think Brian's just got a bit carried away with this, so . . ."

"Well, hang on, Danny. It absolutely *could* have been him. He is as likely to touch the life of *one* man as he is to touch the lives of a *thousand*. But he does so in a form which they can accept. Which is why he appears to some as Jesus, to others as Mohammed, and to others still as . . . well . . . a man on a bus."

"But why?"

"Are you a man of faith, Danny?"

I shook my head. "Not in the sense that I'd call myself a Christian or a Muslim or anything like that," I said. "I believe more in . . . people. The kindness of strangers. Mankind. That sort of thing."

"And that is precisely why Maitreya would have chosen to meet you in the way that he did," said Pete.

And that seemed to be that. It was case closed for Pete. He'd decided. I'd met Maitreya, whether I liked it or not.

"He stands for justice, sharing, and love—no matter what your beliefs are," he said, offering me a biscuit.

"That sounds quite nice, actually," I said, because it did.

"Hey—I'd love to interview you about your experiences with Maitreya, if that's possible," said Pete. "There are plenty of newsletters that would love to hear about it. Is there a number where I can contact you?"

"Er . . . well . . . I'm not sure if I'd be able to tell you much," I said. "But . . . yes."

I wrote my number down on a small pad Pete appeared to have stolen from The Swallow Hotel in Chollerford, and he beckoned me into another room.

"Look at this," he said, and he showed me the same picture of a robed, bearded man that Brian had shown me that day in the restaurant.

"This was taken in Nairobi. Six thousand people saw Maitreya arrive at the Church of Bethlehem at a tiny village called Kwangware. They do miracles there. They heal people, make mad people sane again, that sort of thing. And one day the minister told the congregation that God had spoken to her and that a very special guest would be arriving in a few moments time. Well, the villagers didn't know *what* to expect, but then . . . *then* he arrived. Maitreya. He appeared from absolutely nowhere, and he appeared to be almost *shining*. He blessed them, then got in a car and drove off."

"Goodness," I said. "What kind of car was it?"

I figured if he said it was a Nissan, something odd was going on.

"No idea. Now, if you want to know for certain whether that was Maitreya that you met that day, there *is* someone you can ask."

"Who?"

"A man called Elias Brown."

"Elias Brown?"

"Elias Brown, yes. He is in direct daily communication with Maitreya."

"Really?"

"Oh yes. He has been 'overshadowed' many times, which means that the masters essentially got inside him, spoke through him. He is a brilliant man—kind, generous. Anyway, the masters got friendly with him, and eventually he started to have direct contact with Maitreya himself."

"And this Brown guy definitely exists?"

Pete looked at me oddly.

"Of *course* he exists. I'll check to see if he's in the UK anytime soon. And if he is, I'll call you, yeah?"

"Yeah," I said. "I could ask him if he got home safely that night on the bus."

Pete nodded.

And I finished my tea and, strangely excited, I left.

It was the next morning, and I was on my way to meet Thom, the man I'd met at the party, and to take a look at the car I'd blindly agreed to buy.

He was sitting in the café outside Hendon Central Tube station when I arrived.

"How's it going?" I said.

"Not bad. All packed and ready to go."

"When do you leave?"

"Not for a couple of days. But I'm off up to Liverpool tonight, to say good-bye to my family and friends. I'll stay there until I have to go, and then it's New Zealand . . ."

"Ace. So, what kind of car is this again, exactly?"

"It's a Nissan Figaro," he said.

It still didn't sound particularly glamorous. But that was fine for me. In the few days that had passed since our first meeting, I'd reasoned that so long as it wasn't some kind of bright yellow, turbocharged Porsche, which would both bankrupt me *and* have people pointing at me wherever I went, I'd be okay. And besides, he'd told me he'd give me "an amazing deal." Money wasn't important, he said. Living was.

"And . . . how old is it?"

"Nineteen ninety-one."

"Oh."

Suddenly part of me was wishing it *was* a bright yellow, turbocharged Porsche, after all. A thirteen-year-old Nissan wasn't something that I could see helping my standing with girls very much. Not unless it was made of gold or something.

"And what colour is it?"

"Mint green."

Nope. This wasn't going to help my standing with girls at *all*.

With that said, I'd already decided—a car could be good. And it would get me over a fear, too. I'd always vowed that as long as I lived in London, I'd never own a car. It was just too dangerous. And too much hassle. But that comes from someone who's only ever owned one car in his life—a Mini Metro I'd bought for a thousand pounds after saving up all summer to buy one. And I only passed my test in the first place because I'd insisted on taking it in the town of Trowbridge. Trowbridge, for the uninitiated, has more roundabouts than almost anywhere else in Britain, and I could "do" roundabouts, so Trowbridge it was. I'd subsequently driven the Metro into the ground until every little bit of it was groaning or screeching and had lost the will to live. I sold the car the following New Year's Eve for fifty pounds, and drank it that night. A few weeks later I'd moved to London and convinced myself that I just didn't need another car. For one thing the Tube network took me everywhere I needed to go. And for another I'd been in enough taxis to know that driving in London takes a special sort of skill. And a handgun in the glove compartment. But think of the freedom it would give me—I could go anywhere, see anything, at anytime. Me and my Nissan. Having adventures. Making new friends. Like Michael Knight and KITT from *Knight Rider*. But in mint green. A new car would represent *freedom*.

I had been standing, looking at the car, for about two minutes, without really saying very much.

It was the oddest car I had ever seen.

"What . . . What on Earth *is* it?" I said eventually.

"I told you—a Nissan Figaro."

It looked like something out of *The Jetsons*.

"Is this a real car?" I said. "Or did you make it yourself out of toys?"

"It's real!" said Thom. "It's just a bit . . . unusual."

"I don't see the word 'Nissan' anywhere."

"Look, Danny, I'm not being funny, but this is a collector's item. They're huge in Germany. Only twenty thousand were ever made. Probably only half that still exist. They're imported from Japan."

Which would explain why I'd never seen one before. Well, not unless you count the one I'm sure I saw in an episode of *Wacky Races*.

"So what do you think?" said Thom, sitting in the passenger seat. "Still interested?"

"The thing is, Thom, yes, I'm still interested, but it's not like I can go around just buying random people's cars. . . ."

If only he knew.

"I told you," he said, climbing out. "I'm looking for a quick sale. I put it in the paper at four grand, thinking it would get a definite sale—which it bloody should have, 'cause it cost me six—but no one bit. I'll give it to you at rock bottom. I'm off next week, and it's the last thing to go."

He slammed the car door shut.

"Oh—unless you need a blender?"

I honk-honked outside Ian's front door.

I'd made my way through the London traffic from Hendon to Bow, and I was feeling very pleased with myself. I hadn't at any point felt the need for a handgun, and the whole thirteen-mile journey had only taken three and a half hours!

I honk-honked again, and eventually, Ian came outside.

"What in God's name is that?" he said.

"It's a car!" I said.

"Did you steal it from a fairground? What the hell is it?"

"It's a Nissan Figaro. It's a bit odd."

"Yes. Yes, it is. But, hang on—is it yours? Why? How?"

"A man asked me if I was interested in buying a car. I said yes."

"Jesus! Can you afford it?"

"Just. I got a good deal."

"How good?"

"He said if I bought it, he'd give me a blender."

"Good deal!"

"And he invited me to his good-bye party tomorrow. Do you want to come?"

"Where is it?"

"Liverpool."

"Not really."

Ian walked around the side of the car, took it all in, kicked the tyres, and looked like a real man. He asked me to pop the bonnet open, and once I'd worked out how, I did. He fiddled with things and made sure other things were securely fastened, and then he dropped the bonnet back into place.

"Looks good," he said.

I nodded.

"All the indicators work too," I said. "I checked them."

"You know what this means, don't you, Dan?"

"What?"

"You've got a *Yesmobile*! You're like Batman!"

"It's not a Yesmobile. It's a Nissan."

"It's a Yesmobile! Now, where's this blender? Let's make a smoothie!"

I popped open the boot, took the blender out, and we carried it to Ian's kitchen and plugged it in.

It didn't work.

If only blenders had indicators, I would've been on it like a flash.

I think Thom had only invited me to his party out of politeness. He hadn't really been expecting me to say yes. But that's what I'd done, and now I was stepping off a train in Liverpool after a three-hour journey to attend a party, which began at six. To be honest I felt slightly awkward about travelling two hundred miles to say good-bye to a man I'd only met twice before. It smelled slightly of obsession or, at the very least, infatuation.

As I made my way to the taxi rank outside, my phone rang.

"Hello?"

That was me answering the call and speaking, by the way; not just saying hello to a ringing phone.

"Danny? It's Gareth here. We met the other night at the party."

"Yes! Hello! And can I first of all apologise for taking you through that whole birth-canal-corking thing in quite so much detail?"

"Don't you worry. I mean, the diagrams were probably unnecessary, but otherwise it was a very informative nine-minute monologue."

He was joking. I hadn't even made any diagrams. And I'd talked *way* longer than nine minutes.

"So, listen, I was wondering if you'd like to come into the office for a chat about something?"

"Yes."

"You don't know what it is, yet."

"Oh. Okay. So what is it?"

"Why don't you come in, and I can tell you face-to-face?"

"Good idea."

"Tomorrow morning?"

I looked at my watch. I have no idea why. "Yes."

We said good-bye, and I suddenly realised that if I was going to make it to a meeting in Kennington the following morning, I was going to have to return from Liverpool tonight. What a hassle. Another three hours on a train. I wouldn't be home until the wee hours.

So I trudged back into the station and found my way to the information booth.

"Hello," I said. "Can you tell me when the last train from Liverpool to London is?"

"Last direct train, seven forty-nine," said the man, without even looking up.

I looked at my watch. It was ten to six.

"Seven forty-nine?" I said. "Are you sure?"

The man looked up at me wearily. He was clearly sure.

"But isn't that a bit . . . early?" I said. "Don't last trains usually go at about midnight?"

"Not to London," he said. "And not from here."

"Hi, Thom," I said. "Look, I can't stay long. I'm going to have to leave in about an hour."

"Oh," said Thom. "Where are you off to?"

"London."

"But . . . where have you just come from?"

"London."

I think Thom took a very small step back from me at this point.

"Well . . . it's, um . . . very *nice* of you to come, but you needn't have come all this way just . . ."

"I didn't realise the last train was at seven forty-nine," I said, explaining myself. "And I've got a meeting tomorrow, which I've agreed to, so . . ."

"Why didn't you drive up?"

"Drive up?"

"Yes. In your new car."

He had a point. But I had an answer.

"It took me three and a half hours to drive thirteen miles yesterday. Liverpool is 215 miles away. It would have taken me more than two days."

I don't think he saw the logic, which is a pity for someone who works with numbers.

"Well . . . would you like a beer?"

"Yes."

I was determined to make the most of my hour at the party, and I started by eating a packet of crisps. Just to let the room know I was a *proper* party animal.

We were in a bar called the Baa Bar, and only a few of Thom's friends had arrived so far. It was just after six. But there was one man by the name of Jason, who had clearly been there for some time, waiting for the party to start. He was more than a little bit drunk.

"What do you do?" I asked him.

We'd been sitting next to each other for a few minutes now, and I'd been watching him flick cigarette ash into a pint glass.

"I'm a civil servant," he said. "I work in immigration. Home Office stuff."

"Wow," I said. "That's a proper grown-up job."

"Yeah."

"Do you enjoy it?"

"No."

"Oh. Why not?"

"Because of a lot of things. Because it's my job. It's what I do so I can eat; not what I do because I want to."

"Right," I said, deciding that Jason was on the point of turning from someone who seemed mild-mannered but distracted, into quite an angry drunk. "So . . . what kind of things do you have to do?"

He refilled his glass from a bottle of wine on the table and turned to me.

"Today, right, this woman comes in. She was from Nigeria, and I had to interview her. She's not said how she's got into the country, and I need to know for the forms and that. So I say to her, 'How did you get into the UK?' And she looks at me like it's not her fault and tells me a witch doctor turned her into a peanut and smuggled her into the country under his hat."

He shook his head and smiled, and we laughed.

"Did she think that would work?" I asked, amazed.

"Yeah," said Jason.

"So did you let her in?"

"No," said Jason, quietly. "God knows why she wants to live in this shit of a country. God knows why she thought pretending she'd been a peanut would help."

Usually that's a sentence that would have made me laugh. But it didn't. There was a sadness in Jason's eyes.

"Another bloke came in last week. I said to him, 'Why are you seeking residency in the UK?' He says that he'd been watching TV back home in Cameroon with his wife. It was a lovely, normal evening, he says. And then he turns round and sees a goat standing in his living room."

"A goat?"

"A goat."

"And what happened then?"

"No. That was it. That was his excuse. A goat had been in his living room."

"Was he allergic?"

Jason shook his head.

"Something to do with omens. A goat is a bad one. So that's why he decided to come to Britain."

"Well, there are less goats, I suppose. And did you let him in?"

"No," said Jason. "I sent him back. I end up sending most of them back."

I didn't quite know what to say to this. This was a man clearly affected by his work. He saw suffering, and he heard tales of woe and desperation. He spent his days listening to stories of rape or murder or beatings. Of political pressures and harassment. And at the risk of sounding glib, of ladies being turned into peanuts. Jason was one of the many whose job it was to decide who was telling the truth and who was not. It was a heavy burden.

"I don't know," he said, shrugging. "Sometimes I'm happy with life, and sometimes I'm not. It's like, I know I've got a good job. It's a job with responsibility, and I'm kind of lucky in that way. I've got a good head on my shoulders, and I'm a fair man, when I could easily be some right-wing bastard doing my job and turning everyone back. And it's not a dead-end job. Not really. There are prospects. But . . . I dunno."

"What would you rather be doing?"

"Anything," said Jason. "Pretty much anything. I mean, in an ideal world, it'd be travel. I've never really travelled. My sister— she took a year off before going to university and travelled round the world. She works in a call centre now, but she's happy enough, you know? Because she's *done* something. I sit in a little office with the same people every day, and I think . . . Is this it? Surely this can't be it? My little brother finishes school in five weeks. If there's one thing I'm going to make sure he does, it's travel. Not make my mistake."

"Why don't you go with him?" I said.

"He's asked. I can't. I've got too much going on. I'm the most experienced member of the team. If I go, well . . . I can't. And I couldn't afford it. I've got a mortgage. Pension. No, no. I've made my choices. I've had my fun."

There was something about the way Jason said he'd had his fun that made me incredibly sad. He was in his twenties. And yet he thought he'd had his fun. He thought he'd made all his choices.

"Maybe this doesn't have to be it," I said.

"It is, though."

"All I mean is, maybe you should quit your job. Do something else. See what life brings you."

"Oh, it's that easy, isn't it?" he said sourly.

"Well, I dunno. Why don't you take a risk?"

"Take a risk?" he said. His anger shocked me. "Who the hell are you to suggest taking risks? I can't take risks. I have to be measured and logical and make the right decisions. In my life and with the lives of others. I'd love to have a stupid, risk-free job where the biggest worry is whether or not you'll get down the pub before it gets crowded or not. But I don't. I have a grown-up, responsible job with grown-up, responsible pressures."

"I'm just saying . . . ," I tried before I realised that I didn't know what I was saying. I gave it one more go. "I'm just saying that maybe sometimes it's riskier not to take a risk. Sometimes all you're guaranteeing is that things will stay the same. Sometimes it's more important to say yes to things than it is to say no."

Jason didn't say anything. He just stared into his glass. The conversation had taken a darker twist somewhere along the line, and now I was a child in front of him—a stupid child with a stupid job, who lived his life in a stupid way. And what was I basing my big, superficial sayings on, anyway? I was embarrassed and stood up to leave.

"I'm just saying that yes is as good a word to say as no," I said. "When a chance comes up, I mean. When anything comes up."

"That's the problem," said Jason, still staring into his glass. "I spend all my time saying no, and it's depressing. I say no at work and no at home. I tell people they can't come into the country. And why? Because of a set of rules. I tell them they can't start a new life here. I crush people's hope. And then I take that home with me."

I thought about leaving at that point. About walking away. But I didn't. I had a sudden urge to just tell Jason the truth. Explain the real reason why I'd travelled so far to go to a party and would only be staying one hour. It didn't really compare with the kind of decisions he had to make, but it might mean *something*. I wanted to tell him about all the things I'd said yes to . . . and all the things that had happened as a result. The good things *and* the bad things. I wouldn't leave the bad things out. They were just as important. I would leave Jason under no illusions, but I would show him . . . well . . . that he had a choice. He could do like Thom was doing and walk away and leave his job and sell his car and find a new life. He could do like I was doing. *He could say yes if he wanted.* Yes to *himself*.

He could *say yes more*.

"Listen, you'll probably think that what I'm about to tell you is stupid. Or pointless. Or childish. But I want you to hear me out, because it's something that's become quite important to me. But at the same time, when I tell you, you can't use this against me, okay?"

"I'm not agreeing to anything, mate. . . ."

"No, seriously. If I tell you this, you can't tell *anyone*. You could ruin my life. If Thom finds out, and he tells someone who was at the party the other night, and they tell someone else, I could be in a lot of trouble. So keep it between us, yeah?"

Jason raised his eyebrows and considered it. And then he nodded.

And so I told a complete stranger what I was up to and what I'd done from the start and where it had led me and where I hoped it would lead me in the misguided belief that it would somehow help him.

And when I finished, that complete stranger stood up, swore at me, and walked off toward the bar.

"Thom . . . that mate of yours," I said. "Jason."

"Oh, yes. Jase. Sorry about him," said Thom. "He's, well, he's got the weight of the world on his shoulders."

"Why can't he give up? Do something else?"

"He feels like he's responsible for everything. And that makes him feel like there's no way out. It's no use talking to him. He won't listen. I think he's jealous that I'm in a position to leave, and he's not."

"I guess he's got the kind of job he can't really walk away from."

Thom nodded. And then looked at his watch.

"Hadn't you . . ."

Shit. It was 7:24.

The journey home was an odd one.

I'd wanted to stay at the party, make things all right again with Jason. Explain myself and make it all much clearer. But I knew the rules. I'd said yes to something. I had to go.

And the worse thing was, I couldn't really help but feel that Jason had a point. I was naive. And stupid. I needed to grow up. What was I doing with my life? I mean, really? What was the point

in all this? To waste six hours of my day on a train? To wake up confused and bewildered in a Dutch hotel room? To severely annoy my
ex-girlfriend? What was I gaining from this? Apart from a car and
some mild abuse? Yeah, so I was keeping myself busy and going out
more and having new experiences, but I'd learnt my lesson now.
Maybe I didn't have to be quite so religious about my Yeses. Maybe
I could just calm it down a bit, come clean to Ian, accept his punishment with good grace but know that I had given it a go.

I got home to a cold and empty flat. There was no milk left to
make tea. I didn't bother checking my e-mails.

I just went to bed.

The following morning I lay there, staring at the ceiling. I'd slept
long and hard, and my spirits were lifted only slightly when I saw it
was a very sunny day indeed. For a moment I considered just staying
in bed, convincing myself I was ill. But I'd agreed to go to a meeting.
I didn't want to let people down.

I was at the offices of Cactus TV in Kennington not too long after. I
had driven (yes, driven!) the simple six-mile journey in the Yesmobile in
just ninety short minutes, meaning I was getting a lot better at this driving lark. Soon I'd be able to drive to places like Liverpool again in little
less than a day! Things have really come on since the horse and cart.

Gareth met me at the gate.

"Come through," he said. "We're going to be meeting with Dan,
one of the producers here. Would you like a drink? Tea or something?"

"Yes, please," I said, because even without this whole Yes thing, I'd
never turn down a cup of tea.

We walked through a production office packed with busy, young,
stylish people, setting up shoots, booking guests, researching subjects,
and looking all busy and young and stylish. The carpet was bright
green, and there was a cactus on every corner.

I sat down in the office, and Gareth popped off to get the tea. I
hadn't been told too much about why I'd been asked to come in, but
that was okay, because, hey, free tea.

"Danny, I'm Dan," said a tall man, striding into the office. I stood to shake his hand. His handshake was firmer than mine, and I tried to make up for that by squeezing harder, but I'd done it too late, and I think he thought I'd just liked holding his hand and didn't want to let go.

Gareth was next in with the teas, and Dan shuffled his notes.

"Right, so . . . ," said Gareth. "The reason we got you in was . . . We're coming up with a few new features for the show, and . . . well . . . we're always on the lookout for new people to join the team, and . . . Look . . . have you ever thought about being a TV presenter?"

Eh?

"Eh?" I said.

"Because we're possibly going to do a slot that may or may not be right for you."

What? Was I being asked to . . . *what* was I being asked to do?

"I mean, first of all there was that cult you started. But all the stuff you were telling me the other night, about Jesus on Brick Lane, and the pyramids stuff and the whole—you know—corking theory . . . It fits in with something we've been thinking of doing for quite a while."

Dan took over.

"Basically we want to do a slot about enlightened thoughts and spiritualism. And when Gareth told me you believed that aliens built the pyramids . . ."

"Er, hang on, it's not that *I* believe . . ."

"And you think that men can have babies . . ."

"Um no, I'm just saying . . ."

"And that you think you met Jesus on a bus . . ."

"Okay, yeah, that *might* be true. . . ."

"Well . . . we thought you might be right for this. We needed to find someone who already knows about that side of life, and we were stuck for presenters. So we'd like to possibly take a risk on you."

I shook my head in disbelief. Good lord! I was being asked if I'd ever thought about being a TV presenter! And I hadn't—I was someone who was quite happy being behind the camera, making notes and holding a clipboard and trying to look busy. I was a TV producer—not a TV presenter!

"Look, this may or may not happen," said Gareth, "and if it does, it won't be for a while, but what we might want to do is take you on a couple of spiritualist weekends. Get you to do some Vortex Healing, maybe hug some trees, tap into your psychic powers and try to heal a flower; that sort of thing."

"Like E.T. does in that film."

"Sort of," said Dan. "We thought we could call it *Danny's Path to Enlightenment*. We've already run it past Richard and Judy, and they're going to think about it, because Richard said . . . What was it?"

"You were odd," Gareth told me.

"In a good way," Dan added.

"Yes," said Gareth. "He said you were *odd* in a *good* way."

"Well," I said. "I'm not sure I'd be any use at it, but . . ."

"We can work wonders in an edit, don't worry about that. But the important thing is: If we decide to go ahead with it, are you up for it?"

They were both looking at me intently.

I shrugged.

"Yeah."

Blimey! I was going to be a television presenter! On a national show! A national teatime show! A world of housewives and students awaited me!

"Great!" said Dan. "Well, I guess we'll be in touch!"

That night the drinks were on me.

I met up with Wag and Ian at the Yorkshire Grey, and I told them my good news. I mean, fair enough—it would probably never happen. But even so, things were looking up. My recent spate of slight misfortunes seemed over. The randomness of maybe being recruited onto the *Richard & Judy* team to do a glamorous job like TV presenting—something I had never done before and doubtless never would've had it not been for Yes. It had given me a real lift and a genuine boost.

I was enjoying the ride again.

Wag, however, looked troubled by life. He'd just returned from his trip to Germany, but he didn't seem at all relaxed or rested by it. If anything, he seemed . . . stressed. *Very* stressed. It didn't help that his phone kept going off.

Every time it did, Ian and I fell silent, allowing Wag to answer it. But he didn't. He just looked at the screen, cursed, and ignored them by not answering.

"Wag," said Ian. "Are you in some sort of . . . trouble?"

"I don't want to talk about it."

It went off again.

"Answer it, Wag."

"I don't want to."

"Who's calling you?"

"I said I don't want to talk about it."

It stopped ringing, and we each took a sip of our pints. We sat in silence. We knew the next call wouldn't be far away.

We started to talk about football before realising that none of us really knows anything about football, and the phone rang again, which was quite good timing, really, because it meant we preserved an air of masculinity.

"Okay . . . I'm going to answer it," said Wag, and he did.

Ian and I waited in silence, pretending not to listen.

"No," said Wag with some degree of force, and hung up.

"Who was it?" asked Ian. "What's going on?"

"I know. It won't bloody stop," said Wag. "I'll turn it off."

"But who was it?" I said.

"No one. Never mind. It's nothing."

"Come on, Wag," said Ian. "Who was it? Who keeps ringing you?"

The phone rang again. Wag stared at it, furious.

"It. Won't. Shut. Up," he said through gritted teeth. "It just keeps ringing!"

"That means someone's calling you," I said.

Perhaps Wag hadn't worked out this whole mobile phone thing yet. Perhaps he thought that when it rang, it meant it needed feeding.

"Hang on a second . . ."

Wag answered the call, said another loud and forceful no to whoever was on the other end, and hung up.

"Jesus, this is terrible," he said. "I can't relax. It's been ringing since I got back. Every other bloody minute. It won't stop ringing. They won't stop ringing me."

"*Who?*" said Ian.

Wag took a deep breath. "The Germans," he said.

I took a good hard look at Wag. It seemed he was in the early stages of some kind of paranoid attack. Ian and I made concerned eye contact.

"The Germans won't leave me alone," he said as if that explained all.

I made a sympathetic face and tried some slow and comforting words.

"Yes, they will, Wag. The Germans will leave you alone."

He frowned.

"Why are you looking at me like I'm mental? Why are you stroking my arm?"

"Why don't you tell us why you think the Germans are after you?" said Ian.

"They're not *after* me. They just won't stop calling me."

"Why?!" I said in desperate unison with Ian.

Wag took another deep breath. He was clearly at some kind of turning point in his life. And there seemed to be something he needed to say.

"Because the Germans think I'm Busted."

The words hung in the air. Ian and I blinked at each other a couple of times, and then we both blinked at Wag, and then we blinked at each other again.

"The Germans think you're busted? As in broken?"

"Worse."

What could be worse than being broken?

Oh . . .

"No!" I said in shock. "Do they think you're Busted as in . . . the chart-topping teenage boy band?"

Wag bit his lip, rolled his eyes upward, and nodded his head silently. His phone rang again. Ian covered his mouth with both hands in horror.

"God," he said. "Look . . ."

He showed me the phone. A number was flashing up on the screen. And not a British number, either.

"Another one!" said Wag. "Another German!"

Wag answered the phone, shouted *"Nein!"*, and hung up again.

"Listen," I said, "we may have to backtrack here. Why are Germans phoning you, under the impression that you're a three-man teenage boy band? Because I've known you for a while, now, and you are *nothing* like a three-man teenage boy band . . ."

"I've been working with Busted lately, right? I've been helping out on a couple of tracks. We got on, the four of us. Or I thought we did. They're lovely lads. But they've been on tour lately, and one night"— he took a sip of his pint to steady his nerves—"one night they were doing an interview for a German TV show, right?"

"Right," I said.

"I was backstage setting up some of the technical stuff. And one of them decided it would be funny to give out my mobile number, live, on air."

I tried to suppress a smile. So did Ian. We both failed.

"They said it was *their* phone number and that their fans should feel free to phone up with their thoughts and questions at any time of day or night."

His phone beeped.

"Excuse me," he said, picking the phone up once more, studying it, and then slamming it onto the table.

"They've started bloody texting me now."

Ian started giggling. Wag was clearly deeply affected by this.

"I try telling them I'm not in Busted, but they don't believe me. They say 'Is that Charlie?' And I say, 'No, it's Wag,' and they say, 'Is that you, Charlie?' And I say, 'No, it is Wag speaking,' and they say, 'Charlie? Charlie?' I *need* this phone! It's my work phone! I have to keep it on! Which means I'm being harassed by these people twenty-four hours a day!"

"Look," I said. "It's bound to wind down sometime. How long have Busted got left in them? Five, maybe six years?"

"I can't go about being accused of being in Busted for the next six years, Dan! This is a modern-day nightmare! My phone number is all over Germany! People are even telling me they've found it on the Internet!"

I started to laugh rather loudly.

"Shut up! This isn't funny!"

"It bloody is, Charlie!" said Ian.

"It bloody *isn't*!"

Wag's face went bright red, and he set me off again.

"See how you like it, then, Dan. What's your number?"

"Eh? You're not giving my number to random German teenagers!"

"Yes, I am. Why don't you see how *you* like it, when everyone in the world thinks you're in Busted?"

I started to feel unwell. My laughter suddenly stopped. Was that a suggestion? Was that a Yes moment? Ian's face lit up as he realised the same thing. But Wag hadn't finished.

"Why don't we give *your* number out to everyone in the world, then?" said Wag. "See how *you* like it, eh?"

He started to type my number into his phone. He was preparing a text message.

"Wait . . . What are you . . ."

"I am about to send your number to a bunch of Germans, Dan, to tell them that your number is the new number for the International Fans of Busted club, and that they should feel free to call you whenever the mood takes them . . ."

"Wait . . . ," I said. "Just wait a second . . ."

"Not so funny now, is it?" he said. "Let's see how *you* like being at the centre of a teenage phenomenon. Let's see how *you* respond to being constantly phoned up by people you don't even know, hounding you, wanting to meet up with you, thinking you're in a boy band . . ."

He held the phone up in front of me and showed me his message.

"I'll bloody do it, Danny. . . . If you've anything to say, any apology to make . . ."

I went quite pale. I couldn't work out what to do. I read the message.

CALL ME. I AM NEW BUSTED NUMBER. CALL ANYTIME. 0044 7802 * ***

Oh, Jesus.

Should I stop him? Would that be going against my new way of life? Or should I treat it as an opportunity?

"No apology?" he said. "Fine. Then the question we face is this: Shall *I* press Send, or do *you* want to do it?"

Shit. Two Yeses. Which do I choose? What do I do now? I shrugged, helplessly.

Wag leaned forward, slightly intimidatingly.

"Dan . . . do you *really* want to give your number out to everyone in the world?"

Oh, God. That was it. That was the proper Yes moment. I looked at Ian, who was smirking and slowly nodding and carrying in his eyes the fact that he knew *exactly* what I was going to have to do next. Wag continued to stare at me.

"Well, *do* you, Dan?"

I took the phone from Wag, and—maintaining steady eye contact— pressed Send.

He looked horrified.

"And in answer to your other question, my friend . . . yes. Yes, I *do* want to give my number out to everyone in the world."

A split-second later, Ian's phone beeped. Wag had been bluffing. He'd texted my number to Ian, *not* to thousands of confused Germans.

But as for me . . . well, I *hadn't* been bluffing.

And I knew what I'd have to do next.

It was another level-five job.

CHAPTER 10

In Which Daniel Undertakes a Most Unusual Search

Now, don't get me wrong: I know what I just said.

I know I just said I'd have to give my number out to "everyone in the world." But that was when I was down at the pub. That was during a macho booze-fuelled face-off, when everything seemed possible and nothing seemed like too much trouble. The problem was, when I got home to consider my next move, I realised that I clearly couldn't give my number out to *everyone* in the world. That'd be crazy and would take ages and involve me on the phone to people all over the world, saying, "Hi, you don't know me, but this is my number in case you ever fancy a chat." It just wasn't practical and would take the better part of a lifetime.

No, if I was going to do as Wag said and make my phone number publicly available, I was going to have to do it another way. I would have to get it out there on the streets, where it could be seen and acted upon and used. There was only one thing for it: a clever word-of-mouth stickering campaign. What a great way to make human connections. They say strangers are just friends you haven't met yet. And while that can't be *entirely* true (statistically some of them are *bound* to be muggers), I nevertheless clung to that notion as I ordered two thousand stickers bearing the legend:

CALL ME
Let's have a polite conversation!
07802 * ***

I felt the middle line might put off the muggers and the riffraff, but would leave room for the people like Amsterdam's Jahn, the open-minded and progressive. The people who could teach me something. And so below those two words and that one sentence was, yes, my mobile number. The number I rely on. The number, thanks to Wag's inadvertant suggestion, I would be giving out to the public-at-large. Starting now with Ian in the East End.

"When you think about it," said Ian, walking alongside me, "this is basic psychology."

"What is?" I said, attaching another sticker to the side of a phonebox.

"This. You feel that there's a gap. Am I right? A Lizzie-shaped gap. And you're trying to *fill* that gap. But instead of filling it with *one* person, you're trying to fill it with *everyone*. You not having Lizzie gives you the perfect excuse to do this."

"What do you mean, 'excuse'? I wasn't looking for an excuse to do this! Do you think I've been waiting around for years, hoping desperately that one day someone would say or do something which would allow me to have thousands of stickers printed up, inviting the general public to ring me up for a polite conversation? Is that how you think I live my life?"

"Pretty much, yes."

We stickered Bow, Mile End, and Bethnal Green that day. I kept a wad of stickers in my pocket, too, for whenever the mood took me.

The day flew by, but no one called.

I guess all I could do was wait.

In a large room on the Old Kent Road the following night, dozens of chairs were lined up in neat rows. A woman in a cardigan fiddled with a video camera pointed at the table, which I assumed the world-renowned Maitreya expert, Elias Brown, would call home for the next couple of hours.

Pete had phoned me urgently that morning and said that he'd checked the relevant Web sites, and Mr. Brown was apparently in town to give one of his lectures. Pete seemed to think that there could be something in all this, and now that the people at *Richard & Judy* had decided I could well be an authority on matters of the spiritual, I thought it pertinent to attend. That, and I couldn't exactly say no.

One of the strangest things was, Pete wanted to make sure I knew he didn't believe it was possible that Maitreya, aka the World Teacher, was walking the streets, looking out for people like me, but he'd begun to talk about him in quite reverential tones. So much so that we were both becoming quietly excited by the prospect of learning more about the man who had apparently chosen me—*me!*—to guide and direct. Not that I believed it either, of course. No, no.

There were about forty people in the room now, and most had already taken their seats, but others were busy buying Maitreya post-cards or books or audio tapes of previous Elias Brown lectures. A few months before I'd never even heard of Maitreya. I was surprised to see such an industry revolving around him.

"I've got a few of these books," said Pete. "And I subscribe to Mr. Brown's newsletter, which is *surprisingly* informative."

"He's got his own newsletter as well?"

"Oh yes. He's quite an authority and very nice with it. Genuinely a very nice man. All this is aimed at making the world a better—"

But that was as far as he got. Because just then the man we'd come to see walked into the room. And the room fell silent.

"That's him!" whispered Pete in my ear. "That's Brown!"

He took his seat with ease and smiled a wide and happy smile. For a man in his eighties, he was a bit of a looker. And it's not often you'll hear me say that.

"Good evening," he said in a soft and warm voice.

"Good evening," replied every single person in the room, including Pete, in near-perfect unison. I was a little surprised by the choreography.

"How many of you have been to one of these lectures before?"

Pete and pretty much everyone else put their hands up.

"All I ask is that when I am speaking you keep an open mind," said Elias. He had a kind face. "I am not asking you to believe what you don't want to believe; merely that you keep an open mind. The truly open-minded person is not easy to find. I will give you some statistics later on, if I remember."

This made me laugh. A woman in a pashmina frowned at me, and I shut up.

"What we will do this evening," said Elias, "is in a few moments' time I will be overshadowed by Maitreya himself. He will be here, among us."

Pete nudged me excitedly.

"We will play for you a tape of some of his messages while this is happening. After that I will talk for a while about Maitreya and his mission here on Earth, and then we will finish with a final overshadowing, which will be far more powerful than the first. It should be quite extraordinary."

As he said this his microphone stopped working. The woman in the pashmina whispered something to her friend about rogue energies. Elias continued to talk at a much lower level until one very exasperated man in the second row put his hand up and shouted, "I THINK YOUR BATTERY HAS RUN OUT" far louder than he needed to, given that he was only in the second row.

"Oh," said Elias. "How deeply unprofessional of us. Usually we are *very* polished."

He smiled and looked around the room, and everyone laughed. He was certainly a very charming host, and I was enjoying his company. One of his helpers, however, was going bright red as she struggled to pry the microphone open to replace its batteries.

"I'm sorry." She seemed to be stuttering. "It's . . . oh . . . oh dear . . ."

A moment later a rather strapping man was by her side with a replacement battery. He took full control of the situation, clicked the battery into place, and put the microphone back on its stand, in front of Elias who tapped it and said, "Hello?"

It worked again.

"*Magic!*" said the man in the second row.

"Now let us continue . . . ," said Elias.

Down went the lights.

"I am going to study each of your chakras," he said. "I will look at each of you in turn. But don't worry if you are sitting behind someone tall and it appears that I have missed you by accident, because I won't have."

At this he closed his eyes, breathed very deeply, and then, suddenly, he made a terribly odd noise with his throat, and his eyes shot wide open again. I guessed that this must have been the moment that the spirit of Maitreya had entered into him. Either that or we'd have to start praying that there was a doctor in the house. I found myself sitting straighter, probably subconsciously trying to make a good impression on Maitreya. Someone somewhere clicked Play on a tape recorder and a fuzzy, buzzy home-recording kicked in.

"Prepare yourself . . . to see me soon!" said a slow, deep voice, while Elias Brown looked from person to person, a beatific smile on his face and kindness in his eyes.

"Prepare yourself . . . to hear my message!"

I was. And so, it seemed, was everyone else. I appeared to be the only person in the room without my hands clasped and my eyes closed. Instinctively I clasped my hands together.

"I am the stranger at the door. I am he who knocks. I am your friend."

Elias continued to smile and look from person to person. Somewhere behind me, someone sighed a sigh of pleasure.

"You will see me soon. Maybe . . . you have seen me already."

Suddenly it went a bit odd. I shivered. Elias Brown was looking straight at me. Straight at me, while a tape told me that maybe I had met Maitreya already.

"Those who search me out . . ."

Elias Brown was still looking at me.

". . . are those who *will* find me. . . ."

I fiddled with my watch.

He was still looking at me.

I smiled nervously.

And then he stopped looking at me and looked at the plump woman next to me instead.

"The masters are all around us," said Elias Brown a little later on. "Now, that's a *huge* statement. And one that I can't in *any* way prove. But take it from me: It is true."

I had started to realise some way into this lecture that quite a lot of what I was being told was going to have to be taken on faith.

"Soon you will become aware of their presence and their wisdom. When Maitreya comes, he will appear on television, simultaneously, all around the world. The satellite systems were built purposefully for his coming. You will see a face. A face you will recognise. A face you have seen before. But he will not speak. He will not say a word. But his thoughts will silently take place inside us silently. Each of us will hear him in our own language. Thousands of spontaneous miracles will then take place."

It was half an hour in, and somewhere in front of me, an old woman took a photo of Elias. Pete had his eyes closed and was nodding slowly.

"All those who have shaped humanity are disciples of the masters. Da Vinci, Einstein, Shakespeare, Newton, Freud, Jung . . . they have passed on their knowledge and their inspiration. The masters know what is best for each and every one of us, and they work constantly to help us."

From there Elias talked about Maitreya's thoughts and philosophies on world hunger, the UN, war in the Middle East, nuclear power, George W. Bush, the developed nations, the G8 summit, poverty, disease, and destitution. But at no point did he mention how Maitreya gets home at night, and whether on occasion he's taken the bus rather than the Tube. It was all starting to get a bit disheartening. "Deal with the issues at hand, Brown!" I felt like shouting. "Why cover politics, when we can talk bus routes!"

"One day we will all be immortal," he said. "I *promise* you that."

But even that didn't help.

Mind you it was hard to disagree with Maitreya's general principles. To save the world, he says, we need to share. There are more than thirty million people in the world today who are starving to death . . . and yet the storehouses of the West are overflowing. It was this that I was pondering, when an arm shot up in front of me. It was Pete. What was he doing?

"Yes?" said Elias Brown.

"Is the Maitreya still here tonight?" he said, and I bristled with embarrassment. "In this room?"

Elias smiled and looked around the room for a few moments. He seemed to catch an invisible eye, and then looked back at Pete and nodded.

"Yes. He is here."

Pete nudged me in the ribs and smiled a very wide smile.

"Probably because of you," he whispered.

I was starting to think that Pete *did* believe in all this after all.

"Where does Maitreya live?" asked a man on the other side of the room, and I felt rather smug, because I already knew this.

"He lives among the Asian community in Brick Lane. He doesn't sleep, he doesn't eat, he doesn't have a bed. He works twenty-four hours a day, tirelessly, for the benefit of the planet Earth. For the benefit of each and every one of you."

And Elias Brown once again looked me right in the eye.

"I'm telling you, Ian, he looked straight at me," I said as we walked down Mile End Road. "It was a little bit spooky."

"An old man in a cream suit looked straight at you, and you think that's spooky. It's not spooky. It's just an old man in a cream suit looking straight at you."

"But it was like he *knew* something. He kind of changed my mind, when I saw the look on his face. It was like Maitreya was sitting next to him and pointing me out and saying, 'That's the one . . . *that's* the one I'm helping!'"

"Do you realise how arrogant that sounds?" said Ian as I paused to stick a CALL ME sticker to a phonebox. "Do you think you're the bloody Golden Child or something? Do you think that any minute now, Eddie Murphy's going to burst into the room looking for you."

"Is it really so far-fetched? Why do you automatically assume I can't be some kind of Golden Child? This is precisely the kind of negative feedback that Jesus will get when he makes his Second Coming."

My phone rang. I answered it. They hung up. In the past twenty-four hours, my CALL ME stickers seemed to have permeated London's consciousness, and this had started to happen quite a bit.

"Look, Dan," said Ian. "I honestly don't think the man on the bus was Jesus or Maitreya or *any* of those fellas. I was drunk when I suggested that. And I think it is highly unlikely that you, my friend, are the Golden Child, or the Copper Child, or a child made of virtually *any* metallic substance or element."

"The Starburst Group think it might be possible."

"The Starburst Group think that aliens built the pyramids," he said, and I saw his point.

The only way you're going to get over this, Dan," he continued, pausing only for dramatic effect, "is if you *find* the man on the bus."

Now, I don't know if *you've* ever walked down Brick Lane, attempting to track down and meet an enlightened being from another dimension, but it's really not as easy as it sounds.

Ian had been right, of course: Finding the man on the bus was the only way to confirm once and for all that he wasn't the Maitreya. That said, he hadn't been too keen to join me on the journey. I'd already tired him out with our sticker exertions. No, this time I'd had to persuade him with the promise of a free meal.

"So, what's the plan?" he said as we stepped off the Tube at Aldgate.

I smiled and opened my rucksack.

"This is . . ."

I pulled out a thick wodge of photocopied A4 posters, headed with the controversial and attention-grabbing question: IS THIS YOU?

It was the second great Yes-Man campaign in just one week! I was deeply excited. . . . Here I was, reaching out to the world, exposing myself not just once but twice! This was just what I'd promised myself I would do. Not only did I have my CALL ME stickers out there, circulating in society and spreading my number far and wide, but here were my Man On The Bus posters, proudly displaying the face of the bloke who'd brought me out of the depths of my depression. The only problem was, I'm not very good at drawing, and all I really remembered about my subject was that he was an Asian man with a beard. That, on its own, wouldn't be enough. So I wrote a more detailed explanation of the poster's existence underneath the picture:

Are you a teacher who lives in the Aldgate area of East London? Were you travelling on the bus-replacement service out of Oxford Circus, heading toward the East End on Friday the 6? If so, I'm the man you were talking to on the bus! Please get in touch—there's a story I need to tell you! Either e-mail me

at danny@dannywallace.com or call me on 07802 *** ***. This
isn't a joke! Please call me! Danny

The best thing I could do was plaster Brick Lane—the centre of
the local community—with my elaborate posters and just hope . . .

And so, for the second time that week, we began to stick things up. We
stuck posters on lampposts, over club posters, in phone boxes, and more
while also whacking the odd CALL ME sticker up alongside it. I'll be honest: We got a few strange looks that day. Perhaps it was the quality of my
artwork that was causing concern; perhaps it was the fact that we were
being so very thorough with our campaigning. Whatever it was, I knew
that at the very least, we'd caused a stir. Someone would recognise this
man. They *had* to. Even if the only defining characteristic of my drawing
was a beard.

And then a bell went off, and out of the mosque opposite poured
hundreds of bearded men, and I realised that perhaps this was going
to be a little trickier than I thought.

As we ate our meal, Ian and I pondered the magical possibilities of
what we'd just done. Well, *I* thought they were magical. Ian still
thought they were bollocks.

"It's crazy when you think about it, isn't it?" I said. "You know . . .
about the man on the bus possibly being a god."

Ian laughed.

"What?" I said, offended. "I mean, think about it: What if this
whole Yes thing . . . What if it was *meant to be*?"

"Meant to be what? A waste of time?"

"No. You know . . . *destined*. What if there's a *reason* for it all?"

"If that man on the bus *was* a god, then why does he travel by bus?"

"It's like that song. 'What if God was one of us, just a stranger on a
bus, la la la la la lalala.' In fact it's *exactly* like that. Right down to the slob
reference and the la la las."

"This is a fundamentally flawed concept," said Ian, pointing his
fork at me. A small piece of chicken fell off, but we both politely
ignored it. "For a start, a god would not use the bus. Any god.
Certainly not Jesus or Buddha. They make enough from statuette-

based merchandising alone not to have to slum it with the likes of you. Even the *pope's* got a special car, for crying out loud."

I took a bite of my naan. My phone rang. I answered it. They hung up.

"Maybe you're right. Maybe it's all too much of a coincidence. You know . . . a stranger passing on his wisdom, and then me finding out the World Teacher lives locally."

Ian nearly choked on his tikka.

"A *coincidence?* Dan . . . How is that a coincidence? The two things clearly have absolutely nothing to do with each other. You can't say, 'Oh, I sat next to a man on a bus, and a month later I heard God lives in Brick Lane' and claim it's a coincidence! It's like saying, 'Oh, look, there's an apple, and only yesterday I was on a boat!' How is that a coincidence? You're deluded, my friend. . . ."

I took a sip of my beer and looked at Ian wisely.

"You were probably destined to say that."

When I returned home that night, I considered all the ways I could potentially find the man on the bus. I knew Ian had been right when he said I needed to meet him. And not just to prove or disprove he was Maitreya, but to tell him what I was up to, what he'd done to my life.

I went to sleep that night, excited. But little did I know that, for a while at least, the hunt for the man on the bus would have to take a backseat. Because as it turned out, someone was on the hunt for *me.*

My secret—the secret that was vital I keep as quiet as I could—was suddenly in real danger of being revealed. Because someone knew about it. And that someone was out to get me.

CHAPTER 11

In Which Daniel Finds Himself Central to a Very Disturbing Predicament

I really didn't know what to make of it at first. I really, truly didn't. I assumed, when I first opened it, that it must have been a coincidence. Or, failing that, some kind of joke.

But now . . . now it just seemed *sinister*. I picked up the package once more and carefully, quietly studied its contents.

A very short note:

If you're going to say yes all the time, you may as well give your voice a rest.

And a dark-blue baseball cap, embroidered with one word: "Yes."

The package had been sent from London W1. The label had been printed as had the note. I kept on studying the hat, searching for clues, but then I realised there weren't any, and I was just a man, sitting at a table, studying a hat.

For a split-second paranoia gripped me. What if word had got out? What if Ian had let slip what I was doing? What if someone had overheard our conversations? What if someone was planning and plotting against me? Maybe I had a nemesis now! An evil, mustachioed villain, intent on my downfall! Or what if . . .

Hang on.

Ian.

Of course. Ian. Simple. Mystery solved.

Ian was not only the man who knew, but the man who had something to gain from this. The man who was in on it, and who'd been in on it from the start. The man who'd already told me he was going to punish me.

I laughed and shook my head with what I hoped looked like pity in my eyes.

Oh, he thought he was good, didn't he? He thought he could beat me. He thought that by sending me this hat—this hat-based version of a horses' head under a pillow—he could frighten me. Intimidate me. Make me think what I was doing was wrong or bad or pointless.

But I knew just how to handle this: I would *ignore* it. I would pretend it had never arrived. Sooner or later, he'd start probing, looking for a reaction. It was exactly the same as when he sent me that fake Valentine card, the one he pretended was from Lionel Richie. It wouldn't be long before he'd break down and say, "Look, are you going to *wear* the bloody hat or not?" And then I would look upon him with more weary pity in my eyes, sigh, and say, "Yes."

Which would be all the more frustrating for him, because it would be yet another Yes in the bag. I couldn't lose.

With that said, he's never actually mentioned the Lionel Richie thing.

I was halfway down Regent Street, when my phone rang. I answered it.

"Yeah, mate, who is this?" said a voice on the other end of the line.

"It's Danny," I said. "Who's this?"

"I found a sticker saying I should call you. Why?"

"Oh. Yes. I was wondering if you'd like a polite conversation."

There was a pause. And a laugh. And then he hung up, but not before saying: "Wanker."

I sighed to myself. So far, the Call Me campaign hadn't been a great success. Sure, lots of people had called me, but none so far had wanted to indulge themselves in the "polite conversation" side of my offer.

It was the next day, and I was desperate to meet up with Ian. I wanted to see how long it would take him to try and move the conversation onto hats.

We agreed to meet at the Yorkshire Grey in the afternoon.

I headed into town a little earlier. There was something else on my mind: I knew I should do something to try and make things all right with Hanne. It had been a while since our pleasant three-way dinner, so maybe I could find a small peace offering.

"Excuse me?" said a tall man in what looked to be his sixties. He

was standing outside Pizza Express, and he was clutching a bunch of
leaflets. "I was wondering if you'd give this a read. . . ."

He had a kind face and was wearing a kind of tweed hat and a blue
anorak. I took a leaflet—crammed with tiny, neat print—and began to
read.

Hello
Did you know the fate of the Western world lies directly in
my hands?

I looked up at the man and blinked a couple of times. If the fate of
the Western world really did lie directly in this man's hands, I was
about to start walking east.

I was born in 1938, the seventh son of the sixth duke of
Portland, with a prodigious intellectual ability that developed
quickly and thoroughly. Because of this, I was able to write my
first book of celebrated sonnets 1939.

I didn't quite know what to make of this. Apparently the man in
front of me had written a book of sonnets when he was one year old.
I suppose that was possible. But this was a *celebrated* one. All the sonnets *I* wrote when I was one were *rubbish*.

I was able to quickly rise up the ranks of political power, but
my influence always remained hidden due to concerns about
secrecy and political espionage. My decisions have effectively
saved the world twice, once during the Cuban Missile Crisis
and again when North Korea got the bomb in 1987. I was
responsible for Churchill's actions in the Second World War,
and for those of many of his predecessors.

In the words of Katherine the peace activist, this was quite literally unbelievable. This man, between the ages of one and six, not
only found time to write a celebrated book of sonnets, but was also
busy dictating military strategy to Churchill.

I doubt you would believe the scope and range of my political influence.

Fair point.

You might also find it difficult to believe that not merely have I not been paid for any of this, but the government, in further-ance of their conspiratorial designs, has been paying me less than half of my normal social security.

Aha.

I continue to help bring stability to the world. If you believe this has helped you in your life, you may wish to make a small contribution. . . .

I was overawed. It was all so . . . *unusual*.

"So," I said, looking him in the eye. "Is all of this completely . . . accurate?"

"Yes," he said matter-of-factly. "But people never believe me, which is why I had these printed up."

He smiled as if to show how ludicrous it was that people just wouldn't take his word, and he'd had to go to all this trouble just to prove a simple fact.

"And you really dictated political strategy to Churchill when you were a toddler?"

"Around that time, yes, I did."

My dealings with Omar, Albert Heijn, and Dr. Molly Van Brain had taught me not to take things at face value when money was con-cerned. But I wanted to give the man the chance to prove himself.

"And you *did* actually save the world?"

The man nodded. "Effectively," he said.

I scanned through the piece of paper one more time, trying to find some way out of this. As far as I could see, there wasn't one.

"So you're basically asking me to give you money, because you saved the world and you continue to do so? *That's* your request?"

I was hoping that by repeating all this he might suddenly buckle and say, "Ah, okay, fair enough, you caught me out there. It was actually Churchill who made all Churchill's decisions. You're obviously a politics buff." But he didn't say that. He simply nodded once more, and said, "Well, yes. But only if you think it is appropriate."

I sighed and got my wallet out.

"Have you got change of a tenner?" I said.

"No," he said.

I guess this was one of the downsides of saying yes to everything. You kind of make yourself vulnerable to the whims of the outside world. But being a positive thinker I tried to work out if I could possibly turn my encounter with the toddler politician into a present for Hanne. It had, after all, cost me ten pounds—the precise figure I reckoned I would have to have spent on her. I decided upon careful consideration that I couldn't. It would probably just make things worse. "Hey, Hanne. Sorry about the other night. But I just gave ten pounds to a man involved in the Cuban Missile Crisis. We cool now?"

But moments later the ideal gift would present itself, thanks to a small, laminated A4 sign in the window of a florist: GOT SOMETHING TO SAY? SAY IT WITH FLOWERS!

I would!

So . . . what did I have to say?

Ian was being remarkably coy.

We'd been sitting in the Yorkshire Grey for nearly four minutes now, and not once had he mentioned hats. Or caps. Or headwear in general. The sly dog. I smiled to myself. Ian was obviously playing the long-game. I decided I wouldn't talk about hats, either. That'd show him.

"Why are you smiling like that?" said Ian.

"No reason," I said.

"You're behaving very oddly."

"Am I? Am I indeed?" I said, before adding, "Of course, some would say it is *you* who is acting oddly."

"No," said Ian. "Pretty much everyone would say it's you."

"Would they?" I said, because when you're in a conversation like this, it's all about getting the last word. "Would they indeed?"

"What the hell's wrong with you?" he said. "Did you say yes when someone asked you to act mental?"

I pitied Ian. I was on to him, and he just hadn't worked it out yet. His Yes hat hadn't weakened me as he'd no doubt thought it would. It had made me stronger.

"Listen, I invited Wag along as well," I said nonchalantly. "He should be along when he gets my message."

"Message?"

"My message saying we were in the pub, and he should come along."

"Good. So. How's the project?" he said.

"Not too bad."

"Said no to anything yet?"

I smiled. "No. I have fully embraced every opportunity that has come my way. And I have done it without the use of even a single hat."

I studied his face for a reaction to my subtle hint. There was none. Shit, he was good.

My phone rang. I answered it. They hung up.

"Have you brought your diary?" said Ian.

"You will have my diary, in full in due time, my friend."

"Well, give me details, then . . ."

"I have invented an automatic, self-rewinding video box and entered a competition to be Britain's most German-looking man."

Just then Wag walked into the pub.

"Remember, not a word to Wag," I said, raising a finger to my lips.

"What the hell are you up to?" said Wag. He seemed angry, and he had quite a red face.

"What do you mean?" I asked. I honestly couldn't work out why he was annoyed.

Wag opened his rucksack and pointed inside. There was a crushed bunch of broken flowers with a small card attached.

"You got my message, then."

"You could have phoned me! Why send me flowers with a little note saying, 'I'm down at the pub'? Do you know what the lads at work thought of this? Why didn't you just text me?"

"I wanted to say it with flowers!" I said. It took Ian a second, but when he realised what must've prompted that, he nearly choked on a peanut.

"Well, don't! I'm getting a pint," he said and walked off.

"I wanted to say it with flowers," I said meekly.

My phone beeped. It was Hanne.

THANK YOU FOR THE FLOWERS, BUT YOU MUST STOP THIS UNNATURAL OBSESSION AND MOVE ON.

"Christ," I said. "This is *perfect*. I had something to say to Hanne, and I also wanted to say *that* with flowers, and now she's beginning to think I'm obsessed with her."

"So you gatecrash her date, and then you send her flowers as well? You should *never* send flowers to an ex. Sends out the wrong message."

"Let's just hope she doesn't find out about the small African boy."

"What small African boy? You've not sent her a small African boy, now, have you?"

"No. I had an idea earlier. I gave a tenner to an old man who thought he'd saved the world once or twice, and I thought about doing it in Hanne's honour, but then I thought no, it would have to be better than that, and I saw this thing about sponsoring kids in a copy of the *Big Issue* I bought—my *third* this week, by the way—and so I rang up, and I sponsored one for her. By way of an apology."

"What's going on?" said Wag, arriving back at the table.

"Danny has to apologise to Hanne."

"Oh. Why?"

"Nothing, really," I said, hoping that would be the end of it.

"Danny forbade Hanne from seeing a new bloke," said Ian. "And then when they went out on their first date anyway, Danny gatecrashed and stayed for the whole evening."

Wag looked shocked.

"I *didn't* gatecrash," I said. "I was *invited*. Seb invited me."

"You stayed the whole *evening*?" said Wag.

"Only until I was politely asked to leave."

"They told him to fuck off," said Ian helpfully.

"Are you stalking Hanne?" said Wag, wide-eyed. "This is brilliant. I don't know any stalkers!"

"I am *not* stalking Hanne," I said, and then Ian piped up with "Hanne thinks he's obsessed with her. He just sent her flowers too."

"You're stalking Hanne!"

"I sent *you* flowers, mullet man, and I'm not stalking *you*!"

"Don't try and change the subject by mocking my hair! You don't send your ex flowers!" said Wag. "It sends out the wrong message!"

"And then," said Ian, "he sponsored a small African boy in her honour."

Wag's jaw hit the floor.

"*You don't sponsor a small African boy for an ex!* It *totally* sends out the wrong message! *Never* do that—it's like a *rule*!"

Wag looked toward Ian, and he nodded, eyes closed, in agreement.

"We've got to get you a girlfriend," said Ian. "You could be dangerous."

"Let's talk about something else," I said firmly.

And after ten or twenty minutes we did.

It was a couple of days later, and I'd been staying in a bit more. It wasn't that I'd stopped saying yes. It was just that I'd stopped looking quite as hard for them. I'd annoyed Hanne, and Ian was clearly trying to scare me off with his Yes hat. Wag too had seemed annoyed with me, and I was growing tired from all the going out. Several more strangers had rung me up, and I'd nearly managed to engage one of them in a polite conversation. But then they'd lost their nerve and hung up like all the others. Plus Hanne had clearly had a thank-you letter from the Sponsor-a-Child people, because she e-mailed me to ask whether it had been me that had sponsored a small boy in her honour. I wrote back and reluctantly said yes, and that she should let me know if I should sponsor one in honour of Seb too. She told me that wouldn't be necessary.

• • •

I pottered about in the flat. My phone rang. I answered it. They hung up. I ran a bath.

What did Ian think his hat would achieve, anyway? Did he really think I'd crack under pressure? Was he hoping to catch me out and make me say no to something, before pouncing on me from out of a bush and dealing out his as-yet-unspecified punishment? Well, I had to stay one step ahead of him—that much was certain.

I got out of the bath an hour later to find a new e-mail waiting. It was from Tom the BBC man. He wanted to know what my plans for the Edinburgh Festival were—was I going to go up this August, and if I had no plans, did I want to help with his team? He needed an extra pair of eyes up there, seeing shows, scouting for talent, developing ideas. Did I want to pop in and have a chat about it? Too bloody right I did!

I'd been going up to the Edinburgh Festival—the world's largest arts festival—for years, but just hadn't planned on it this year. Too much had been going on as of late . . . But now that there was an opportunity, I had to grab it. Particularly as it all stemmed from a Yes.

I had another new e-mail.

```
To: danny
From: whoisthechallenger
Subject: Like the hat?
Hello, Danny . . .
    It is me again. . . . Hopefully you received the
hat. . . .
    I have something to suggest to you. . . .
    Why . . .
    Not . . .
```

I scrolled down.

```
    Go . . .
```

What was going on here?
I scrolled farther down.

To . . .

Down.
And down.
And down.
And there I saw it.
One word. One, confusing word.

Stonehenge

And that was that.

Stonehenge?

What? What was I supposed to do at Stonehenge? Who was this?! *The Challenger?* So Ian was calling himself the Challenger now, was he? And he was making anonymous suggestions, was he? Suggestions he knew I'd have to say Yes to? Upping the stakes? Stepping over the line? Ordering me about? Doing precisely the thing I'd told him not to do!

I read it again. *Why not go to Stonehenge?* But why *Stonehenge?*

I was filled with a sudden rage. Who the hell did he think he was, setting up a free e-mail address, and calling himself the Challenger? Did he think he could beat me? Did he think I'd just roll over and stop, opening the door wide open to his punishment?

The thing to do was surprise him. Shock him. Demonstrate my abilities. Demonstrate my commitment. I'd do this. I'd go to Stonehenge. Not tomorrow. Not next week. I'd do it *now*. I could be there and back in just over five hours, if the wind was behind me and the traffic forgiving. And then I'd find Ian, I'd show him the evidence, I'd throw him into submission, and I'd put an end to the immature silliness of the type of man who'd call himself the "Challenger."

"The Challenger," I muttered to myself as I walked to the car. "Who calls himself the Challenger?"

I was right. It was a *pathetic* way for a grown man to behave.

I jumped into the Yesmobile and started to drive.

CHAPTER 12

In Which a Friendship Is Brought into Doubt, and Daniel Buys Some New Spectacles

I was driving at full-pelt back toward London.

I'd been to Stonehenge. I'd gotten out of the car. I'd had my picture taken. And now I was on my way to find Ian, confront him, show him the evidence, and tell him he was getting in the way.

His interference was actually quite annoying. He knew why I was doing this. He knew it was something for *me*. This wasn't a stupid boy-project; this was important. Sure, it felt a little pointless from time to time, but that's only because I hadn't worked out what the point was yet. And how was I supposed to do that when Ian was prancing about in his flat with a mask on, pretending to be the Challenger and probably spending his time designing little Challenger logos and sewing a special lycra Challenger suit?

I pulled up at a service station somewhere in Wiltshire and got my phone out. I texted Ian.

WHERE WILL YOU BE IN TWO HOURS?

I'd been sitting in my small green Yes-related car for several hours and needed to stretch my legs. I got as far as the mini-mart. By which I mean I walked across the forecourt; not that I have magic extendable legs.

Inside, the man behind the counter put down his paper and said hello. I said hello back.

"Is that your car?" he said despite the fact that I was the only person for miles around, and he'd just seen me get out of it.

"Yes," I said.

"Odd, isn't it?"

"Yes," I said.

"Where did you get it, if you don't mind me asking?"

"I bought it at a party," I said a little grumpily.

"Oh. A car party?"

I have no idea what a car party is.

I found a pasty, shoved it in the petrol station's microwave, set it for thirty seconds, and thought about what lay ahead of me. But my thoughts were instantly interrupted by the beep of my phone.

I'LL BE IN STARBUCKS, CARNABY STREET. WHY?

There was no time to reply. I was on a mission. I had to get going, move fast. I was out the door and in the car before the microwave even pinged.

"Excuse me," said a man, suddenly to my right. "Would you have a moment to talk about Save the Whales?"

I was striding down Carnaby Street toward Starbucks, and I wasn't in the mood for conversation.

"Yes, yes I would," I said, stopping dead in my tracks. This joker was no match for me. "But can I go first?"

"Er . . . how do you mean . . . ," he said.

"Did you know that the UK is the world's fourth richest country, and yet more than two million pensioners live below the poverty line?"

"Um . . ."

"Did you know that there are more than eleven million pensioners in this country?"

"Sorry, do . . ."

"Did you know that a third of pensioner households lived in poverty in the year 2000?"

"Uh, no . . ."

"Just a few pounds each month can keep a pensioner warm and fed all year round. Is that something you might be interested in?"

"Er, yes, I guess . . ."

"See that man in the green Adopt-a-Granny bib over there?"

"Yes?"

"He'll give you the appropriate forms."

I strode on, leaving a confused and bewildered whale saver behind me. Strode on, toward Ian. Toward vengeance.

When I arrived, he was just sitting there, all sweetness and light. He'd ordered a latte and a tiny muffin.

"Well, I'm back," I said, standing over him. "And I've got the evidence."

I handed him the digital camera. He put his newspaper down and studied it.

"You appear to be showing me a picture of you with a small sign saying 'Happy Now?'"

"Yes. So are you? Are you *happy* now?"

"Is that Stonehenge?"

"Of *course* it's Stonehenge. So are you happy now?"

"Am I happy that you've been to Stonehenge?"

"Yes."

"Why would that make me happy? Because unless you won it in a raffle, you standing in front of Stonehenge isn't at the top of my make-me-happy list."

"Oh, so it *doesn't* make you happy? I suppose it's because I'm not wearing a hat, is it? I can wear a hat if you like. I can wear it right *now*, in fact."

I whipped the baseball cap out of my jacket and fixed it onto my head. I stared at Ian and pointed at the hat. He took it all in.

"Now you appear to be wearing a baseball cap with the word 'yes' on it."

"This must be a pretty great day for you. You must be over the bloody moon."

Ian sat back in his chair.

"Danny . . . I haven't got a clue what you're on about."

And annoyingly I believed him.

"So if *you're* not the Challenger, then who is?" I said.

We'd moved the conversation into the pub opposite Starbucks.

"Well, I don't know," said Ian. "I mean, why would they send you to Stonehenge? It's a bit bloody mysterious, that. Stonehenge must be a clue."

I thought about it. Had I met any Druids along the way? Maybe the Starburst Group had realised that there was more to my Yeses than I'd let on, that I wasn't just "being more open" as I'd claimed. Or maybe they thought aliens had built Stonehenge and wanted a second opinion?

"Have you told anyone, Ian? Anyone at all?"

"No."

"Not even Wag? You haven't told Wag, have you?"

"No. Have you?"

"Why would I ask you if you'd told Wag if I'd already told him?"

"I don't know, Dan. This is all very confusing. It's like someone's out to get you. I guess it *could* be Wag. I mean, he's *bound* to suspect *something*."

"How come?"

"How come? Because he was out with you right at the start, when you told that bloke you were looking at his girlfriend. You always say yes when he suggests going for a pint, when you'd done pretty much the opposite for most of the year. You sent him flowers because you saw a sign saying 'Why Not Say It With Flowers.' He knows about all the trouble you've had by saying yes to Hanne. It could be him, Dan. It really could."

Oh my God.

It was *blatantly* Wag.

"So what should I do?"

"You've got two options. Confront him, or confound him."

"I'm going to confound him," I said. "I'm going to display the very essence of Yes."

"The Yessence," said Ian.

"I'll show him the way."

"The way of Yes. You can teach him a Yesson. Take him on a Yescapade!"

And then I took my phone out, dialled Wag's number, and casually asked him if he fancied a night out.

We arranged to meet at 6 p.m. at the Pride of Spitalfields—a tiny pub just off Brick Lane, packed with old men and London hipsters—and from there we would grab some food. And food wouldn't be a problem. Brick Lane is *lined* with curryhouses. It's a street in which dozens of men take to the pavements to greet you and persuade you in with promises of free wine and discounts that they conveniently forget about when handing you the bill.

We found one such man the moment we left the pub.

"My friends, come in . . . ," he said, making insanely welcoming gestures with his hands. "Fantastic food here . . ."

Oh, this was going to be sweet. I was going to challenge the dark and brooding presence of the Challenger himself. On my terms. And my turf.

We did as he said and sat down to eat. I had the dansak as is right and proper. Wag had a bhuna, the mullet-haired idiot. And then, tummies full, we asked for the bill.

"This is on me, Wag," I said, and he looked impressed when I very purposefully showed him a wallet full of new Yes-related credit cards. I paid up, and we left.

Another man was on our backs almost immediately.

"Food? You come in here, very good discount for you . . ."

Wag patted his stomach—the international sign of "I've eaten, thanks"—but I was having none of it. I bellowed "Yes!", dragged Wag into the curryhouse, and immediately ordered some poppadoms. Wag had a beer.

"Jesus," he said. "How hungry *are* you?"

"I'm not hungry at all," I said, snapping a poppadom in two and trying to look mysterious. "I'm not hungry in the *least*." Wag looked at me a bit oddly.

From there we jumped into a black cab and headed into town. I had a little surprise lined up for Wag.

"What are those?" he said, looking at the items I had whipped out.

"Tickets," I said.

"What for?"

"A musical."

"A *musical*?" said Wag, alarmed. "*What* musical? Why?"

"I was walking through Leicester Square today, Wag. A ticket tout offered me two tickets for the price of one for tonight's performance. So that is why we are going."

"But I don't want to go to a musical! *What* musical?"

"*We Will Rock You*."

"The *Queen* musical? I don't want to go to the Queen musical!"

"We are going to see the Queen musical, because I have already said yes to it, and then we are going to do whatever you want. Do you understand? *Whatever* you want . . ."

Three hours later we were leaving the theatre and walking toward Soho. I started to sing a medley of Queen numbers. Wag didn't. He seemed to have been stunned into silence by the raw power of tonight's theatrical experience.

"So what do you want to do, Wag?" I said, stopping to hand my *We Will Rock You* T-shirt to a homeless person. "Suggest something! Anything!"

"I dunno. Pub. Whatever."

We found the first pub we could and left after the first pint. I was keen to show Wag what else was out there.

We crossed over the road and through Soho Square.

"Why are you so jolly?" said Wag. "And where are you taking me?"

I started to sing another Queen number, and we passed a man standing in the shadows saying what seemed to be the words "Hash, coke? Hash, coke?" very quickly and very quietly.

I stopped in my tracks. Wag continued on until he noticed I'd stopped, and he turned around.

"You want hash, coke?" said the man.

"All right, then!" I said in a loud and dramatic voice, so that Wag could hear. I wanted him to know that Yes had opened my horizons, made me a man of the world. I'd already had a drag or two on a comical cigarette in Brixton as well as a psychotropic mindbomb. I knew what I was doing, all right!

"Dan, what are you doing?" he said in a kind of shouted whisper, and instantly I realised I didn't really know.

"How much you want?" said the man.

"Um . . . I'm not sure," I said, suddenly out of my depth. "A pound's worth?"

"Danny!" said Wag again and walked toward me. This made the man in the shadows a bit nervous, and he started to back off.

"Wag, I am *trying* to buy a pound's worth of drugs."

"Why?"

"Because this nice gentleman asked if I'd like any."

"Danny. Pub. *Now.*"

Minutes later we found ourselves in a late bar on Frith Street. We'd arrived there on a high-speed ricksha—because a driver had asked—and our cheeks were red and our hair windswept.

"What the fuck is going on?" said Wag. "Why are you so keen to move on? Why the *ricksha?*"

I simply smiled enigmatically. Now I was matching Wag drink for drink and making sure he knew it. I was showing Wag how to live. How to grab the Yeses!

At closing time we left the pub, somehow both with balloons, and both of us singing. Unfortunately we were singing different songs.

"Come on, Wag . . . let's go to a bar . . . yeah?"

"No, Dan. I've had enough . . . 'fun.'"

"Come on! It'll be brilliant! We can stand in the corner and awkwardly look at girls! We can say yes to *life!*"

"Stop bullying me! I feel a bit sick. . . ."

"One more, Wag! Yes?"

Wag looked a broken man. I had truly taught him a lesson.

"One more," he said.

Now we were in Madame Jo Jo's, deep in the heart of seedy Soho. We were drinking out of cans, and Wag had begun to sway. I was worse. Only the adrenaline of each Yes moment was keeping me on my feet. Another novelty tequila man was here, though, and Wag and I forced a shot each before Wag grabbed my arm and said, "Enough . . . enough . . . *please* . . ."

Was it a cry for help? Or—more likely—an admission of *guilt?* I knew the time was near.

Minutes later we were stumbling down the street toward a cab rank. Wag could hardly speak. I had started to be able to see properly, but only if I closed one eye.

"So then . . . ," I slurred, "that was an interesting evening. What are your conclusions? Do you have anything to say? Is there anything you wish to apologise for?"

Wag looked a little too shellshocked to apologise, if I'm honest.

And then the words we really didn't need to hear . . .

"Looking for fun, boys?"

I looked up to see a woman, sitting on a stool under a sign that read

MODELS. I tried to focus my eyes. Her hair was elaborate and her dress sense revealing.

"Good show on downstairs. Five pounds each."

Shit.

I looked to Wag. He shook his head. I nodded mine. For a second it looked like he was about to cry.

I'm not proud of this. Particularly as I can't blame it on the booze.

But I gave the woman ten pounds, and I dragged Wag in with me through some red velvet curtains and into the seedy lair within.

It would be the final proof he would need of my commitment.

I awoke the next morning and tried my best to understand what was going on. I was lying in a position I'm not sure anyone's ever been in before; at least not by choice or not during wrestling.

I knew I was on my own, but there seemed to be too many arms for that to be possible. I was facedown on the sofa, my cheeks wet with dribble, and both the TV and the radio were on. As was my computer. As were all the lights. And I mean every single light I had. The ceiling lights, the lamps, a small anglepoise . . . I'm sure if I'd checked the cupboards I'd have found all the torches and Christmas lights on too. I had clearly come home drunk and happy and wanting to keep the night going— despite the fact that all I'd done was turn everything on, check my e-mails, and pass out on the sofa.

I was fully clothed, intensely dry-mouthed, and I was aching all over. I was also boiling . . . The sun was streaming in through the windows, and I was half-hidden beneath a spare duvet. I started to wonder why on Earth I was on the sofa. Perhaps I'd had a fight with myself in the night and banished myself to the living room. That seemed unfair to me. In relationships I'd always been the one who'd ended up sleeping on the sofa. You'd think living on my own would mean I got the bed. But a vague memory reached me, clouded and slow. I began to remember that in my drunken state I'd decided it wouldn't be all that wise to try and start negotiating the stairs up to the bedroom. But worrying that I would get cold in the night, I knew I'd need to fetch a duvet. So I ran upstairs to get one and bring it down. At no point had the all-too-logical idea of just staying up there hit me. I'd even gone for the spare duvet—the one hidden away at the back of a cupboard, the one I'd have to stand on a chair to get. Worse, I could remember feeling rather proud of myself for being so sensible as I stumbled back down the stairs, duvet in arms, ready to pass out.

The world was still blurry, and so I reached out to grab my glasses. I grabbed a pen instead. I reached again. A remote control. I gradually worked out that in order to find my glasses, I would have to *find my glasses*. Say what you like about me, but I'm bloody good at problem-solving.

But it was proving a difficult problem to solve. I knew my specs had to be somewhere, and they had to be somewhere in here. I tried the coffee table, making huge sweeping gestures with my arms, but couldn't find them. I tried the sofa, the side table, and then the floor, scuttling over to any object I could make out and sticking my face a mere inch away from it in order to see what it was. At one point I imagined a shoe could have been my glasses. It wasn't. It was a shoe. Moments later I was up close to a tiny, carved wooden elephant, studying it just in case it had a couple of flip-out arms I could use to rest on my face.

I was starting to panic now. My glasses were the one thing I needed to function in this world; the one thing I couldn't do without. They were the only thing that stopped me from having to stand a little too closely to strangers, the one thing that helped me retain my Britishness. How drunk had I been last night? Had I said yes to someone who wanted my glasses? Could I have eaten them? Or had I lost them earlier on in the evening but not noticed? Perhaps I'd put my blurry vision down to drunkenness, when in fact it was because I'd lost my specs?

With growing desperation and a thudding head, I checked the bathroom and the stairs and the living room again. I tried retracing my steps from the night before, but what with them being drunken steps, they would have made me quite dizzy. And in my current state I could do without being dizzy. You'll know what I mean if you've ever spun a blind man.

Finally, with great sorrow and confusion, I was forced to admit it: I had lost my glasses. *I had lost my glasses!*

This, as the bespectacled among you will know, is a horrifying prospect for anyone low on sight. The world's a big place. It's full of . . . you know . . . *things*. Big, blurry things. It's easy for a spectacles-wearer devoid of spectacles to get lost in a world like that. To mistake buses for dragons. Short people for goblins. Men with beards for wizards. This was going to be terrifying! How would I know what I was wearing anymore? How would I know what I was cooking? How could I pretend to be considering an important problem without some glasses to pop into the corner of my mouth while staring into the distance? I had to find them!

The phone rang. I was thrown into panic again. The phone! My God, the phone! How would I ever find the phone!

And then I remembered the phone was where it always was, so I ambled over and picked it up.

"Hello?"

"Dan, it's Ian."

"Oh, Ian, thank God!"

"What's the matter?"

"What's the *matter*? Can't you *tell*? I've lost my glasses!"

"Oh," said Ian. "Never mind."

"Never mind?" I said, outraged. This was typical of the full-sighted. And of the way people with disabilities like mine are treated by society at large. "What do you mean, never mind? I'm going to Edinburgh in a couple of days! I can't set off without my glasses! I'll never get out of London!"

"Get some new ones."

"'Get some new ones'?" My God, this man had a cheek. How did he . . . well, yes, I suppose I *could* get some new ones, actually.

"Hey! What a great opportunity to change your look!" said Ian. "Go to an optician and say yes to the first pair of glasses they make you try on!"

"I don't *want* a new look!" I said. "I just want my glasses back! They're like a part of me, Ian!"

"Where did you last have them?"

"On my face."

"Have you checked there?"

"Have I checked my face?"

"All of it, I mean."

"Oh, not all of it, no. Just the lips. Hang on, I'll check the *rest* of my face."

"All right, all right . . . don't you have a spare pair?"

"No. Oh, hang on, though . . ."

Now, a spare pair I *didn't* have. But I did have *a* pair. A pair I used to wear as a kid. Surely my eyes couldn't have changed that much in the last twenty years? They'd still work, wouldn't they?

"Ian, you're a genius," I said.

I was sitting on a chair in front of the mirror, considering the problem.

I appeared to be a grown man, wearing the spectacles of a small boy.

If there is indeed an afterlife, and our ancestors do, as is claimed, pop back every now and then to check up on us, then I hope they choose their moments carefully. The last thing I needed was word of this getting back to the afterlife.

"How was Danny?" one of them would say.

"Oh, fine," the other would say. "Although it appears he is now a simpleton." And what would Maitreya make of it all, if he'd popped in to have a look-see? Surely this couldn't be part of his grand plan?

The phone rang. It was Ian again.

"So, I just talked to Wag," he said. "What the hell did you do to him last night?"

"Nothing! I just showed him the way of Yes."

"He says you took him into a strip club, where you were both robbed."

"We were *invited* in. And it wasn't a strip club. It was a 'gentleman's parlour.' It was very classy."

"Where was it?"

"In an alleyway."

Ian made some kind of overly dramatic "tsk" sound.

"And you were robbed?"

"We were *not* robbed. We simply walked in, and after seeking firm assurance that there was nothing illegal or immoral going on, sat down in a small room where a woman in a negligee poured us two warm beers, before a fat Moroccan in a suit walked in and told us the beers were fifty quid each, and we would have to leave, because the show was over."

"It was a clip joint! They're made for tourists! Not you!"

"I don't understand it. Why invite us in at all, if all you're going to do is take our money and kick us out again?"

"Wag thinks you're on the verge of a breakdown."

"I'm not!"

"I know you're not, but he doesn't. He says you were ordering curries and then going into the restaurant next door and ordering even more."

"Exaggeration! I had poppadoms."

"He also says he thinks you might have a . . . *thing* for him."

"A *thing*?"

"He says the obsession with Hanne is a front. He says he first started to suspect something was up when you sent him the flowers. But he says you always agree with everything he says now, and you're always so eager to hang out with him."

"That's hardly enough evidence to question my sexuality."

"He also says you've got a newfound interest in musicals and have talked more than once about how men can have babies."

"Oh."

"Essentially," he said, "Wag thinks you may want to have a baby with him."

"Ah."

"I don't think Wag *is* the Challenger, after all."

"No. I don't think he is, either."

So Wag was off the list. Which was fair enough. He had proved himself to be no more than a confused friend in my ongoing battle with a shadowy and secretive enemy. No matter.

Two hours later I had braved my hangover and was in the optician's office, trying to get new glasses and hoping to God the woman behind the counter wouldn't try and suggest any fancy new children's frames.

"Okay," she said. "A few questions. First, your name please . . ."

"Wallace," I said.

She very slowly typed "Wallace" into her computer.

"Okay . . . Wallace . . . and your surname?"

"Oh. Sorry, that *was* my surname. Still is, in fact. My first name's Danny."

She sighed and made quite a show of having to press the delete key seven times.

"Okay. We'll start again. Name?"

"Danny."

She typed "Danny."

"And your surname?"

"Er . . . Wallace."

"Now . . . ," she said, obviously coming to the next prompted question on the screen. "Is it 'Mister'?"

Eh? Of *course* it was "mister." Look at me, woman. I'm not exactly the most feminine-looking man in the world. Not unless you like your women unshaven. And . . . you know . . . *male*.

"Sorry?" I said.

"Is it *Mister* Wallace?"

She wasn't looking up. But she'd seen me come in. She could hear my voice. How could she not know? Was she afraid to guess? Despite myself, I considered her question carefully, before answering: "Yes, it's *Mister* Wallace."

Perhaps it was the fact that I was wearing a small boy's pair of glasses that confused her. Perhaps she assumed I was going to say, "No, it's *Master* Wallace, but I'm a big boy now, because mummy's sent me down to the shops on my own."

"Right . . . *Mister* Wallace. And is it spectacles you're after?"

"Yes."

I watched her click *yes*, before the screen changed, and she asked her best question of the day. . . .

"And are you a spectacles-wearer already?"

That is an entirely unmissable fact. I am a spectacles-wearer, and I am a *mister*. You might as well call me "Mister Four-Eyes Spectacles-Wearer, the Male Boy-Man Who Wears Glasses on His Face."

"Am I a spectacles-wearer already?" I tried, just in case I'd misheard her.

"It's for the system," she said, looking up for the first time since sitting down, but still not registering that all the information she needed for "the system" was literally staring her in the face.

"Yes, I am. I am already a spectacles-wearer."

"Well, great!" she said, standing up. "Let's get you sorted out, then."

My new glasses would be ready in one or two hours, and thanks to the power of Yes, I'd also agreed to undertake a free thirty-day contact-lens trial. With some free time suddenly in hand, I took the opportunity to run some errands to fully prepare myself for my trip up to Edinburgh.

I bought vitamins and six pairs of black socks and a pair of white ones too, in the unlikely event of some surprise exercise being sprung on me up there. I wandered around TopMan for a while, but I kept catching glimpses of myself in the mirror, and it was a little disconcerting. So I decided to head off and undertake another much-needed errand—one that would not require me to wear a pair of children's glasses. A haircut.

I found my way to a hairdresser's on Great Portland Street, but as I was about to enter, I received a most annoying text message.

YOU OWE ME FIFTY QUID.

It was from Wag. I hadn't really wanted to call him before now—the whole "him thinking I have a thing for him" thing made that a little uncomfortable as a prospect. And anyway, you're supposed to wait two days before calling someone after a first date.

But, oh well. I suppose I had to give him his fifty quid—the fifty quid I'd made him spend on one warm beer in a Soho clip joint. You'd think he'd have let me off, what with the ticket to *We Will Rock You* and the bhuna, but I guess that's the risk you take when you're a Yeser. I texted him back, and we arranged to meet briefly, later on in the afternoon.

"So . . . ," said Scott, the kiwi hairdresser. "The question I'm asking myself is, what are we going to do for you today?"

"Same basic shape," I said, "except I would like you to cut it so that it is a little shorter."

"Understood," said Scott, who I'm suddenly worried you will think is not simply a hairdresser from New Zealand (a kiwi *hairdresser*), but instead a hairdresser who cuts the hair off kiwis (a *kiwi* hairdresser). "I can do that for you very easily indeed."

But then Scott did something rather odd. He put both hands on my shoulders and leant down to my level. We made eye contact in the mirror.

"Or . . . ," he said, "do you want to try something *new*?"

Scott certainly seemed to be putting his back into this haircut. I'd had to remove my glasses—something I was only too pleased to do—while he did something fancy with a razor down the sides of my head, but it gave me a few precious and welcome moments of contemplation. That's the good thing about being near-sighted. When someone takes your glasses off, all you can do is think—not much good in a fight, admittedly, but *perfect* for the hairdressers. And so that's what I did. I thought about the new cast of characters who'd come into my life of late, some of whom I knew, and some of whom I . . . well . . . didn't.

The thing was, if Wag wasn't the Challenger, then who was? Who was sending me odd things and taunting me? What was their objective? To tease me? To scare me? Had they really expected me to go to Stonehenge? Did they know I'd been? Was I too hasty in ruling Ian out of the equation? And where did the man on the bus fit into all of this? I suppose if the man on the bus was, in fact, Maitreya, as Brian and Pete and the Starburst Group had suggested, maybe *he* was the Challenger? Maybe I was merely a pawn in a very odd game of chess. Hey, "yes" rhymes with "chess." Maybe that was a clue. But who knew about my very important quest? Who had I . . .

"Okay, we're all done!"

Scott stood back from me, and I reached for my glasses.

"Great," I said, putting them on. And then I didn't really say much at all.

I just looked.

I now had very, very short hair at the sides. The top had a kind of mohawk effect, but it was much more spiky than it had ever been before, and there seemed to be something still tickling my neck. . . . But after a moment or two I liked it. Kind of. I *kind of* liked it.

"I'll just show you the back," he said, holding up a mirror, but then whipping it away again before I could really see what was going on round there.

"Er . . . could I just see the back again?"

"Sure," said Scott, and he held the mirror up longer this time.

And I nearly swallowed my tongue.

Scott had given me . . . No, he couldn't have . . .

Could he?

I thought that . . .

Christ.

Scott had given me . . . a *mullet*.

I was now a man with a mullet, wearing the glasses of a boy.

I waited in the Yorkshire Grey for Wag. I'd picked up my new specs, thank heavens, and I'd tried to make my new haircut a little less manic by going to the toilets and smearing water all over my head. It just made the wax Scott had put in there go all runny, and my hair had now set in a much more unfortunate style than before. I winced. Somehow I had found the one hairdresser in all of Great Britain who shared Wag's conviction that the mullet was a somehow acceptable haircut.

Oh god! *Wag!*

Moments later he walked in and just stared at me.

"What the hell's happened to you?"

"I got . . . a haircut."

"Let me see," he said, and reluctantly I let him.

"What do you think?" I said.

There was a slightly awkward pause.

"So you decided to get a mullet."

I nodded, a bit self-conscious.

"It appears that way," I said.

"Right," said Wag. "Only . . . well . . . *I've* got a mullet."

Bollocks. He'd noticed. He'd noticed that we'd *both* got mullets.

"So, now we've *both* got one. We are two men, both with mullets."

I smiled awkwardly. Maybe that would trick him into thinking this was a good thing. I don't know if you've ever turned up at a party, wearing the same top as someone else. It's much the same when it appears you have specifically attempted to base yourself on someone else's entire look.

"Well . . . mine's not really a mullet," I tried. "I mean yours . . . Yes, that *is* a mullet. And a fine one. But mine isn't a mullet. Not really."

"Well, what is it? It *looks* the same as mine."

"It really isn't the same as yours. Believe me. It's mulletesque, certainly, but it's really only a very *small* mullet. If anything, it's a mull*ette*."

There was a long and cavernous pause.

I cleared my throat.

Somewhere a floorboard creaked.

I could see deep concern in Wag's eyes. I thought about what Ian had said. I thought about how this must look to a man who already suspected I had a crush on him.

"It doesn't mean I want to have babies with you," I said.

Another substantial pause.

"I have to go now," he said.

I walked into my flat that night and immediately found my glasses. They were on the floor next to the sofa.

Minutes later Ian sent me a text message.

WAG JUST PHONED. HEARD ABOUT YOUR NEW IMAGE. LOOK WHO'S STALKING!

Oh God.

Still. Wag wouldn't have to worry about me for a while. I was off to Scotland the next morning, after all, and looking forward to it. My train was booked, my socks were packed, and I couldn't wait to get up there and begin my important BBC duties.

But I was feeling chirpy for another reason, too. I'd returned home that evening to find a small white box outside my door. A small white box that had made its way all the way from Tucson, Arizona, to my flat in London's glamourous East End. I'd ripped it open and found a world of wonder within: a video, a CD, some incense, a small laminated clip-on badge, and a book of handy speeches.

At last . . . I was a *minister*!

The reverand Amy E. Long from the Universal Life Church had sent me everything I needed to set up a church of my own, including a small sign, which I could stick on my car, that read: THE DRIVER OF THIS CAR IS A LICENSED MINISTER ON OFFICIAL BUSINESS! This was great! Now I could break the law, whenever the urge took me! Thank you, God!

I even had my own certificates of marriage, commitment, and baby naming to hand out to people after my special ceremonies! I could *name babies*! I don't think I've ever been so excited. But what would I name them? Was that my decision, or the parents'? Could I just walk about, naming them as I saw fit? That would be brilliant.

"I name thee Mister Chubby!"

"But his name's Tim!"

"Not anymore it's not. And that other one next to him—let him forever be known as Chao Lee, Child of the Stars . . ."

Parking wherever I wanted, naming whoever I chose . . . I would be a maverick minister on the edge.

I wanted to know more about the Universal Life Church, though, and so sauntered over to my computer and fired it up.

Ten minutes later, and I'd decided I was going to buy a cassock. I was feeling deeply spiritual. But this was to stop the very second I checked my e-mail.

I was pleased to see that I had one from Lizzie. But I didn't understand it.

```
To: Danny
From: Lizzie
Subject: RE: soho ho, ho, ho
Danny,
Okay! I believe you! So get me a ticket, then!
xo,
L
```

Eh?

What was that supposed to mean? She believes me about what?

She'd clearly sent an e-mail to the wrong Danny. . . . I hadn't asked her to believe *anything*. . . .

I nearly deleted it, but then stopped in my tracks. I studied the subject line. *Soho ho, ho, ho?* And it had *RE:* before it. It was a *reply*.

When was the last time I'd e-mailed Lizzie? And about what?

Oh, God, what had I done? My cheeks started to burn.

I knew that feeling, and I hated it—the feeling that creeps up on you, side-by-side with a hangover, the feeling that you may have started sending e-mails at the worst possible time to be sending e-mails . . . when you were drunk. E-mails that, at nine o'clock on a Monday morning, may have lost some of their Saturday-night vibe. E-mails that were hilarious or fascinating when they left your flat at four in the morning, but which had somehow lost their appeal or relevance the second they flew down the wires. What had I written? What had I said? Had I poured my heart out? Had I proclaimed undying love? Had I bored her to tears?

No. No, I couldn't have.

I found my Sent Mail folder.

Oh, shit.

Shit, shit, shit.

I *had*. I *had* sent her an e-mail. I had sent her an e-mail at 4:26 that morning. . . . I'd mailed her after stumbling in from that Soho clip joint after a night of careless and determined Yeses . . .

I clicked my e-mail open and held my breath, readying myself for the worst. And I instantly saw that it was pretty bloody bad.

> To: Lizzie
> From: Danny
> Subject: Soho ho, ho, ho
> Lizziiiiiie!
>
> How is australia is austrlia good? Sems like it woul dbe good in australian. Have you met any australians yet haha-haha.
>
> I am havin a great time here in london englan an have just had a night out with wag remember wag he is ok. we ended up in a place, it was a gentleman parlour in case anyone ask you and a moroccan man said get out you tossbag.s

```
    hey listen i an going to the edinburgh festival to work
for a bit you would love it their. it is big and funny
and loadsa people. why don't you come, it'll be brilliant
if you come there you could get a train like me. do you
have trains in australia.
    okay maybe see you in edinburgh its good there let me
know
    you are really cool an pretty an i miss you
    danyy
```

Christ. No wonder I didn't understand the e-mail from Lizzie. I didn't bloody understand the e-mail from *me*.

My first reaction was embarrassment. Embarrassment at my drunken, pointless ramblings. My second was one of sickly realisation. . . .

Because slowly, slowly I was piecing it together. . . .

I had said Lizzie should come to Edinburgh.

And Lizzie had said . . . *yes*.

Yes, even though she was in Australia.

But not just yes.

She'd said, *"Okay! I believe you! So get me a ticket, then!"*

Which was, in effect, a suggestion.

A jokey one, yes, and a silly one, true—but *a suggestion nevertheless.*

Let's face it—there was no way in the world that Lizzie could think I was serious. I was a drunk man, suggesting she take a train—a *train!*—from Australia, on the basis that Edinburgh was "good" because it was "big and funny and loadsa people."

She was humouring me. In a sweet and gentle way. But still only humouring me.

I paced the flat.

Okay, okay. Let's say I did it; let's say I got her a ticket. She would never in a million years get on the plane. Why would she? She hardly knew me. She'd almost known me, once, but that was months ago and miles away. She was on a different continent now. She had a different life now. And anyway, with Wag and Hanne, I already had *two* people who thought I was obsessed with them. I wasn't trying to make up the *set*.

What if I got her a ticket and on some mad whim she *did* come?

What then? Why spoil a beautiful friendship? Sure, something could have happened, once, but not now. And if she turned up, and we didn't get on anymore, well, what then?

It was stupid. It was stupid. It was so bloody stupid.

But it was a *suggestion*.

No. Sod that. A ticket from *Australia*, for God's sake! *And* she'd probably want a return one! I couldn't afford that. No way. They were . . . *how* much were they?

I scrambled onto the Internet and did a search.

Five hundred and forty-five pounds! Minimum!

I can't go around spending a minimum of five hundred and forty-five pounds on girls I'm not even going out with! I can't even go around spending a minimum of five hundred and forty-five pounds on girls I *am* going out with!

Somewhere, sometime, I would have to draw a line with this Yes thing. It was starting to cross financial and emotional barriers. And not just mine—how would Lizzie feel about this? It'd be a hell of a lot of pressure to put on her.

I couldn't do it.

I sighed.

I had failed.

I would tell Ian in the morning. I would tell him that he was right. That I was afraid. That there are some things you just can't say yes to no matter *where* they might lead.

I zipped up my bag, put my credit card–sized ministry ID in my wallet—just in case there were any baby-naming emergencies in Scotland—and, with a heavy heart, popped the wallet in my pocket.

And then . . . I took it out again.

Something had caught my eye.

A silver, shiny, gleaming credit card.

A new *type* of credit card.

A virgin, unsullied, never-before-used type of credit card. With a substantial credit limit. And six months at 0% APR.

CHAPTER 13

In Which Daniel Receives a Very Pleasant Piece of News

Edinburgh crept up on me outside the window of the train. I packed away my book and notes and tucked myself into my jacket.

The book, which arrived that morning, was called *Embrace Yes: The Power of Spiritual Affirmation* and had been sent to me anonymously by, I guessed, the Challenger in a bid to encourage me to stop my Yes-related nonsense and come to my senses. My heart sank as I'd opened it up. There had been a note with the book, saying, simply "Maybe you can pick up some tips." I'd read as much of it as I could without going insane—the back cover describes it as "a journey to the very heart of acceptance and aliveness through affirmation," and "an opportunity to meditate and reflect on the aliveness of affirming reality and to live with the attitude of Yes." I figured that was an attitude I was already living with rather nicely, thank you, and stopped reading to concentrate on who might have sent it to me.

I'd compiled a list as we'd trundled through Berwick-upon-Tweed.

Suspects
Ian (he may have been cleverly bluffing)
Brian and the Starburst Group
The man on the bus/Maitreya/the Baby Jesus
Elias Brown (if he is psychic or something)

People who *might* have it in for me
Hanne's new bloke, Seb (?)
The man I beat up (sort of) in that club
Hanne (for ruining her date)
Wag (who may think he's copyrighted the mullet)
Ian again (chance for him to punish me, if he ever comes up with something)

But try as I might, I couldn't quite see any of them fitting the bill.

It was a crisp and brisk August afternoon as I stepped off the train and into a taxi. I stared out of the window as we drove from Waverley Station to the Travelodge I'd booked myself into for the next couple of weeks.

I tutted to myself. The Challenger was clever, wily. The Challenger was using psychology to intimidate. The Challenger was vindictive and bitter and was taking an active stand against my behaviour. The Challenger had knowledge and was using that knowledge to gain power over me. The Challenger liked Stonehenge.

It was, all in all, a puzzling case, but one that I was determined to solve. It just didn't seem fair. I'd only been doing this about two months, and already I'd picked up a mortal enemy.

But I also had far more on my mind.

What had I done where Lizzie was concerned?

Well . . . I'd bought her a ticket, of course. I had to. A ticket from Melbourne to Edinburgh via London. It was there for her, if she wanted it. It was up to her, now. Up to Lizzie. I was taking no more responsibility for having no responsibility. I had simply forwarded her the airline confirmation e-mail, attached a short note saying "Here y'go, then . . . ," locked the flat up, and headed for the train, my neck prickling with awkward British embarrassment. Another foolish foray into level five completed.

Yes, I'm well aware it was stupid. In fact my trip to see Dr. Molly Van Brain aside, it was perhaps the stupidest thing I'd ever done. The thing is, it would almost have been romantic, had I done it of my own volition. But I knew me and Lizzie were doomed. I knew it from the start. And now I'd spent five hundred and forty-five pounds just to prove it. But a yes is a yes, and in some ways, by saying that one little word, I'd rid myself of a problem. By saying yes to that ticket, I'd made it not my responsibility anymore. I didn't have to think about it. Now it was *her* problem to deal with. Now *she'd* have to sit there and worry about what to do . . . whether to get on a plane or ignore me forever or break it to me gently or ridicule me to her friends for the rest of her natural Australian life. Getting that credit card out wasn't as brave as I would like to think it was. If anything, it was typically male—push the problem to her side of the fence. The way inept, immature blokes one

day decide to treat their girlfriends badly in the hope that they'll get
dumped before they have to do the dumping.

And as well as cowardly and embarrassed, I felt slightly . . . I
dunno . . . *creepy* about having done it. I'd definitely lost any sem-
blance of cool, now. I'd bought a ticket to Britain for a girl I hardly
knew. She would now either think I was some kind of misguided man
of means or an *incredibly* lazy stalker. The kind of stalker who'd say to
his stalkee, "Um, look, I'm a bit busy at the moment—any chance you
could come to *me* this time?"

So here I was in Edinburgh, in a black cab on my way to the hotel,
and for a while, at least, I could pretend my troubles were behind me.
Maybe without Ian on my case, without Hanne and Seb to bump into,
with no Wag to clash hairstyles with, no Elias or Pete to claim Jesus
had been spotted in the Pilau bloody Palace and—fingers crossed—no
Challenger to breathe down my neck, I could treat yes just as I had in
the beginning. I could start afresh in a whole new city.

"Danny! Take a seat, mate!"

I was in the courtyard of the Pleasance Theatre, and I was with
Tom. There was a buzz in the air. The festival was still in early days,
and all around us were theatre-goers, journalists, comedy fans, actors,
artists, and—mainly—drunkards. The weather had lifted, slightly, and
the air was warm.

"So the plan is this: We want to find the next generation of enter-
tainers. You know? But not the obvious ones that there's already a
buzz about. People we can work with. Develop. So see as much as
you can. We're looking for . . . *quirky*."

"Quirky. Right."

"See things you wouldn't normally see. Shows that no other broad-
casters will be looking for. We want to find talent in the hidden places,
and then see what we can do with them. Have you got a brochure?"

"No, not yet . . ."

"Here's mine . . . Have a look through it, see what grabs you. I've
got to go to a show now but you've got my number . . ."

"Yep."

"Okay. See you in a bit."

And with that he was off. I ambled over to the bar to get myself a pint and sat down to make my way through the brochure and decide how I should go about my day. My mission was to see shows—and that wasn't a bad mission as missions go. I cheerily opened it at a random page and took in a show's blurb.

Death is death, but life is death—you are already dead! Or dying from so many things!! Life is a struggle, grief is a pool in which you drown. The insanity and violence of love abounds. The madness of struggle. The conquest of death.

Now, there's quirky, and there's utterly bloody terrifying. I didn't feel this show fitted with the former. I flicked to another page.

Together we are yet together we can't be. Togetherness and the togethered—together they are as one, but Together seeks to explore not oneness, but twoness . . . a play in two halves, sewn together and shown as one. A physical and metaphorical exploration by Brendan Fealey.

I decided to have a baked potato instead.

But before I could even stand up, someone had slammed a leaflet down on the table in front of me.

"Are you looking for a show?"

A girl with dreads in her hair and glitter on her face looked at me with hope in her eyes.

"Yes," I said.

"Gilded Balloon, five thirty. We got three stars in the *Scotsman*."

"Oh," I said. "Is it quirky?"

"It's a play about hope, love, betrayal, rape, and death."

"Right," I said. "A bit of everything, then."

"Well . . . mainly betrayal, rape, and death."

"Hmm. I'm kind of looking for . . . *lighter* stuff."

"It's very light," she said. "It's very funny."

"Is it?"

"Yes . . . but also . . . *not*."

I looked at my watch. Five o'clock. That would give me just enough time to go and get my food. I could pop down to the Tempting Tattie on Jeffrey Street and be sitting, satisifed and alert, in what she had now decided to assure me was a frankly hilarious play minutes later. I folded the flyer and popped it in my pocket, thanked her, and was just about to stand up, when from another angle I heard the words: "Hello. Are you looking for a show to see?"

Dear God, the leafletters.

I had managed to make it out of the Pleasance Theatre with only six new flyers stuck in my pocket, but now, approaching the Royal Mile, I saw them.

Leafletters. Everywhere. Like a wide and rampant pack of wolves.

I had forgotten what Edinburgh was like. For one month the entire world descends upon the city for the largest arts festival on the planet. There are literally thousands of shows to see, each one usually performing more than twenty-five times. That's a lot of tickets that needed to be sold. And that's a lot of leafletters trying to sell them.

The desperation in the air was palpable. And for miles around, all I could see were leafletters . . . leafletters with leaflets. There were leafletters dressed as dogs. Leafletters dressed as ballerinas. One leafletter who appeared to be dressed as a giant, grinning apple. And they were closing in. It was like the nightmare of the charity bib people in London—but without the oh so-lovable excuse of "doing it for the children. Sorry, I mean the commission."

"Are you looking for a show? Ten past eight at the Assembly Rooms. It's about—"

"Looking for a show? Clowning and Russian dance! Six forty at the—"

"Would you like to hear about my play? It's a powerful one-woman piece about—"

I was striding quickly down the Mile, my head down and my hands out, taking every leaflet that was offered to me, stuffing them in my pockets and watching any free time I might possibly have had disappear before my eyes. I was beginning to realise that if I wanted to get through this festival alive, I was going to have to be very, very careful about where I went and at what time of day. I could be the first person killed under the weight of a thousand leaflets. I decided I'd need to sit down with my diary and work out how to see as many of the shows I had leaflets for as possible. And then I would need to work out a system of not actually taking any more leaflets. And how was I going to explain my choice of shows to the BBC? Was this what they were paying me for?

Finally I made it to the Tempting Tattie. I had a baked potato with cheese. And then I went to watch a play about the lighter side of rape.

It was late. I was in the bar of the Assembly Rooms, catching up with Tom.

"Good day? What did you see?"

I took a deep breath.

"A disturbing play about betrayal and death; a powerful one-woman piece about the search for identity in an identityless world; a clown; and a late-night close-up magic show by an inept Dutchman. You?"

Tom counted in his head.

"Ross Noble."

I had worked out my professional itinerary for Edinburgh fairly quickly, and I was feeling quite pleased with myself. I'd noticed in the *Scotsman* that they had a daily list of "Five Recommended Shows You Really Must See." This, I decided, would be my system. I would see whatever they recommended, time slots permitting, while at the same time working my way through the leaflets I already had. And I'd also worked out my new system for avoiding the rampant terrorism of future leafletters. Sure, it wasn't quite in the spirit of being the Yes Man, but neither was spending eighteen hours a day in tiny, black rooms, watching American students adapt Shakespeare to Bhangra. So what was my system? I bought a pair of cheap, black headphones from Argos and permanently had them in my pocket. Upon spotting a leafletter, I would pop them on, people would see me coming, realise I was immersed in a world of loud and inpenetrable music, and leave me alone. It couldn't fail.

It did.

• • •

"What did you see today?" asked Tom the next night, once more propping up the bar at the Assembly Rooms.

"A play about famine, a ninety-minute monologue about a pension book, a Canadian dance troupe who were clearly hungover, a man who just sat there and said we should think, the 'Oxford Revue,' and a Bhangra version of Shakespeare by some guys from Nevada."

I was tired, and I looked it. "How about you?"

Tom held a ticket up. "Adam Hills."

Oh.

"How about tomorrow, Danny? Anything on?"

"Yep," I said heavily. "I've got my tickets already. Seven shows. Five of them *Scotsman*-recommended. First one's at ten."

"Seven shows," said Tom, under his breath. "Goodness."

"And you?" I said.

"I dunno," he said. "I thought I might have a night off."

There was, of course, another reason for throwing myself into the Edinburgh Festival with such gusto. While I was sitting quietly in the back room of a pub watching Bavarian physical theatre ("Crucial," said the *Times*), I couldn't be out there roaming around, getting myself into too much trouble. And, more important, I couldn't be in an Internet café, risking the wrath of the Challenger and, well, the rejection of Lizzie.

That, probably more than anything, was what concerned me. The Challenger I could maybe take. The fierce, blunt punch of rejection, on the other hand . . .

If Lizzie *had* written back, my heart would doubtlessly sink. And if she *hadn't*, well, there was a chance it would *break*.

Suddenly my phone rang.

"Dan? It's Ian."

"Hello, Ian."

"Are you enjoying Edinburgh?"

"Yes, thank you."

"Seen any shows yet?"

"One or two."

"Good. Well, listen. I was thinking . . ."

"Go on."

"I was trying to work it out. And I reckon I may know who the Challenger is."

And, after a moment or two, he told me. And it made complete and utter sense.

I said good-bye to Ian, got my diary out, and found the scrap of paper on which I'd already tried to solve the case. I added one more line.

Jason, the bloke from the party.

Jason!

Jason, the bloke from Thom's good-bye party! A man who could *easily* have gotten my details from Thom! A man who not only *knew* about my Yeses, but *despised* them! A man filled with an unquenchable rage that he would be only too pleased to unleash on me! A man who said no for a living; a man who was my opposite! A Lex Luther to my Superman! A No Man to my Yes Man!

I knew just what to do next. I had never replied to Jason's initial e-mail—the one that sent me to Stonehenge. But I still had it. I could e-mail him back. I could e-mail Jason!

I was filled with confidence and power. It was time to strike back before he upped the stakes. I found an Internet café just off Princes Street and ordered myself a cup of tea. It was time to check my e-mail and to send a couple of them. I reasoned that if Jason had indeed issued any more demands or instructions, I now possessed the strength to deal with them. The upper hand would soon be mine. For I was about to unmask him. There would be no more hats, no more books, and no more impromptu trips to Stonehenge. There would just be one very embarrassed man in a Lycra Challenger suit.

But this wasn't without its emotional risks. Checking my e-mail would leave me wide open to Lizzie. And if she'd written back to tell me I was a tit and I should never contact her again . . . Well, I didn't know how I'd handle it.

I logged in and instantly noticed two things: There was nothing new from the Challenger . . . but there was something new from Lizzie.

My stomach turned.

I couldn't open it. Not yet. Not *first*.

So I wrote to Jason.

> To: whoisthechallenger@hotmail.com
>
> From: Danny
>
> Subject: I know who you are
>
> Hello "Challenger,"
>
> You can stop now. The game's up. I know who you are and why
> you're angry with me, and I'm sorry, but this has to end.
>
> Thanks,
>
> Danny

But, just to make sure, I also wrote another e-mail to Thom, the
man who'd inadvertently introduced me to my nemesis. . . .

> Thom,
>
> It's Danny here. The bloke who bought your car.
>
> Listen, I'm sorry to be brief, but I need you to e-mail
> me back. I don't know if this e-mail address still works
> for you, because you'll be in New Zealand by now, but if
> it does, please get back to me
>
> I need to get a number for Jason, the bloke from your
> party. The civil servant. I think I did something to annoy
> him when I met him, and I think he's punishing me for it
> in quite an obscure and weird way. Did you give him my
> details? Please get back to me asap.
>
> Danny

I clicked back onto my list of messages and knew that now was the time
I'd have to deal with Lizzie. What would she say? What would a girl like
Lizzie say to a show of childish stupidity and apparent borderline obsession?

I clicked on her name and flinched as I read . . .

> What?!

Just that.

Just that one word.

My heart sank. But at least it didn't break.

I wrote back, "I know. Sorry." And went to find a pub.

Edinburgh by night is a city of warming beauty.

The castle, lit up and towering. Parliament Square. The Balmoral—the most impressive hotel I've never stayed in—with every light in the window a sign that wealth had come to town. The Canongate Tollbooth, Fettes College, the Ramsay Gardens tenements . . .

But I wasn't bothered about any of it. It could have all been built with LEGO blocks for all I cared.

I was grumpy and embarrassed, and now regretting the moment I'd decided to take a shortcut through Fleshmarket Close—the only short-cut in the known world which cuts down on distance but multiplies both the time your journey takes *and* the effort it takes to get there. Finally, breathlessly, reaching the last of the million or so stupidly steep steps, I looked up to see a woman, holding out a flyer.

"Interested in a show?"

I took her leaflet just as she said, "It's a play about betrayal, rape, and death."

Bugger.

A short while later I was nursing a pint in the Greyfriars Bobby, a pub named after a small dog of Scottish legend that had lain faithfully on his master's grave until he too had passed away. It seemed a fittingly melancholy place for me to drown my sorrows. I toasted the dog. By which I mean I raised my glass to it, not that I got a lighter and a spit out.

Around me were students on a pub crawl, a couple of rugby boys, a smattering of tourists as well as a tall, tanned man, who had just looked up at me and now approached . . .

"Danny?"

I jumped, slightly.

"Yes?"

There was something very familiar about this man.

"Danny Wallace?"

"Yeah. Hello."

"It's Hugh. Hugh Lennon."

Hugh Lennon! Hugh Lennon the Hypnotist! Hypnotist Hugh Lennon!

I hadn't seen Hugh Lennon in years—not since we'd had a drink after I'd reviewed a show of his for the *Scotsman* in . . .

Oh, God. I hope I gave him a good review.

"Great to see you!" he said.

Evidently I had.

"How long's it been?" I said.

"Must be . . . 1996? How strange to bump into you here!"

Hugh is a hypnotist who has the distinction of owning the world's only hypnotic dog, Murphy. Together they travel the world, hypnotising people. Like a magic version of Shaggy and Scooby.

"Murphy's at the venue," he said, "so I'd better go in a minute. Just popped in for a Coke and a pee. How are you? What are you doing up here?"

"Working. Seeing shows for the BBC. You know . . ."

"Seen anything good?"

Probably best to change the subject.

"So, what are you doing up here? A show?"

"Not really . . . I mean, I'm doing a one-off tonight . . . just the hypnotism and stuff . . . Hey, do you fancy coming along? It's a kind of warm-up. . . . I'm doing the Leeds Festival soon, you see. . . ."

"Um . . ."

"We could have a drink or two after. . . ."

"Yes. That would be great."

I drained my pint, and we left the pub. This was good. Some company. It was quite easy to spot Hugh's car. It was the one with HYPNODOG written across the side in great big letters. I wondered whether I should attempt something similar with the Yesmobile.

Hugh's venue was the back room of a pub on the outskirts of town, and I sat myself down with a pint. Hugh's in his early fifties now, but has the personality and energy of a man thirty years younger. He travelled to Britain from Mauritius when he was eighteen, and his faint accent and tanned skin add hugely to his onstage mystique. I hadn't quite been in the mood for comedic hypnotism, to be honest. It's rare for me as moods go.

Twelve people were now on the stage—old, young, male, female—
and all had fallen under Hugh's spell. For more than an hour I watched
as he somehow crafted a show out of them. And it was hilarious. And felt
good. And communal, somehow. I forgot all about what had been trou-
bling me earlier, and laughed a lot as Hugh's volunteers suddenly thought
they were Madonna or invisible or that a tiny duck kept on stealing their
drink. I can honestly say: If you're ever feeling blue or tired or down, try
and find a fat Scottish man who thinks he can fly. I don't know why more
agony aunts don't recommend them.

But it was what Hugh did in the final few minutes of the show that
truly astounded the room.

"I would ask you all to be very quiet, now," he said, looking very serious, "as I bring out a very special guest . . ."

I knew the story behind this very special guest. One day, many years
ago, Hugh came across an old and wise farmer, who talked in mysterious,
awestruck tones of a Labrador puppy not like the rest of its family. It kept
itself to itself, he said, and had a remarkable ability. . . . Hugh was
intrigued and went to visit the puppy. . . . The puppy that was later to
become . . . the *Hypnodog* . . .

Immediately the music started up (the theme from *2001: A Space
Odyssey*). The crowd fell silent as Hugh disappeared offstage and
returned moments later with Murphy. . . .

And ten minutes after that, the crowd cheered as twelve Scottish volunteers lay fast asleep on the stage, having stared deep into the abyss of
Murphy's chocolate-brown eyes. . . .

After the show Hugh sat next to me with a cup of coffee.

"Great show," I said.

"Thanks. They loved Murphy tonight, eh?"

On cue Murphy walked into the room, sniffed about a bit, and
walked out again. When he wasn't staring people into oblivion on stage,
he seemed fairly harmless.

"I lost him one year, you know," said Hugh. "He wandered off, and
I couldn't find him. It made the papers. The people in Scotland were
terrified. The headlines were screaming 'Do Not Approach This

Dog!' Journalists genuinely thought he was going to be walking around, staring at people, convincing them they were chickens. I thought that'd be the end of it, but we started getting calls from European news agencies, and then America, and then Japan. The phone wouldn't stop ringing. It was big news in China. 'Hypnotic Dog on the Loose in Scotland!' We were bigger than Nessie."

Suddenly we were interrupted. A lady who'd been watching the show wanted a word.

"Mr. Lennon . . . um . . . I've got a fear of spiders. . . . Is that something you can help with?"

"Yes," said Hugh. "You can cure pretty much anything with hypnotism. So long as it's in the mind. Which is where most problems are."

"Really? So I should see a hypnotist?"

"If you've got a problem in your head, a hypnotist can solve it, whatever it is. Here . . ."

He handed her a Hypnodog flyer with his number on it.

"I'm sure Murphy and I can solve your problem."

The woman smiled and took the flyer and walked away, satisfied.

"You'd let her come round your house?" I said.

"Yes," he said. "But only once I've got my spider costume out. I'll jump out at her at the train station. That'll fix it."

I laughed.

"But, no," he said. "It's good to be able to help people, when you can."

I was impressed.

"Christ, look at the time . . . I'm going to have to get going, Danny," said Hugh. "We've got a long drive ahead of us. But here"— he pulled out another Hypnodog flyer and handed it to me—"if you're ever in Wales, look me up, okay?"

"Cool," I said. "And thanks, Hugh."

Hugh smiled, and we looked at each other for slightly longer than we should have done, and for a second I worried he was hypnotising me. I averted my eyes and looked at the dog, but he was staring at me too.

"Well, see you soon," I said and left rather in a hurry.

I slept soundly that night.

I'd bought a bag of chips on the way home and reasoned that life was pretty good, all things considered. I fell asleep with the TV on and would have slept for days had I not, at four in the morning, been woken by a curious beep.

I looked around and saw that my phone was lighting up the room. I had a text message.

I yawned, knocked the telly off, rummaged around to find my glasses, and then picked up the phone as its light began to fade.

It was probably Wag, drunk and lost in London, texting me in case I happened to be close by.

I squinted to read it. There was a message, but no name. And it was an unrecognised number.

Zero-zero-six-one?

Who was that?

I read the message.

And then I sat bolt upright.

RING ME. I'M COMING TO EDINBURGH.

It was from Lizzie.

Four days later I was waiting in the arrivals lounge at Edinburgh International Airport with butterflies in my stomach and a flower in my hand.

And then there she was, pulling a suitcase behind her and smiling. I couldn't believe it. It was *Lizzie*.

"Hi," I said.

"Hi," she said.

And then we hugged. And we laughed and looked at each other. And then she said the words that I'd been longing to hear.

"What's with the *mullet*?"

CHAPTER 14

In Which Daniel and Lizzie Climb a Mountain, Visit a Brass Rubbing Centre, and See a Bad Play

I had been waiting for what seemed like days for Lizzie to wake up.

After I'd realised she was going to take me up on my offer, I'd phoned her straight away. Was she *sure*? I'd asked. Could she *really*? She told me she'd been hoping to come back for quite some time. This was the perfect excuse. Her work was sorted; she was her own person. She could do it. Especially now that she had a ticket.

I was overawed—and nervous. I mean, who does something like this?

"I got your postcard from Amsterdam," she'd said in the taxi on the way back. "The one which said sometimes you've just got to do things like that. I thought you were right."

So she'd travelled for twenty-four hours to London. And then an hour more to Edinburgh. And now here she was asleep in front of me in a slightly murky Travelodge in the centre of town. The power of postcards.

She'd arrived in the morning, and it was now getting on for nine at night. Edinburgh was orange and phospherous outside my window. The streetlights blushed through the condensation on the glass. I watched the news with the sound down. Eventually I fell asleep too.

"I can't believe you bought me a ticket," said Lizzie, buttering her toast.

It was the next morning. We sat in front of two fry-ups in the City Café round the corner. I was unbelievably happy.

"I can't believe you came here," I said.

Things were just as they'd been eight months earlier in London. Nothing seemed to have changed or shifted. It felt . . . natural. But exciting.

"Don't you think it's a bit . . . odd . . . though?" I asked.

"What? That I got on the plane or that you bought me the ticket?"

"Well . . . both."

"Yes. It's very, very odd," she said. "But that's good, isn't it? Life *should* be odd."

I thought about it. And I agreed.

"I brought you a present," she said.

"What is it?"

She opened up her bag and pulled out a picture. It was of a Big Cow.

"A Big Cow! Brilliant!" I said.

"Geek," she said.

I suppose it must be a boy thing. I suppose in Melbourne or Adelaide or Canberra these Big Things must attract boys from miles around, while the girls just sit there in the car, wondering what on Earth they're doing with their lives.

"So . . . ," she said. "What are we going to do today?"

"Absolutely anything you want," I said. "The whole festival is ours."

We went to the zoo.

The days flew by in the best way possible.

We did whatever came up, whenever it came up. We walked down Princes Street and accidentally ended up following a ghost tour. We walked by the shore in Leith and down by the sea, she made me buy cod. We moved out of the Travelodge and moved into the grand old Balmoral just because the mood took us, and we wore dressing gowns and sipped whiskey, and then we moved back to the Travelodge the very next night. She wanted to buy haggis and a deep-fried Mars bar and looked a little green after a mouthful of both. We had fun.

I marvelled at the power of Yes.

One time over a hot chocolate, Lizzie took the brochure of shows out. She flicked through it. She read some of it. She slammed it shut and threw it down on the table.

"You know what we should do?" she said.

"What?" I said.

"We should walk out that door and just go to the first show we get a flyer for. Whatever it is. No matter how bad it sounds."

I laughed. I'd kind of been doing that anyway, of course, but now it seemed like *fun*. Because we'd be *sharing* a Yes.

"Okay," I said.

A couple of hours later I had seen a show about betrayal, rape, and death for the third and hopefully last time.

As the days progressed we clambered up the sixteen thousand steps of the Scots Monument and sampled the brew in all two million of Edinburgh's pubs. On a rainy morning we bought a guidebook, and Lizzie stuck a pin in the museums section. We spent an hour in the Museum of Early Keyboard Instruments on Cowgate. Later we passed the Oxford Bar and sat there and drank tea and felt like characters from an Ian Rankin novel. I taught Lizzie words like "stushie," "bampot," "weejie," and "youze." She taught me "barrack" and "doodle."

One morning days later at 5 a.m., we were weaving our way home through a deserted city, carrying a half-full bottle of wine, when I suddenly became completely and utterly convinced that I could make this more special for Lizzie. I decided there would be snow on top of Arthur's Seat, the extinct volcano that watches over Edinburgh. I was drunk, yes, but I was determined too, and I told Lizzie I had a surprise for her, and she was to follow me at once. We walked and laughed for what would have been more than an hour, but didn't seem half that, until we were eight hundred feet up, standing at the top of the hill, overlooking the Firth of Forth and Fife and a city so splendid in the early morning sun that I didn't know what to say. There was, of course, no snow. It was late August, for God's sake, of *course* there wasn't. But that didn't matter. Because this had surprised us *both*.

I realised that in all the years I'd been coming to Edinburgh, I'd never once walked to the top of Arthur's Seat. I'd never been to the galleries, I'd never been to the museums, I'd never been to the things that are there all year round. They were always there for me, but I'd never used them, never said yes to the opportunities I thought would *always* be there. It was like I'd discovered a *new* Edinburgh through Lizzie. But somehow it meant more than that.

It was like the world was full of Yeses or something. But what I want you to understand—what I think it's *important* you understand—is that I wasn't saying Yes because I was playing the Yes game. I'd all but forgotten about that. I wasn't saying yes to prove anything to myself anymore, or to Ian, or to anyone else. I was saying yes because I *wanted* to. I was saying yes because all of a sudden it was coming naturally. I was saying yes because when you're in love, the world is full of possibilities, and when you're in love, you want to take every single one of them.

And that's my roundabout, slightly awkward way of telling you that . . . yeah . . . I was . . . you know . . .

In love and that.

"In love?" said Ian over the phone.

"Yeah," I mumbled shyly. "In love and that."

"Wow," said Ian thoughtfully. "Cool."

"I mean, I must be. I can't stop saying yes to things."

"Oh. Well. What a turnaround."

"But I don't even think about it when I'm with her. I'm saying yes because I *want* to. *Everything* seems like a good idea, so long as I'm doing it with *her*. It's like I've gone Yes mental."

"Or . . . Yental."

"That doesn't work."

"No, it doesn't. But all this is great, isn't it?"

"Yes," I said. "So, maybe Yeses are meant to be shared. Maybe that's what all this is about. Maybe life's about finding opportunities to share with someone. That's all it is, when you think about it. A series of opportunities to share."

Ian sounded like he'd need more convincing.

"Weirdo."

But maybe Lizzie felt differently. Not about me being a weirdo—God knows I hoped she felt differently about that—but about the other stuff. I don't know. Maybe this was how she *always* led her life. Open to opportunity. Spontaneous. Ready to go somewhere, do something. Maybe she was *always* a yes girl. With or without me.

I flew back down to London with Lizzie a few days later. I took her to the same terminal I'd taken her to when we'd last said good-bye. I knew, somehow, that this would be the last time I ever saw her. Saying yes had bought me another ten days with Lizzie. Ten days I'd never thought I'd have. But it had also cost me a little bit more. I'd had to say bye to a girl I once liked but now loved. But I wouldn't truly realise that until the next day, in fact, when Lizzie would already be thousands of miles away, and I would wake up and look around and for the first time see just how alone I really was.

CHAPTER 15

In Which Daniel Receives Some Unexpected News

For a couple of weeks and a day I did very little.

It felt like I was back at square one.

Nothing much was happening anymore. The whole Lizzie thing had kind of knocked me for six. It's better to have loved and lost, they say. Yeah, maybe. But not that bloody quickly.

I'd started putting in more time at the BBC. I threw myself into my work. I wrote a detailed and comprehensive report on all the shows I'd seen while at the festival, using words like "powerful" and "evocative," and telling Tom who I thought it was worth him getting in for chats and so on. I said yes to all the meetings I was asked to go to. Not because of Yes, but because I wanted to do a good job for a fine company. I turned up and worked even when my contract said I could be sitting at home, larking about. Work was becoming my focus. Because as long as I was working, I was . . . well . . . *safe*. Work couldn't hurt. So I worked.

The Challenger seemed to have disappeared off the face of the earth. My e-mail to Jason had clearly worked. The e-mail I'd sent Thom hadn't bounced back, but it hadn't been returned, either. And his mobile number had been disconnected, presumably to make way for a New Zealand number. Still, no matter: The Yes Man had conquered. I couldn't help but feel that should have made me happier than it did. In actual fact I was a little disappointed that it had been so easy. Now I had neither a love life nor a nemesis— and life's exciting when you've got a nemesis.

But my work at the BBC had clearly paid off. If nothing else, a couple of months' worth of Yeses and my impressive commitment to whatever I could at the festival had marked me out as a man of dedication and positivity. Tom asked me if I'd like to come in to talk about a new position that had opened up over at TV Centre. He said he thought I could well be the man for the job, but he just wanted to have a chat first.

I said yes.

That weekend Ian was desperately trying to work out what I wanted to do. I was slouching, unshaven on the sofa in my boxers and a T-shirt, and he was sitting on the chair opposite, smartly dressed and smelling of aftershave.

"So . . . do you want to go the pub?" he said.

I shrugged.

"Yeah," I said.

"Or . . . do you want to go the cinema?"

I nodded. "Yeah."

"Or we *could* go and play pool."

"Great," I said flatly.

"Yes to that as well," said Ian. "Right. Well . . . do you want to . . . I dunno . . . go for a bloody *jog*?"

"Yeah." I shrugged again. "Whatever, really."

Ian was perturbed.

"Jesus, Dan. You don't have to keep on just saying yes. It's me."

"Mmm-hmm."

"I'm just trying to find out what you want to do."

"Cool."

However distracted I may have been, I suppose I was still at least saying yes to things. I just wasn't enjoying it anymore. The thrill was gone. It was automatic. But I couldn't see the point of it all in the way I once had, in the way I'd hoped I always would. And I didn't want to think about it.

"I suppose now would be a bad time to tell you I've come up with the perfect punishment for you, if you don't do this?" said Ian.

I glared at him. He looked frightened.

"This is worse than when you always used to say no," he said. "At least then I didn't have to hang around with you."

We went to play pool.

Ian had managed to pot nearly every ball on the table. I was finding it hard to muster up the energy to compete.

"Dan . . . you're not going to slip back to how you were, are you?"

I looked up from my shot.

"How do you mean?"

"Well . . . you're not going to give up and revert back to how you were a few months ago are you? Because if you are, I will be able to put the punishment into action a little sooner than I'd thought . . ."

"Oh piss off with your punishment talk. You blatantly haven't thought of one yet."

Ian looked genuinely hurt.

"I have so."

"What is it, then?"

"Okay, I haven't. But I will. And it will be excellent."

I thought about what to say and leaned against the table.

"When I won that twenty-five thousand pounds, and then lost it again, it didn't really bother me. You know?"

Ian nodded.

"Because Yes had *given* me something. The fact that I lost it didn't matter. But then Yes gave me something *better* than twenty-five thousand pounds. It gave me Lizzie. And that was a cruel thing for Yes to do, because I couldn't keep her. It gave me someone who lives on the other side of the world, and it made me fall in love with her. And then she was gone. *That's* why I'm in a foul mood. That's why I think Yes is stupid. That's why I'm playing pool in this pub with you, thinking life is a mess, a sad fucking mess, and I wish I'd just said no a bit more. No's all I want to say, now, Ian. I don't want to be like I was, but I'm so sick of saying yes. All it does is tire me. It was supposed to *help*. It was supposed to be *exciting*."

Ian put his pool cue down and nodded sadly.

"What Yes giveth," he said, "Yes also taketh away."

Ian must have told Hanne what had happened.

The next day she wanted to meet up at a café near Old Street.

"Hey," I said, sitting down.

I was twenty minutes late, but she didn't say a thing. She was clearly in sensitive mode.

"Hey," she said softly. "So I just thought we should meet up. It's been awhile. I wanted to see how you are."

"I'm fine."

"Are you sure? You don't look fine."

"Honestly I'm good. I've just been a bit distracted lately."

"Something else is wrong. I can tell."

"No, you can't. And no, it isn't."

"It is. I can read you, Dan. I know you better than anyone."

"I've got a lot on my mind, that's all."

"Look, I know things are a bit funny, because of me and Seb, but . . ."

"Hanne. Honestly. That's not what this is about. And you don't have to worry. I'm absolutely not obsessed with you, and I didn't want to go on your bloody date with you, and I'm sorry about the flowers and the small African child. It was odd behaviour, I know, but please, if you don't mind, let's put it behind us. I moved on ages ago. Seriously. You and Seb are fine. You're great. And you and me—well, we're friends. Great friends."

Just then Hanne's phone rang. She was about to turn it off, but I gestured for her to take it, pleased for the interruption. It was her mobile phone company. I could hear them, tinny and loud, from where I was sitting. They wanted to know whether Hanne had a few moments to talk about her mobile phone bill. She said not really. I smiled. It must be nice to be able to say that. But again I gestured for her to continue. I had nowhere I needed to be. I had my meeting with Tom at the BBC, but that wasn't for hours yet.

"Okay . . . ," she said, mouthing *sorry* to me between answering questions. "Surname is Knudsen . . . ," she said, before giving the first line of her address, her date of birth, and her security password.

"Norway. N-O-R-W-A-Y." She rolled her eyes. "Yes. Like the country."

Well, what *else* was it like? The colour?

"Sounds good," she said. "Okay, thanks . . ."

She hung up.

"They've moved me to a better call plan. Free text messages, twenty percent off my bill. Glad I took the call . . ."

At least saying yes was working out for *someone*.

"So, listen . . . ," she said.

"I'm going to be fine," I said, cutting her off. "Life's just a bit . . . strange right now."

"Strange how?"

"Well, it *was* very uneventful. And then it *wasn't*. But now it . . . *is* again. But I like it that way. I'm just tired, Hanne."

She wrinkled her nose, struggling to follow my babbling.

"I never thought I'd say this, but . . . it sounds like you need to get yourself another stupid boy-project," she said, and I considered the irony. "You know you're allowed to now? You can do whatever you want. You're free! You know . . . You could count all the hairs on your legs again. It's been ages since you did that. You could see if you've got any new ones. Photograph them. That kind of thing."

I nodded. That sounded okay.

"I'll be fine, Hanne. Anyway. How's Seb?"

"He's good. He's still a little confused as to why you joined us for dinner that night."

"He asked! I felt I *had* to say yes!"

"Oh, sure, you *had* to. And I suppose you'd have said yes if Seb had asked you to jump off a cliff, would you?"

I opted not to answer that one.

"There's . . . another reason I wanted to meet up with you," she said.

"What's that?"

"Well . . . there's someone I'd like you to meet."

"Eh?"

"A girl I know."

Oh, no.

"Hanne, I'm fine. . . ."

"You said you were bored!"

"I didn't say I was bored. I just said things were uneventful."

"Look, do this for me. Just have a drink with her. What have you got to lose?"

"Hanne, ex-girlfriends aren't supposed to set their ex-boyfriends up on dates."

"Danny, ex-boyfriends aren't supposed to sponsor small African kids for their ex-girlfriends. And yet they do. All the time. It's really very common."

I blushed a little. "But I don't want to." I sounded like a child and I knew it.

"Oh, go on. Live a little. You seemed like you'd got back into the swing of things until just recently. You seemed like you were really enjoying yourself."

"I was."

"So have a drink with Kristen. Just a drink. I think you'll get on brilliantly. And you'll feel better for it."

Maybe Hanne was right. I mean, obviously, I'd have to say yes, but on another level it might be good for me. I knew the situation I was in. And I knew the solution too. Get over it. And how do you get over something like that? You get on with life. You don't look back. You look forward.

"Fine. I'll have a drink with Kristen. I'll give her a call."

Hanne smiled an oddly satisfied smile and wrote the number down on a napkin.

"That's great," she said. "That's really great. And listen . . . tell me to get lost if you think I'm being too nosey, but . . . I was talking to Ian, and . . . well, don't get annoyed, but I think maybe you should see someone."

"Well, obviously you do. That's why you're trying to set me up with your mate."

"No. I mean, *see* someone. A psychologist. A psychiatrist. A counsellor. Just . . . *someone*."

Oh.

"What the hell did you tell Hanne?" I said to Ian.

"What?"

"Did you tell her I was saying yes to everything?"

"Of course not! Why?"

"Because she wants me to *see* someone! A psychiatrist or something!"

"I think, to be fair, she may want you to see someone, because she *doesn't* know about your Yes thing. She must just think you're mental, that's all."

"I'm not mental!" I said, probably a bit too loudly.

"Keep your voice down," said Ian. "Shouting 'I'm not mental!' only makes you sound more mental. And anyway, think about how it looks to *her* . . . You live for months in your flat in some kind of cocooned depression, then suddenly you're out every day and night, you buy a weird car, you seem on top of the world, and then *bang!*— you're all depressed again. It's like schizophrenia! Or the beginnings of a midlife crisis! No wonder she wants you to see someone. You've got to snap out of this. It's been weeks since you got back from Edinburgh. You're in danger of undoing all our good work."

"*Our* good work?"

"Look, you have to get a grip. Jesus, think about what saying yes has done for you. Think about all the good things that have happened, if there *are* any. And then learn from it and put it to bed, if you have to."

"Put it to bed?"

"Yeah. I'll let you off the punishment. You can stop right now, and that'll be that. No repercussions. Just you. Cheered up."

I thought about what Ian had said. And I thought about what I'd achieved so far. Life *had* been more fun. I'd met some interesting people, I'd done some new things, and, all in all, Yes had been a minor success. But that had been in the early days, when the consequences hadn't seemed to matter so much. Now, I was in a lull. I wanted life to be normal again. We were only just coming up to October, for God's sake. October! If I was going to do this properly and stick to my Yes Manifesto, there was still a long way to go. An *impossibly* long way. Could I really only be halfway through? I felt like crying. I felt like grabbing someone—*anyone*—and telling them the whole story, start to finish . . . but I already knew I didn't like the way the story finished. Not if it ended like this. Hanne had said she wanted me to see someone. Maybe she was right. She wouldn't have said something like that if it wasn't important.

I lay in bed that night, thinking and thinking and thinking. Did I stop now? Or did I see it through? In what direction should I take my life?

I needed a sign.

The next morning my phone rang. I answered it. The person didn't hang up.

And I had the sign that I so badly needed.

• • •

"I need a bottle of champagne, please. Cheapest you've got."

"How much are you looking to spend, sir?"

"Um . . . a fiver?"

"We've got two pounds off Dom Perignon at the moment, at twenty-six pounds and eighty-eight pence, if you're interested?"

I relished the moment.

"Yes!" I said.

"Would you like to buy a cooler with that?"

"Yes!" I said. "Yes—whatever you like!"

"What are we celebrating?" said Ian, standing at the door. "And why are you grinning like that?"

"We are celebrating some shocking news," I said, pushing past him. "And a new beginning."

"What news?"

"My promotion," I said.

"Your *promotion*?!"

"My promotion."

"But you're never at work!"

I ignored Ian's childish comment and found two mugs in his cupboard.

"Blimey. Dom Perignon . . . feeling flash, are you?"

"Not really. I wanted the cheap stuff, but the man suggested this."

"Why have you brought a corkscrew?"

"It was on offer."

"So . . ."

"Yep. Just when I thought I was out, Yes pulled me back in."

I poured the champagne, and Ian opened his packet of nuts.

"So what's the job?"

"Well . . . it's in a small department over at TV Centre—*tiny*, really—working up new ideas, finding new talent, developing stuff, that sort of thing."

"What's your job title?"

I took a deep breath and told him. "Head of Development."

I was beaming. Absolutely *beaming*.

"*Head of Development!?*" said Ian. "What? You? A *head* of something? That's *ridiculous*!"

"I know. But if it makes you feel better, there's literally no one beneath me. It's like being made Head of Stationery just because I've got my own pencil."

Ian shook his head.

"As far as I can tell," he said, "you've just got an executive-level promotion at the BBC, the most respected broadcaster in the world, essentially on the basis that you say yes a lot."

We clinked mugs.

"Yes," I said.

"So you're still going to say yes?"

"Yes!"

What Ian didn't realise was what this *really* signified.

There was a reason for this. I knew it. It had come just at the right time—just when I was doubting the validity of what I was doing and considering another change in life. A change to the sensible. To the more predictable. To the more comfortable. And it had confirmed to me that that choice was *right*.

An optimist would say that Yes had given me another big chance, and I should stick with it. I would have said the same a month or two earlier. And it's true—saying yes to that first meeting had set off a chain of events that had somehow led me to buying a bottle of champagne and toasting a new start. But a realist would see what this really meant.

I realised now all too clearly that you can't live life as a total optimist. I saw the underlying reason for this promotion. The secret reason. It was there to encourage me to say good-bye to my stupid, carefree ways. To say good-bye to living life like it was all about fun and frolicks and adventure. At some point you have to grow up, move on. Hanne had always told me that. And now I'd realised it for myself. Jason had been right that night at the party. Responsibility comes to us all. Life can't just be about fun. We have to sacrifice our freedom sometimes, so that we can progress. I would e-mail Jason once again. I would thank him for the lesson. Who'd have thought it? The Challenger won after all. No was best.

And what do I mean by "No was best?" I mean No is power. No

says, "I'm in charge." Think about how many times you've said yes in the past year, and how many times you would've liked to have said no instead. Maybe being able to say no is the one thing that keeps us sane. Some people go through their whole lives saying yes over and over again—yes to things they don't want to do but feel obliged to; yes to things that allow other people to take advantage of them, just because that's the way things are, the way things have always been. Some people need to learn how to say no. Because every time they say yes, they say no to *themselves*.

All those Yes moments, when I'd done something I didn't necessarily want to do, all those Yes moments that hadn't led anywhere, hadn't done *anything* . . . what if I'd said no to those? It would've meant I could have said yes to things I *did* want to do. . . . Saying no gives you access to a process of elimination that can lead to a better life. If I could say No to the part of me that wasted his time doing things he knows he shouldn't, I could say yes to the part of me that wanted to move on.

I explained all this to Ian, and he ended up agreeing with me.

"I suppose you're right. I suppose this is the first good thing that's happened to you since you started saying yes. I mean, you won and then *lost* that money, which I've always said is *worse* than never winning it at all. You've loved and lost, which I don't think *is* better than never having loved, actually. You *thought* you were going to be a telly presenter, but that hasn't materialised, either, which is more disappointing than never thinking it. You owe thousands of pounds on credit cards you shouldn't have applied for. You are constantly phoned up by strangers who hang up as soon as you answer. You bought a car you don't need and got a haircut which was last fashionable in 1985. In Hungary. Your inventions don't work. Your . . ."

Suddenly I was a little offended. "Actually the inventions are pretty good. Maybe not the spoon one, but the Incredible Automatic Self-Rewinding Video Box is sound."

"Your design worked by placing a magnet on the inside of the box. It would wipe the tape as it rewound. It's basic science. Anyway in a few years videos will be obsolete, and no one will even use them."

My God . . . things were even worse than I'd imagined. I'd banked on that rewinder being my nest egg. But the only way to deal with it was to treat it like a lesson. So I left Ian that night feeling positive about pessimism. These things happen for a reason. Thank heavens I'd seen the sign. Maybe there *is* a grand plan after all.

I suddenly thought of the man on the bus, and then, slowly, of Maitreya. It sounds outlandish to say it, but maybe there was something in all that. Maybe Maitreya really *was* the man on the bus, the man who'd kick-started this whole thing. Maybe I really *was* being looked after by some higher power. A higher power who wanted me to grow up. Suddenly *anything* seemed possible.

The thing was Yes had started off as a way of getting back into an old, carefree life. Turns out it was a way of making me realise the *errors* of that life. It represented the end of an extended adolescence. And surely . . . that was a good thing?

So I would do this. I would get this Yes thing out of the way. I would do it, and then move on. I would start the new job in January. And then I would put a stop to this chapter of my life—not just the Yes chapter, but everything like it.

But it was important to *succeed*. I never wanted to think I'd moved on because I'd *failed*.

For now I got on with the work at hand, knowing for sure that this would be the last stupid thing I ever did. I had a clear run ahead of me. This would be easier than ever.

But less than one week later, I received another package.

CHAPTER 16

In Which Daniel Is Tempted by Evil

The Challenger was back, and I was a furious man.

I'd sorted this out! I'd already sorted this out!

The fact that Jason had lulled me into a false sense of security, and then slapped me in the face with yet another package did nothing but infuriate me. My decision to continue the way of Yes as a good-bye to my stupid, carefree past was a noble and pure one—and all he was doing now was sullying it. Spoiling it. Making it more about *him* than *me*. This was supposed to be self-help, a personal odyssey. This wasn't supposed to be a game of cat and mouse with me as the mouse.

I was thundering out of Oxford Circus Tube toward the Yorkshire Grey, my face a picture of concentrated anger. I needed, once again, to speak with Ian.

"Buy a Big Issue, mate?" said a man, standing outside of Boots.

I turned to face him as I strode past.

"No!"

Yes. That's right. No.

The really infuriating thing was, once again, the Challenger had upped the stakes. What made it all the more painful was that it was *all my fault*. I'd e-mailed Jason to tell him about my new frame of mind, that he'd been right all along. That I'd realised the true danger of Yes and the true power of No. And now . . . now he'd sent me *this*.

A man asked me for spare change as I walked past McDonald's. I had no time, but I had the correct answer: I barked a no as quickly and sharply as possible. He looked slightly shocked, but I didn't care. I had to get to the Grey.

As I burst through the doors of the pub, I saw Ian, sitting by the fireplace in the corner. I paused by the bar to compose myself.

"What can I get you?" asked the girl behind the bar.

I maintained perfect eye contact with Ian as I said, "Nothing, thank you. I do not want a drink."

Ian's eyes widened. He had heard my answer. He knew something was very, very wrong.

I sat down next to him, and he didn't say a thing, just stared at me.

I reached into my pocket and took out a letter. On it was one type-written line. I put it on the table and slid it toward him.

He leaned forward and read aloud.

I saw this and thought of you.

He looked at me again, shrugged, and did that little shake of the head people do when they don't know what's going on.

"Who sent you that?" he said.

"Guess," I said.

But he knew. He knew *exactly* who had sent it.

"But what does it mean? What did they send?"

I unzipped my jacket and revealed a bright, blue T-shirt.

On it were three simple words:

JUST SAY NO

Ian looked at me in horror.

He recognised the slogan from the old antidrugs campaigns of the eighties . . . the ones you'd usually get underneath a picture of a crack-addled teenager or next to a beautifully crafted charcoal portrait of a man with a tiny dog on his shoulder. But he also knew what its meaning would be to *me* . . .

"No!"

I nodded silently.

"You look surprised," I said.

"I thought they'd decided to stop all that!"

"Me too."

"So what do you think it means?" he said.

"It means I should just say no."

"Instead of yes?"

"Well, that's the problem. Do I say yes to just saying no, or do I just say no to saying no? Do I make a stand and say no, or is that exactly what they want?"

"Or does it mean you should just say no to just saying yes?"

"Yes. No. I don't know."

"But if you just start saying no when once you would have just said yes," said Ian desperately, "you'll have failed! That goes against everything the Yes Manifesto stands for! I should know! I've got it stuck to my fridge! I can't make a cup of tea without being reminded of your plight!"

"But if I just say no to saying no, I'll still be saying *yes* to just saying no, because I'll have just said *no*. Maybe I can just say no to just saying no, thereby cancelling it out."

"That's a no-no."

"A double no, yes."

"No. A no-no in that you can't just say no to saying no. You'll still just have to say yes to just saying no, otherwise you'll have said no!"

"So I should just say no from now on, and wait until the Challenger sends me a T-shirt saying, 'Okay, you can just say yes again now'? It's not going to happen!"

I was starting to wish I'd ordered a drink, and looked at Ian's beer longingly. Ian caught me looking.

"Pint?"

I sighed. "No."

Twenty minutes of intense crisis talks later, we had a solution of sorts.

It was a fair and worthy solution to an unusual and tricky problem. I clearly had to do what the Challenger said . . . especially now that Ian was so heavily involved. But part of me couldn't help but wonder if Ian was now in cahoots with Jason. Yes, Jason would have taught me a lesson by messing with my life, but who really stood to benefit? Whose punishment would I have to ultimately undergo? Just where was Jason getting his information? How would he know I was going through with his demands? I decided to sit on my worries for now and see how it all panned out before making any untoward accusations.

So the solution was: I would spend *one day* just saying no. That's how this whole Yes thing had started—one day of utter positivity. I would do the same with negativity. I would spend today saying no to everything—*anything* and everything. And I would show the Challenger the way of the righteous.

So, with confidence I stepped out of the Yorkshire Grey with a whole new adventure to get stuck into. I knew it wouldn't make me feel as good as my Yes adventure once had, but I knew it was part of the deal. Sure, I couldn't say I'd enjoy it, and yeah, so it would grate on me, but . . .

"Excuse me, sir . . ."

It was a man with a green bib on.

"I was wondering if you'd have two minutes to talk about Help the Aged?"

I smiled.

"No."

Hey.

That felt . . . *good.*

I was sitting alone at home, almost cackling.

Why had I never realised just how good it felt to say no before?

I'd arrived home and immediately opened the rest of that morning's mail—the mail I'd forgotten about as soon as I'd found the new package. I saw that the people at American Express wanted to offer me a new credit card. I wrote them a postcard, saying no. I specifically didn't do as the ad said by not ringing up to ask where my nearest WeightWatchers meeting was. I got the invite for Paul Lewis' stag weekend and howled with joy as I wrote back and said I couldn't be there to watch him and his army pals destroying barges and levelling whole towns with their raucous, witless behaviour (then I scribbled that out and wrote a more polite version—I'm not an idiot). I didn't buy the "five greatest albums you really must own," I declined the offer of a free no-obligation quote from Kitchens Direct, and I shouted a cheery "no!" when the advert on cable TV said, "Isn't it about time you learnt to cook pasta like the professionals?"

Something was happening to me here. Something strange. I was really enjoying myself.

A text message came through from Hanne.

I HAVE AN EXTRA TICKET FOR DAMIEN RICE TONIGHT, IF YOU WOULD LIKE TO COME.

Damien Rice! I *love* Damien Rice! I gleefully texted back.

NO!

Minutes later Hanne did the same.

RUDE.

Rude. Yeah. But I didn't care. Because I was the No Man. And this was *just* what I needed.

It was like the Dark Side had taken over.

The Challenger had reared his Darth Vader–like head once again, but this time he had turned me. A battle between good and evil had started to rage inside me. Well, not *evil*, exactly. More like *grumpy*. Yeah, that was it: A battle between good and grumpy had engulfed me. No was suddenly *good*. No was *great*. I *felt* that now. But could I let it take over? It was tempting. What if I just extended the period of No-ness? I'd done it with the Yes side of things. . . . It'd be only fair. Did I want to go back to the Good Side at midnight tonight, or did I want to see where a healthy dose of negativity could take me? Sure, it was dangerous, and no, it wouldn't be much use in January, when I started the new job, but the thought was intriguing. Obviously, I didn't want life to be exactly the way it had been before, but that had been when I hadn't been in control. Now, the world of No wouldn't control *me* . . . *I* was in charge! After all, I knew how to use the word properly now. I knew how to handle it. And I could give up any time I wanted.

Ian had thought maybe I was overreacting to the Challenger's demands. He said I was blowing it out of all proportion, letting him get the better of me and turning him into an evil genius figure, when actually it was probably just someone I knew, winding me up without realising the effects.

Evil genius, I thought. *Probably just someone I knew . . .*

Interesting choice of words, Ian. Ever been to Liverpool?

I continued to suspect it was Jason. No—not suspect. *Knew*. This was a man I'd seen as an enemy but should now treat as an ally after all he'd done for me. I'd made him furious by denying his way of life was healthy, and so now he'd made me taste it. And it was good. I would e-mail him again. . . . E-mail him for the third time. E-mail him to tell him that soon I would be like him. Soon I would walk among the rest of the No-bodies. Soon I would reclaim my No. Soon I would run with the Dark Side.

I was excited. I switched on the telly just in time to hear Graham Norton say, "Join me after the break . . ." So I shouted, "No, Graham Norton, I will *not!*" and switched the telly off again.

This was *brilliant!*

That evening I stayed in. Nothing could tempt me out. Each option I came up with in my head was greeted with a pure and resounding no. Great. This was great. Exactly what the doctor ordered.

I stared out of the window for a while, watching the trains go by and the people off on their nights out. When the advert for Domino's Pizza came on the radio, and the voice of Tony Hawks suggested I try their new two-for-one combo value meal deal, I just switched off the radio, and tried not to think about how hungry I was.

I sat, staring at the digital clock, from 11:37 p.m., waiting . . . waiting for midnight.

It was taking *ages.*

I weighed up what it all meant by writing in my diary, and realised in an instant that it meant, well, nothing. No achievement. No living. *Nothing.* I tried to feel good about it. Tried to remember that No meant freedom, choice, discretion. But I yearned for the early days. The simple days. The days when I was winning on scratch cards and enjoying an extra pint and seeing my friends. When had things started to go so wrong? When I bought the car? When I went to Liverpool? Why did this mean so much to me? Why did I have to continue? Couldn't I resign myself to the fact that a new job and a new life were only round the corner? Couldn't I just stop and . . . *wait?*

No was wrong. It didn't fit. It was a flirty, evil temptation to take me away from the real work that had to be done. And I had to *succeed* in this work. If I didn't, perhaps I would never be able to move on. But

I was beginning to realise and reluctantly decide that maybe I'd need some help. And not just the kind of help that Ian brought. Professional help.

It had been Hanne's suggestion, of course. She'd meant for me to see a psychiatrist or a counsellor or someone who could guide me.

Well, I would get some guidance. Because I'd had an idea. A way of making this all so much easier. A way of guaranteeing success. With this man's help, I couldn't fail. I would be rejuvenated. Enthusiastic. Ready to fight the good fight, the final fight. Full of Yes.

I opened up my diary again and pulled out the flyer on which this man had written his number. In the morning I would make a phone call and book a ticket.

I was going to see a man about a dog.

CHAPTER 17

In Which Daniel Meets with Hugh the Incredible, a Tiny Soldier, and a Magical Dog with a Hat On

I had informed Hypnotist Hugh Lennon that he was to prepare himself for the toughest case of his professional career. He was to meet me at Cardiff Central train station that very afternoon and immediately begin work on resolving a delicate matter of both the heart and mind. Hugh, in return, had decided this meant one thing.

"It looks like we'll be needing some takeaway."

And so there he was, waiting for me as I stepped off the train with a small box of wonton he'd bought on the way from a Chinese restaurant.

"Snacks for later!" he said enthusiastically. "Very necessary when dealing with tricky psychological problems. Keeps the energy levels up. I find wonton does that well. I love a bit of wonton. Pork wonton, especially. I don't think there's much that beats it, really."

I nodded in absolute agreement. I felt this was a matter it was vital we were unified on.

"But prawn toast is good too," Hugh went on.

I nodded again, even more enthusiastically this time. Basically I'd decided that I needed this man, and I was willing to go along with *any* of his opinions on Chinese food, no matter *how* controversial.

Hugh would simplify things for me. He was already involved in this, after all; he was part of the adventure of things. Yes had led me to him that night in Edinburgh, and now it had led me to him again. I needed him to help me focus my mind. Clarify things.

I clambered into his Renault, and we began to drive out of Cardiff and toward Mountain Ash, the tiny, former mining town Hugh now calls home.

"So . . . ," he said as we found ourselves deeper and deeper into the blustery, bruised valleys. "All I know so far is that you need my help. But with what?"

"Well . . . it's a tricky one," I said. "I made a decision to do something.

And I think I need to keep doing it. I know I do. Just until the year is out. But I've kind of lost my willpower."

"Aha," he said. "Willpower."

He said the word "willpower" in the way that wise, old sea captains often stare into the distance and say the word "wind," like it's their old enemy or something.

"Willpower," he said again wistfully. "So what is it . . . smoking? I can stop you from smoking in five minutes."

"No, not smoking."

"Drinking? Is it drinking?"

"No. It's not drinking."

"Well . . . what, then?"

I thought about how to put it.

"I need to say yes more."

Hugh nodded.

"Fair enough."

"It's a fascinating problem," said Hugh, munching on a wonton. "Usually I get asked to help people say no more. You know . . . no to whatever they're addicted to. Are you sure you'd want to just blindly say yes to things?"

I thought about it. Even without the help of hypnosis, I'd already run up an intimidating debt on credit cards I should never even have applied for, let alone used, I'd found myself some kind of masked enemy figure who was out to torment and ruin me, I had the haircut of a hick, I'd bought a car, and I'd loved and lost.

"Yes," I said with a small shrug. "I just need to know if there's an easy option. You know? A better way of going about things? I've still got a couple of months of this left before I move on forever, and I thought it would get easier the more I did it. But certain . . . things . . . have happened which have made it harder."

"What things?"

"A girl. A girl, for one thing."

Hugh nodded and said, "Ah."

"And a . . . well . . . a nemesis."

"A nemesis?"

"A nemesis. Someone keeps winding me up and making me do things because they know I'll say yes. But I don't know who they are, and I'm afraid that if I say no to them, it'll ruin everything, and all my hard work will have been for nothing."

"So you want to say yes, so that your hard work means more?"

I nodded. My phone rang. I answered it. They hung up. I was getting really bloody sick of these polite nonconversations. Whatever happened to having a good old chat?

"It's interesting," said Hugh, leaning forward to make a roll-up. "I suppose in some ways all this is about confronting fears. People sometimes go through their lives having fears and never realising they can be removed in just a few minutes, forever. People are always saying no to things, aren't they? They're frightened of change, used to routine, used to doing things a certain way. Like, the people who take risks in business are the people who don't fear change, and ultimately they're the most successful."

"I think this started through fear," I said. "I was living quite negatively, and I was missing out on things. I guess I'm afraid of what you can miss out on in life. Every single day."

"So," said Hugh, licking the rizla. "It's a kind of fear of the unknown, in your case. It's a negative form of thinking. People do miss out on so much by instantly and unthinkingly saying no. . . . They don't realise they're putting a real limitation on their lives. Take my wife, for example. When we were first friends, I offered her wonton and she said, 'no way.' And then she tried it, and she *loved* it."

"That's true!" shouted Arlene from somewhere in the house. "I *love* wonton now!"

I didn't know how to respond to a sentence like that coming from someone in a different room. Usually a smile would have done, but she couldn't see that, so I just said quite loudly, "I like wonton too."

Hugh lit his roll-up and continued.

"It's the same with travel. People decide to stay at home. They say, what would I want to go to Spain for? What's in Spain for me? I've got everything I need right here in Pontypridd. And they miss out on a wonderful new experience. It's all they ever know. They just say no."

I considered Hugh's words.

"Tom Jones used to live in Ponty!" shouted Arlene. "He used to walk around the pubs, singing for pints. My granny booed him one night."

I smiled and once again realised that she couldn't see me. So I said, "Tom Jones is a good singer."

Hugh nodded.

"*Bloody* good singer," he said.

Murphy's fez had fallen off, and he hadn't bothered to pick it up and put it back on again. That's dogs for you. Lazy.

He was sitting with his paws on my lap, staring up at me with the big, brown eyes that have made him the toast of the transcontinental animal-variety circuit. I was on the comfy chair, ready to "go under." We were watching videos of Murphy and Hugh's various television appearances around the globe. Hugh wanted to show me what I'd be in for, if we went ahead with the hypnotism.

We'd already watched their appearance on American tabloid shows *Hard Copy* and *Inside Edition*, and now we were watching a Discovery Channel show called *Animal X*.

"This . . . is the Hypnodog!" bellowed an American man over some slowed-down footage of the slavering Labrador, bounding toward the camera. "Few stand a chance against his mysterious stare!"

Some sinister music started up. And then there on the screen was Hugh, sitting on a sofa in a softly lit room, with his dog on his lap.

"I must admit . . . It *is* unusual," he said.

"Unusual indeed!" bellowed the American man again, who must be a nightmare to sit behind in the cinema. "*Animal X* tracked the Hypnodog down . . . to Luton, England!"

"It was actually Harrow," said Hugh.

I suppose saying it was Luton gave it more mystique.

"But other dogs are said to have mysterious powers too!" said the American. "This terrier"—they showed a picture of a small terrier—"became famous in the United States for bringing a young boy out of a coma!"

"What did he do?" I said. "Jump on his bollocks?"

Hugh and I laughed for ages, which was fair enough, because it was a quality gag.

"But the Hypnodog is said to have the strangest powers of all . . .

the power to control the human mind! Animal expert Dr. Roger Mugford has come across other animals with the same skill. . . ."

The camera cut to Dr. Roger Mugford.

"A mongoose can hypnotise a snake!" he said with some enthusiasm. "And a tiger can hypnotise a monkey!"

I made a mental note to remember these sentences for the next bring-a-fact party I attended.

"The Hypnodog is said to have hypnotised a man into handing over his lunch. And those who fall under his spell tumble like a row of dominoes at the sight of the deep, brown pools of his eyes . . ."

I looked down at Murphy. I wasn't sure I wanted to tumble like a row of dominoes. For starters there was only one of me, so I'd have to keep getting back up and knocking myself down again. Murphy stared up at me. Suddenly it was a little disconcerting. I had definitely caught sight of the deep, brown pools of his eyes. What was going to happen to me?

Suddenly, Hugh was by my side.

"If you're still feeling nervous, read one of these . . ."

He handed over a cuttings book. There were hundreds of articles, from all over the world.

"Paws for Thought!" screamed the *New York Post*. "Trances with Wolves!" read the *Mail*.

"It should reassure you. Murphy and I have hypnotised many, many people. You're in safe hands."

It wasn't the hands I was worried about. It was the paws.

"Hang on," I said. "What's this headline here about?"

I pointed it out. "Hypnotist's Spell Made Girl's Boobs Swell!"

"Ah, yes," said Hugh. "I enlarged a German girl's breasts."

And he left it at that.

"So you just want us to make you more open, then . . . ," he said, his hand on my shoulder.

"Well, yes. That, and I suppose . . . to give me a total and utter inability to say no. At least for a couple of months. Until December 31."

Hugh balked and took a step back.

"Ah. Well. Wow. That's different from just an openness to saying yes. . . . That's . . . well . . . you could get into a lot of trouble in two months."

"Well . . . could you put a limit on it?" I said. "Could you perhaps make me stop short of murder and robbery?"

"You won't do anything that's against your moral code. That's not how hypnotism works. But it *will* mean that you'll lose your inhibitions. . . . I'll have to get into your subconscious."

"Is that dangerous?"

"Well . . . the subconscious is an amazing tool. People don't realise that you can literally ask your subconscious any question, and when you're at your most relaxed, it will give you the answer. You literally ask it out loud, you go away, and it'll work on it."

"Do you do that?"

"All the time. Like . . . last week. I was trying to come up with a title for a competition to find another Hypnodog. You know, an audition for another dog that can hypnotise people, like Murphy can. But I was trying so hard to come up with a title that I just couldn't. So I asked my subconscious."

"And?"

"Well, sometimes it takes a little time."

"Oh."

"Now, when I get into your subconscious, I'll remove the self-doubt you have. That fear of saying yes."

"It's not just fear that used to make me say no, though. Sometimes I just couldn't be arsed. Someone would say, 'Come and see this band tonight,' and even if I was free, I'd say, 'Ah, I can't. I've got something on.' And then I'd go home and watch *Neighbours*."

"So you need to regain your childish enthusiasm . . . that's fine. We can do that. I suppose in some ways we have to find your . . . *reset* button."

"Right, well . . . how are we going to do this?" I said, and I clapped my hands together to try and show I meant business. But I was actually becoming more and more nervous. Murphy rested his head on my lap. Was this part of it? If Hugh did the same, I was in trouble.

"I'll play some music. I generally use Baroque music, because that's sixty beats a minute, like the heart. Or failing that I've got a Richard Clayderman CD, and you'll relax for a little while. You'll stare into Murphy's eyes when I tell you to, and we'll take it from there. What I'd like to do is rid you of your preconceptions. Make your Yeses new and wonderful again."

I wondered what preconceptions he thought I had, given that I had already agreed to be hypnotised by a man and his dog. I think Hugh saw that in my eyes.

"What I mean is . . . it's like with danger. You put a plank of wood between two buildings, and no one will walk across it. You put that same plank of wood on the ground, and they won't have a problem doing it. I'm going to put all your Yeses on the ground."

I saw what he was saying. If every option seemed secure, and every opportunity felt like a safe bet, I'd be far more likely to take them. I wanted to ask Hugh a little more about what we'd be doing, but I was a bit distracted. Murphy had started to sniff me, and it was slightly intimidating. Plus I didn't want to wake up and discover that while I'd been asleep, he'd given me a pair of huge German breasts. Although I suppose then I would at least have a chance of winning the contest held by the people looking for Britain's most German-looking man. Who, by the way, still hadn't phoned back.

Murphy whimpered, and suddenly I wasn't so sure about any of this. Sure, I needed a booster, and yes, this was the perfect cure-all for my particular predicament, but was it . . . right? Was this cheating? Would it really be me saying yes to things, or would it be Hugh saying yes for me? If I couldn't *help* but say yes, that wasn't *choosing* to say yes, was it? Or was it?

Hugh switched the video off and tried to find the right remote for the telly. He'd already found the right CD and dimmed the lights.

What was I doing? I was about to be hypnotised by a stormtrooper and his spacedog! I needed more time. . . . I glanced about the room, desperate to find a distraction.

"Hugh, did you paint that picture?"

I pointed at a poster hanging on the wall.

"No . . . ," said Hugh. "That was Rembrandt."

What else was there in here? What else could I use? And then I noticed something . . . something on the TV. Something that actually genuinely intrigued me. A strangely familiar view. When Hugh had turned the video off, the picture on the screen had turned into . . . well . . .

"Hugh, what's that?" I said.

"What's what?" said Hugh.

"That view on the telly"—I pointed at it—"that's the view out of your front window, isn't it?"

This seemed very odd to me, whether buying time or not. Why close your curtains to block out the view but purposefully have the view piped into your TV? It seemed like something an extravagant rapper on MTV *Cribs* would do. Perhaps Hugh was more showbiz than I thought.

"Oh, that, yeah," said Arlene, suddenly there. "There's a camera on the windowsill."

"Right. What, like a security thing?"

I was very grateful she'd arrived. She'd just bought me some time.

"No, no . . . nothing like that. It's very safe here."

"Well, why, then?"

"There's a little boy next door," said Hugh, studying the back of another CD. "Dean, his name is. He's great fun, but he wants to come in all the time. *Literally* all the time. He always knows when we're in, and so we close the curtains and put the camera on so we know if it's him at the door. Otherwise I'd end up doing magic all day, every day. Usually we'll hear a knock, so we'll turn the telly on, and his face will be filling the whole screen. He presses his face right up to it so we can see it's him."

"So, he knows it's there?" I said. As a distraction technique this was working wonderfully.

"Oh, yes," said Arlene. "Doesn't stop him. He loves watching magic, and Hugh just can't turn him away."

"I'm too polite. So that's why I had the camera installed."

This was brilliant. They had actually installed a camera in their window so that they could avoid the little boy next door. And they'd had to do it, because they were too polite to say no to him. They were trapped in their own home by a Yes.

"Can't you just tell him to come back another time?" I asked, wondering what else I could use to stall for time.

"He's crafty," said Hugh. "As soon as you open the door for him, he puts his foot in the hallway so you can't close it again. Sometimes we have to hide behind the sofa and keep quiet, like if we've forgotten to close the curtains, and he stands there with his face pressed up against the window for ten minutes or so, waiting for us to move."

"Last week," said Arlene, "he knocked on the door and when we turned the camera on, he was holding his school report card up to the camera so we could read it. I mean, you can't really turn that away, can you?"

I loved Hugh and Arlene for this. I loved the fact that they were essentially being terrorised by a little boy who just wanted to be friends with them. I loved the fact that they wouldn't just tell him to go away or complain to his parents or jade him for life by rejecting him outright. And I loved the fact that when they talked about him, they smiled broadly and with real love and enthusiasm in their voices. They loved the kid next door. They just wished he'd stay there.

"Look," said Hugh. "He gave me this the other day. . . ."

He pulled open a drawer and took out an A4 certificate. He read from it.

"It's a Best Mate Award. It reads: 'It's hard to find a friend like you. Lucky people have just one or two. However, many good friends are rare. And you for me are always there!'"

"But you're not!" I said. "You're usually hiding behind the sofa!"

Suddenly there was a knock at the door. A loud one.

"Sh!" said Arlene, putting her fingers to her lips.

There was another knock now.

Bang.

Bang, bang.

Hugh sat perfectly still. Arlene sat perfectly still. I sat perfectly still as well. We all stared at the TV. Suddenly, he stepped into frame. A little boy, of around eleven or twelve, with short, blonde hair and big, blue eyes. He was staring at the camera now. He stepped closer to it and just stared and stared, and then tapped the window, and then stared.

No one said a thing. It was genuinely one of the most terrifying moments of my life.

And then the little boy shook his head, crossed his arms, and walked off.

"Anyway," said Hugh. "He's a lovely lad. But sometimes when he comes in, he'll take his jumper or one of his shoes off, and he'll hide it in here, so he can come back to get it later. And he'll leave little presents. He gave me an ashtray he'd nicked from the pub the other day."

"We call him 'The News of the Valleys,'" said Arlene. "You tell him something, and the whole valley knows before the end of the day."

"Just before Christmas," said Hugh, "I told him he was doing my head in, so I'd decided to move to Bosnia. The next day he turned up with a card that read 'Bon Voyage' and a biscuit for the trip. I couldn't move, because people kept coming up to me in the town and wishing me good luck in Bosnia."

Suddenly, and with no warning whatsoever, we heard the letterbox flip open quite violently. It was Dean. He was trying to catch us out. The letterbox remained open for ten or twenty seconds, while we all sat in our chairs, wide-eyed and silent. It started to close, but as it did so, Murphy let out a short sneeze, and the flap slowly opened up again. It was like something out of *Jurassic Park*. I held my breath. Moments later it slammed shut, and we watched the screen as a little boy, who'd obviously tried to avoid the camera, walked sheepishly away and headed, grumpy-faced, back down the road.

"Anyway," said Hugh. "Are we going to get you hypnotised or what?"

And then, out of the blue, it hit me.

"Hugh! That show you need a title for!" I was excited all of a sudden.

"Which show?"

"The one where you audition dogs to try and find a new Hypnodog!"

"Yes?"

"You should call it *Pup Idol*!"

Hugh's face lit up.

"*Pup Idol*! Brilliant! I told you! The subconscious! You concentrate on something else, and the answer comes to you! Right, hang on. I'm going to make a phone call. . . ."

An hour later, and I had just woken up.

My *Pup Idol* revelation had bought me some time . . . but nowhere near enough.

I had undergone hypnosis.

I couldn't tell whether the dog had been involved at any point—

which is always worrying when you wake up in a stranger's house—
but he was certainly staring at me now. And so was . . . a little soldier.

The tiniest soldier I had ever seen, in fact.

I recognised him more or less straight away. It was Dean. The kid
from next door. He was sitting on the sofa opposite me.

"Hello," I said.

"Hello," he said back.

He was wearing a large, black beret, camouflage gear, and shiny
black boots. I wasn't sure quite what was going on, to be honest with
you. It was like I'd fallen asleep, and next door had invaded.

"Hey, Danny, I thought I'd let you wake up naturally," said Hugh,
walking into the room and throwing Murphy the last spare wonton.
"Have you met Dean?"

"Yes," I said. "But have you hypnotised me to make children look
like soldiers? Because if you have, you should stop that right now."

"Dean's on his way to ACF."

"ACF?" I said.

"Armed Cadet Force," said Dean.

"Oh," I said, impressed but yawning. "What are you armed with?"

"Nothing," Dean said.

"His wit!" said Hugh. "Hey, he nicks all my jokes, this kid."

"They're not yours," said Dean. "They're Tommy Cooper's."

"We like watching Tommy Cooper videos, don't we?"

Dean nodded and smiled. Suddenly the fez made sense. And it was
brilliant, seeing the way the two bantered. They were clearly great mates.

But while all this was lovely, there was only one thing on my mind:
Had it worked? Was I now a Yes Man, whether I liked it or not? I
tried asking myself a question in my head. *Shall I have a cup of tea
later? . . . Yes.* It certainly *seemed* to be working.

"Danny, did you know Tommy Cooper lived down the road in
Caerphilly?" said Hugh. "Quite a few people lived around here.
Tommy Cooper, Tom Jones . . ."

Suddenly Arlene poked her head around the door.

"Dean, you'd better be off to ACF . . . ," she said.

Dean nodded, gave us all a little salute, and said he'd be back round
later, at which Hugh secretly rolled his eyes.

He walked toward the door, and I was about to ask Hugh how the hypnosis had gone, when he turned around.

"By the way, I came round earlier, but you didn't answer," he said, accusingly.

"I was out," lied Hugh.

"But your car was here."

"I . . . walked."

"No. You were in."

"How do you know?"

"Because I looked through the letterbox, and your keys were in the door."

Hugh went a bit red.

"Okay. I was in. Now get out."

Dean shut the door behind him.

"You let him in, then?" I said.

"Arlene was putting the bins out, and he ran in while her back was turned."

"Nice kid, though."

"The best."

There was a slight lull in the conversation. I knew what I wanted to say, but I didn't quite know how to put it.

"So . . . um . . . I don't . . . y'know . . . feel all that different."

"No?"

"Nope. I mean, since the . . . you know. Since you . . ."

"Since you fell asleep?"

"Yes. Well, no. I mean, since you put that Richard Clayderman CD on and . . . *hypnotised* me."

Hugh sat down.

"Danny, listen. Don't be annoyed, but . . . I decided not to hypnotise you. Not properly, anyway."

"Eh? Why? I thought that's what you did? You and Murphy?"

"Well, it's mainly me. Murphy's a dog, after all. And I decided not to."

"But why?"

"I talked to you when you were under, and . . . well . . . you don't need it. From everything you've told me, you're doing this because you want to, and because you need to. It takes a certain amount of dedication, and that's what you've done . . . and it means more if you can fail. Because if you can fail, then you can also *win*. The way I see it, it means more if you do it yourself. As humans we seem to go to more effort to avoid trouble and pain than we do to make things better. Avoiding rather than *doing*. Am I anywhere near the mark?"

"I think so," I said, knowing he was. If I was going to do this, if I was going to survive until the end of December, I was going to have to do this myself. What good is sorting out your own life, if it's not you that's sorting it? Where's the achievement in being *programmed* to do something? What's the lesson? That someone will always be there to help? If I was going to act irresponsibly, the least I could do was be *responsible* for it.

Hugh dropped me off at the station half an hour later. We sat in the car as rain began to spatter the windscreen. Hugh offered me a carton of Ribena as we waited for my train to arrive.

"When you think about it," he said, "probably some of the best things that have ever happened to you in life, happened because you said yes to something. Otherwise things just sort of stay the same."

We let the thought hang in the air.

"I mean, just ask Arlene. She can't get enough of bloody wonton now. She wants me to pick some more up on the way home."

I smiled. I'd never realised that wonton could be a real symbol of hope in this world.

"But some things we have to do for ourselves," said Hugh. "I mean, take me . . . *I* had a fear once. A terrible one. But I conquered that fear. Through hard work and self-belief. Not hypnotism."

"Oh. What were you afraid of?"

Hugh blushed.

"Dogs."

SELECTED EXTRACTS FROM THE DIARY OF A YES MAN

September 28

On the way home from Wales the other day, I noticed an advert in the paper, reading, DO YOU WANT TO BE A WRITER? and then dutifully sent off for the information pack. They asked for a three-hundred-word sample of my writing in any genre. I chose science fiction and wrote the following this morning. I have called it, rather ominously, "Future War."

Tex McBellamy cast his eyes to the skies and smiled the smile of victory. He had done it. He had single-handedly taken on the entire Kraxxon race with only his trusty friend and robot, Figgy5000, for backup.

"I don't think they'll be coming back for more," said Tex, which was true, because they were all dead.

"MEEP. I think that—MEEP—we should both go to the—MEEP—" said Figgy5000, but he was stopped from saying any more by the sudden sound of an explosion on the horizon.

"What the . . . ," said Tex, never intending to finish the sentence and actually leaving it at that.

"MEEP," said Figgy5000. "MEEP."

It was a heli-chopper, a futuristic cross between a helicopter and a chopper. It was the vehicle of choice for Senator Greenglove, the evil senator who had first imprisoned Tex all those years ago in that cell he was in.

"Greenglove," said Tex. "So, he's come back to finish the job himself. . . ."

"McBellamy!" screamed Greenglove from out of the big tannoy on the front of the heli-chopper, and shaking his trademark green-begloved fist at Tex. "So, we meet again! Well, prepare for your doom! You know that it's a crime now that we're in the twenty millionth century for you to have your own thoughts and ideas! Well, you've had far too many of them, and you've had your last! So it's back to the big prison made out of ice that I made for you!"

Tex groaned. He hated that big ice prison.

"You dumb bastard!" he shouted. "Why don't you and your frozen cell just melt off! I will not return there!"

"Yes, you will!" retorted Senator Greenglove.

"Figgy5000," Tex whispered. "On my order, reverse the polarity on your positron deactivators."

"MEEP—okay," said Figgy5000, who, by the way, was shaped like a beautiful woman.

"Well, Senator Greenglove, I suppose I'll have to come quietly, then . . . ," said Tex, but Greenglove couldn't hear him, because he was still miles away, and Tex didn't have a tannoy on his front like he did.

I enclosed a note with the words "To Be Continued . . ." and I told them that this was merely a small part of an epic Tex McBellamy trilogy I have in the pipeline. Hopefully they will like it and we can publish sometime early next year.

October 5

Paul Lewis was the boy at my school who used to bully people. He has just found me on *Friends Reunited* and said we should go for a pint sometime. I had to say yes.

My most vivid memory of Paul Lewis is from the end of every school day, when he used to give Anil Patel, a boy in a wheelchair, a dead arm—just because he liked "watching him go round in circles."

We are meeting next Thursday in Bath.

October 7

Saw something in the *Standard*. WOULD YOU BE INTERESTED IN PARTICIPATING IN A CLINICAL TRIAL, INVESTIGATING WOMEN'S SEXUAL LIBIDOS AFTER MENOPAUSE?

I rang the number, but it turned out I was ineligible.

Sometimes it surprises me how deep the discrimination in this country runs.

October 13

Paul Lewis thinks we should stay in touch and become great friends. He is in the Territorial Army now. He says it gave him goals and focus and changed his life. He thinks I should apply too. That way we could be comrades as well as great friends. He has invited me to his stag weekend, which will take place on a barge with his army pals. I think Paul Lewis may be planning to abduct and kill me.

October 14

A reminder e-mail from celebrated bully, Paul Lewis, about my joining the Territorial Army. He says I should fill in their on-line application form to get more details. I go to the site and fill in the boxes. At one point it asks me if I would like to offer any particular skills to the TA. I click yes, and it presents me with a huge list of options. I choose "receptionist."

October 15

I have three hairs on my chest—but not for much longer. Today I accepted a no-risk, thirty-day, money-back-guarantee trial pack from the people at HairBeGone, an "amazing new product that says good-bye to shaving, tweezing, and waxing!" I will receive my two tubes of hair-removal cream and a hair growth-inhibitor spray very soon. However, I noticed no recommendations from doctors and no safety notices, either, so who knows what it will do to my hair. It is at times like this that I wish Stuart the cat was real. I know animal experimentation is wrong, but something that hairy *has* to get self-conscious every now and again.

Plus: *Result!* If I say yes to upgrading my mobile phone to a new, fancy Siemens one, my phone company will give me a free return flight to any major European city! What a cracking Yes!

Also sent off for an information pack on learning Flemish within twenty-eight days. I guess I could have chosen a different language, but I had a waffle yesterday, and I suppose the feeling just stuck.

October 16

Paul Lewis has e-mailed again. Just to say hello.

October 17

Another e-mail from Paul Lewis. He wants to know if I want to meet up again soon. I am a bit scared of Paul Lewis.

CHAPTER 18

In Which Daniel Finally Has a Polite Conversation

It was 7 a.m., and my phone was ringing. What kind of society do we live in, when someone can make your phone ring at 7 a.m.? There should be rules.

"Hello?" I said, my voice gruff and my eyes bleary.

But no one spoke.

"Hello?" I said again.

I could hear what sounded like trains in the background, and the *bing-bong* of a tannoy.

"Who's there?" I said, but there was no answer. I was about to hang up, when . . .

"It's Paul," said a man. He had a northern accent and what sounded like caution in his voice. "Why? Who's this?"

"It's Danny."

"Right . . . ," said Paul. "And what do you want?"

I was confused. What did I want? I thought about it. I didn't know. Why was I speaking to Paul? What *did* I want?

"I don't know," I said. "I thought you called *me*."

"I did," said Paul. "I wanted to find out what you wanted."

This isn't the kind of conversation I'm used to having at seven in the morning.

"I'm afraid I am very confused," I said. "I'm afraid I don't know what I want. Why? What do *you* want?"

"Er . . . Well, I found this sticker, saying 'Call Me,' and then this number, and it was playing on my mind, so . . ."

"Oh!" I said, sitting up, suddenly on top of the situation. The mere mention of my sticker was like a slap on the face. "Yes! That's mine! Don't hang up!"

Amazing! It was someone who genuinely wanted to have a polite conversation!

"Right . . . so . . . what's it all about?"
And I told him.

It turned out that Paul didn't want to have a polite conversation. At least, not right then. He'd love to have one at some stage, but it'd have to be a bit later. He had to get on his train to go to work, he said, and he had a meeting first thing, which was about European strategies and business integration, and he had to go to it, because he was going to be taking the next meeting, and he wanted to make sure he knew the form, because they had a very different approach at his last company, but he did wonder whether I'd like to have a polite conversation after work, when his train got back in, which should be about a quarter past six, but could just as easily be a quarter past who-knows-when these days, what with one thing and another, but he's been putting the hours in after work a lot recently, so he should be able to get away without any problems, really, oh look, there's his train, he should be on his way.

To be honest I somehow felt like I'd had about six polite conversations with Paul already, but he sounded like a nice man who just wanted a chat, and I was excited to have finally had some success with the scheme. So we quietly and politely arranged to meet.

I was happy. That was precisely the kind of thing I should be doing with my life. Throwing open the doors. Seeing who walks in. Saying yes to a new friend.

I'd been doing a lot of thinking about things like this these past few days.

And much of it had been to do with what Hugh had told me. *When you think about it, probably some of the best things that have ever happened to you in life happened because you said yes to something. Otherwise things just sort of stay the same.*

It was true. The more I thought about it, the easier it was to trace almost any of the best things that have ever happened to me back to one single moment of Yes. Maybe you can too. I mean, think about the best thing that ever happened to *you*. And now think about *how* that thing happened.

I tried it one night with Wag, over a pint.

"Wag, mate . . . What's the best thing ever to have happened to you?"

"Nineteen ninety-eight. Newbury. The hour was late. Domino's brought the wrong order round. We got four pizzas instead of—"

"Apart from that?"

He thought about it. "My girlfriend."

"Your girlfriend. And how did you meet your girlfriend?"

"A stroke of good luck. I happened to be at a gig, and so was she, and that was that."

"Why did you go to the gig?"

"Someone asked me to cover for them. I was playing bass."

"Okay. And you said yes?"

"Yeah."

"And did you really want to do it?"

"No. But it was a favour."

"Right. And who asked you?"

"Ben."

"Who's Ben?"

"A guy I met at a party."

"Who invited you to that party?"

"Neil."

"How did you meet Neil?"

"University."

"You nearly didn't go to university, though, eh?"

"Well . . . yeah . . . but . . ."

"So, by saying yes to going to university, you ended up meeting Neil, and he in turn helped you end up with, in your words, the best thing that's ever happened to you."

Wag looked a bit affected by it.

"Do you think I should get him a card?"

The thing I instantly realised was that at first, Wag had blamed all this on luck. But *he'd* made that luck happen. He just hadn't realised it. He'd made a series of "correct" choices, which led him, bass in hand, to his girl. Maybe we can *all* do that. Maybe we can all change our fortunes. Maybe there's no such thing as destiny. There's just a series of choices we create ourselves. I guess it's only when we look at how a No could have changed our lives for the worse that we realise the value of the tiny Yeses that fly at us each day.

It was a revelatory moment—maybe we really did all have the power to change our lives for the better by using this one simple word. Yes had made me fall for Lizzie, true, but rather than mope around, pining after a dream, maybe a Yes could help. Maybe it could at least help me get over her. Maybe it could even work again. There was now a hole where she'd been, and somehow I felt I needed to fill it. It was down to me to say yes.

I found the number Hanne had given me for her friend Kristen, I took a deep breath, and I gave her a call.

I found it difficult to sleep that night. I was anxious. There were a few things to be anxious about. I'd had a slightly stilted conversation with Kristen, and she'd suggested a time and a place, and I'd said, "Yes, great, that'd be nice." But was it the right thing to be doing? It was something I would never, ever have done before—a blind date, essentially. Hanne seemed to think it was for the best. But then Hanne used to think it was okay to make smoothies at five in the morning with the loudest blender in the world. But what would Lizzie think? Fair enough, we had no future, but wasn't it all a bit . . . soon? Something else was on my mind too. I couldn't help but wonder what the Challenger had up his sleeve next. The need to unmask him was pressing. Every couple of weeks there was something else—something worse—and I was due for another sometime soon. Plus it was clear that Jason—if it was, indeed, Jason—was slowly upping the pace of his challenges. From "wear this" to "drive there" to "change your rules," I had to find him quickly and efficiently, and before he reached the next level of mischief and intrigue. And what would that be? "*Fly* there"? "*Run* here"? "*Kill* that"? It was time to be proactive. To *stop* him rather than just react to his whims.

I got up and switched on my Mac. First, I e-mailed his Hotmail address again.

To: whoisthechallenger@hotmail.com
From: Danny
Subject: Stop
Look here,
Why aren't you writing back to me? I know exactly who you are and what you're up to. I've done everything you've asked so far, but once I've unmasked you, you will have no choice but to stop. So you may as well stop now and avoid my wrath, which can be quite considerable once I'm riled. So there.
Danny

And then, to make sure I was covering all the angles, I e-mailed Thom again.

Thom,
It's Danny again. I'm sorry to bother you, but could you let me know if you get this e-mail? Did you get my last one? I think your mate, Jason, is still playing pranks on me. I need to get in touch with him, but I don't know how.
Please get back to me!
Danny

I pressed Send, then sat back in my chair with a sigh.
This was a mystery I needed to solve.

It was two evenings later, and I was sitting in a pub just off Oxford Street with Paul, the man who'd phoned me up for a polite conversation.

He was a pleasant chap in his forties with neat hair and a blue suit. He wore a chunky watch and slightly raised shoes. Our polite conversation had started well, but somewhere along the line had taken an odd turn.

"There's a lot of shit talked about Border terriers," he said.

And that's where I have to interrupt. Border terriers was pretty much all Paul and I had talked about tonight. . . . Well, pretty much all Paul had talked about. The phrase "let's have a polite conversation" does, I hope you'll agree, imply two people exchanging opinions and viewpoints. Paul had clearly misread that and had taken it to mean, "please deliver some lengthy monologues on subjects only you have an opinion on." It just went on and on and on.

"The number-one thing people say about Border terriers," he said, which instantly made me terrified, because I knew I was in for a list, "is this: 'Border terriers do not shed their hair.' Well, that is a total fallacy. They *do* shed, and some of them shed very heavily. Contrary to popular belief, they are *not* a nonshedding breed."

"Okay," I said. "Got you."

But Paul clearly wasn't finished. He pointed his finger in the air and continued.

"Also, the number-two thing people say: 'Border terriers are easy to train.' Well, how exactly are we defining 'easy'?"

He laughed like this was the most common and ridiculous mistake a rookie in the Border terrier field could make, and he laughed as he carried on. "Do you know what I mean, Danny? How does one define 'easy'?"

"That's right," I said. "There are probably a lot of variables."

"Precisely, Danny. That's right. There are a lot of variables."

Saying "there are probably a lot of variables" is my number-one tip for appearing to be on top of a conversation when you are really six miles out of your depth. Consider it a gift from me to you.

"Number three: 'Border terriers are good around small children.' Well, to a certain extent that *is* true. But Danny . . . no dog should *ever* be left unsupervised with a child. That is a definite no-no."

"Definitely."

"Do you know why?"

I didn't even know what my name was anymore.

"Er . . . lots of variables?"

Paul just looked at me. I never said the variables thing would work twice in a row.

"Well . . . I suppose so."

Oh. I guess it does.

"Another pint, Danny?"

Inwardly I collapsed.

"Sure," I said.

"Your round, then, maestro!"

And I went to get them in.

I liked Paul—he was a nice and gentle man—but after another ten minutes I do have to admit that I did wish he would stop talking about Border terriers.

We agreed to meet again in a week or two. He said he'd call me. I didn't doubt it. I was now the world's second-foremost authority on Border terriers. Who *wouldn't* want to hang with me?

There was huge and explosive excitement upon my return home that night for two reasons.

The first was a message on my home phone. It was from Gareth, at *Richard & Judy*. He was apologising for the delay, but they'd finally decided to go ahead with what he called *Danny's Path to Enlightenment*! He wanted to know if I was free this coming Saturday to go up to Yorkshire to film a report with a load of Buddhist monks! Of *course* I bloody was! Although, as I'd decided to play it cool, the e-mail I sent him read, "Should be fine, yeah, talk soon."

But how cool was that? My yes had come good! I was going to meet some monks! On *telly*!

The second exciting event was that Thom had finally replied to my e-mails.

```
Danny!
How's the car?! Got your e-mails about Jason, sorry,
things have been manic here with the move and all. Tried
e-mailing him, but he's apparently not there at the moment.
Annoying! Have another couple of avenues to chase up, think
his sister works at Lancaster Uni, will get back to you.
What's your address, by the way? And what's Jason been
doing? Sounds naughty!
     Thom
```

This was fantastic news. I mean, fair enough, I was no closer to catching Jason out, but at least now I had an ally. Thom was aware of the situation and would help me bring Jason to justice. The Challenger was nearing his end.

I went to bed, happy. Things were on the up again.

I think Kristen had been looking forward to our intimate tête-à-tête. And so, I think, had all her friends.

"I'm Kristen," said a tall, attractive, Sloaney girl, when I walked in. "And this is Dan, Michael, Bri, Jane, Rudi, and Nick."

"Hello . . . everyone," I said.

"Hello," they all said back.

Kristen had suggested the time and the place. A slightly grubby pub in Islington. During the Arsenal versus Tottenham match. With just about everyone she knew. It wasn't classic date material.

"When Hanne suggested I meet up with you for a drink," she said, "I was, like, *oh, you fucking wankers!*"

Kristen was on her feet now, shouting at the telly. As were Dan, Michael, Bri, Jane, Rudi, and Nick. Arsenal had just scored.

"But then I thought about it," Kristen continued, sitting back down, "and, you know, I thought, sometimes . . ."

"*Get a fucking grip, ref. You blind bloody bastard!*" shouted Nick, next to her, and she patted his knee.

There is little I find more terrifying than girls in pubs who are really, really into football. For one thing, they are the loudest, angriest women in the world. They're up and out of their seats quicker than my eye can move. Many's the time I've thought the girl in the seat next to me had evaporated, when in fact they were now on their feet, screaming obscenities I didn't even know existed. As you can probably guess, I'm not really very big on football. International games I love, but your normal, run-of-the-mill pub-based Arsenal versus Tottenhams I tend to leave alone. Maybe it comes from having a dad who supports Carlisle United, a team who scored once, sometime in the eighties. It somehow wasn't enough to enthuse me to the merits of league games, although I remember the occasion well, because Dad bought some biscuits to celebrate. You can still see him to this day in empty, windswept stadiums up and down the country, standing wet and silent with half a dozen or so other retired men also old enough to remember the glory days—though old enough to know better, too.

I sat in near-silence as the group stared intently at the screen, but I couldn't shake my feeling of awkwardness. It felt like I was . . . cheating, somehow. But hey—this was only a drink. And it was only a Yes. I remembered something. I could *choose* to be okay. So I turned to Kristen, and I started to talk to her.

"So is it reds versus whites?" I asked, only partly in jest.

Kristen looked at me. "You're not into football, then?"

"Not exactly. Who's the guy in the black? One of their dads?"

She smiled. A nice smile. All of a sudden this wasn't so bad.

"The referee," she said. "But I think you knew that. To tell you the truth, I'm not all that into football either . . . force of habit from my dad."

"Ah. Me too. What does your dad do?"

"He's retiring next year."

"Oh. Are you going to get a new one?"

She laughed. I'd scored a point.

"Oh, come on you *utter wankers!*" she suddenly shouted. I guess if she's not all that into football, she must just really love swearing in public.

"This is bollocks," she said. "Do you want to get out of here?"

Kristen and I sat in a bar on Upper Street.

My phone rang. I answered it. They hung up.

Kristen leaned forward.

"Don't you find it a bit weird that Hanne's set you up on a date?" she said.

"Yes," I said, turning my phone off. "Do you?"

She sipped at her wine.

"Pretty much. So why have you come?"

"You could call it . . . open-mindedness."

"That's a good thing," she said. "It's good to be open-minded."

There was a pause, but not an awkward one. I took a breadstick.

"Relationships are tricky," she suddenly said. "Sometimes you know where you are with them or you think you do, and then one day you realise that you just don't. All of a sudden. Like it happened in an instant. Don't you find that, sometimes?"

"Yeah," I said. "Sometimes."

"My last boyfriend, Ben. Everything was cool. We'd been seeing each other since university. And then one day he met someone else. And that was that. Four years, over in an evening."

"Oh," I said. "I'm sorry. That must have been—"

"It was. It was shit. But . . . probably for the best. Better now than when we had kids or something."

I nodded.

"It just makes me . . . I don't know . . . Now that I'm single, I'm worried that I'm always missing out on something. . . . I felt more *content* before. I guess it's just because I don't—"

"Is it like you're not grabbing opportunities? Ones that could lead somewhere? But you're not sure where?"

"Exactly!" she said. "Yeah . . . like I could be missing out on the important things . . ."

I didn't quite know what to say next. I knew exactly what she meant, but saying I did would cheapen it, somehow. Make it seem less unique to her. Because until now, I'd thought it was unique to me.

"How about you?" she said. "Last relationship? Or was that Hanne?"

"Well . . . kind of. There was a girl. But it couldn't work. Long distance. I mean, it *could've* worked, but . . ."

"Sure," she said. "That's tough in its own way. The not knowing. Worse than the knowing, in a sense. No matter how many friends you have, sometimes you just want to be with one person."

I liked Kristen. And I felt sorry for her. Things were still raw for her. And me? Well, I'm sure she felt sorry for me, too. I took another breadstick and realised that my heart just wasn't in this. The date, I mean, not the breadstick. Kristen was right—sometimes you *do* just want to be with one person.

And then she smiled.

"Do you want to get some food?"

• • •

I felt like I'd made a new friend in Kristen. It was good to meet someone who . . . *understood*. I was glad I'd said yes to this.

We bought ourselves a fine meal of pasta and wine, and chatted and laughed, and the time didn't seem to matter anymore. We hit another bar, and soon we'd forgotten our woes and our pasts and absolutely everything else, and as the bar closed, and we prepared to go our separate ways, she suddenly said, "Coffee?"

Christ. What did she mean by that? But it was a Yes moment. A moment to be grabbed, just like Kristen had said. But all I could say was "Um . . . ," before Kristen jumped in with, "Come on. I *actually* mean coffee. I live round the corner. You can have a coffee and call a cab. You can also have a biscuit if you're lucky."

I smiled and said, "Cool," and we made our way to her place.

I heard her open a bottle of wine in the kitchen, and I laughed when she brought it through, and we talked some more—about holidays and childhoods and families. She told me she was going to try to get tickets to a gig in Camden soon, and should she get one for me, and even though I'd never heard of the band, I smiled and said yes.

And then, when I was putting my coat on, getting ready to go downstairs to find my way home, she tilted her head and said, "Look, I don't normally do this . . ." And my heart leapt and my shoulders tensed as I realised what was coming next.

"Would you like to stay with *me* tonight?"

CHAPTER 19

In Which the Reader Is Required to Read Between the Lines

I probably shouldn't talk about it.
And I'm not sure I really want to, either.
For now.
Just for now.
Sorry.

CHAPTER 20

In Which Daniel Travels to the Goodly Castle of Dobroyd, and Chances Upon More of the Wisdom of Maitreya

Now, if there's one thing that we all learnt at school, it's that the towns and villages of England's West Yorkshire region make up the global centre of international Buddhist activity.

Which is why I was now on my way there to meet some monks.

My new and unexpected employers at *Richard & Judy* had charged me with an exciting mission: go to West Yorkshire, hang out with some Buddhists, and film a five-minute documentary. It sounded easy enough. And exciting enough. I still couldn't really believe that I'd been asked to do this. I mean, there were *plenty* of people far more qualified than I was. Su Pollard was advertising *steam cleaners*, for God's sake. Surely *she'd* have been free? I can only imagine that, after meeting me, Gareth and Dan had decided that out of everyone who could possibly benefit from a series of enlightenment courses, I was probably the one who needed it most.

The journey from London to Yorkshire is a long one. I was driving up with Robin, the researcher, and Ricky, the sound recordist, and we'd been on the road for several hours already. We'd spent much of that time stuck on a narrow road behind a blue car with a sign in the window that read BABY ON BOARD. It had taken me nearly forty minutes to realise that unless that baby was *steering*, I really didn't need to know it was on board at all. Eventually we managed to pass the car, and to our joy saw a sign marked TODMORDEN.

I'd be meeting the director and cameraman from *Richard & Judy* at a secluded castle in this small town. But this made me a little nervous. After all, as I slowly worked out, Todmorden is made up of two basic words: "tod" and "mord." "Tod" means "death" in German. And "mord" means "murder." I'm not sure about you, but spending the day in a secluded castle in a town called Deathmurder doesn't sound like the ideal weekend to me. I decided very quickly that if I was approached by any monk named either Professor Plum or Colonel Mustard, I'd be out the door, in the car, with a five-iron. Which is a scenario Clue never seemed to cover.

"So you're the man looking for enlightenment, eh?" said Jim, the director.

"Well, I suppose so," I said, shaking his hand. "If there *is* any enlightenment. So this is the place, eh?"

We were standing outside Dobroyd Castle, an imposing but friendly castle surrounded by trees and woodland. It was built in 1865 as a symbol of love from a husband to his wife, but things hadn't quite worked out. He'd been the rich mill owner's son; she a poor mill worker. He'd fallen deeply in love with her, and she'd said she would only marry him if he built her a castle as a present. In a grand gesture of love, he did just that. She didn't like it very much. She moved into a little chalet on the grounds instead. The man was heartbroken; the woman died an alcoholic. It can be no coincidence that soon after, someone invented gift vouchers.

"So," said Jim. "Here's what we're going to do. . . ."

He took me to one side.

"I've had a look about the place. There are some great locations. This should be easy. So what we'll do is this: We'll film you arriving, and then we'll film you meeting a couple of the monks, and then we'll film you leaving."

"Right. Sounds easy enough."

"Yes. The whole thing shouldn't take more than six or seven hours."

"Oh."

"Have you presented much TV before?"

"No. This is my first time."

Jim went a bit pale.

"Right. Well, the whole thing shouldn't take more than nine or ten hours. Robin will brief you on what else we'll be doing, and Ricky will put a mic on you."

"Basically," said Robin, who was wearing a baseball cap and had the chin of a superhero, "we want you to get *under the skin* of the Buddhist monk. Find out if Buddhism is the way for you. What makes a monk tick? And we need to work in the stuff they do here—the courses, the things you can learn, the people you'll meet. Sound good?"

"Yep. Just point me at a monk, and let's do this."

Ricky sprang into action. He pulled my jumper down and attached a microphone to my chest with a piece of tape.

"Good. Smooth chest," he said. "I won't be ripping any hairs out, then."

"It's all thanks to HairBeGone," I said, and he laughed, because I don't think he believed me.

"Right," said Robin. "We've arranged a meeting for you with"—he paused— "Samten."

"Who's Samten?"

"Samten's the man. He's the big monk on campus. He's in charge. And he's agreed to let you talk to him."

"Great."

"But first, why don't you take a bit of a walk around? Get to know the place?"

Dobroyd Castle was bought by the monks in 1995 for a few hundred thousand pounds. It was in total disrepair. The monks decided to use it to start up a centre, the Losang Dragpa Centre, which would offer cheap courses, teachings, and meditations to anyone who decided they needed it. It's a remarkably giving attitude, seeing as all they want in return is some help with rebuilding the castle. Anyone is welcome at any time of year. If you're stuck for something to do, I'd genuinely recommend it.

"Oh," said a man suddenly in front of me. He had a shaved head and was wearing a long, red robe. I guessed he was probably a monk. "Hello."

"Hello," I said. "Nice place."

"Thank you. Are you with the TV people?"

"Yes," I said.

"Welcome," he said.

And he started to walk with me.

• • •

His name was Liam, and he loved it here.

"This is a place to nurture inner peace," he said. "Anyone can seek refuge here. They don't even have to be Buddhist. You can just come along and free your mind from the negative. We just want to help increase peace and happiness in the world."

Liam and I talked more as we walked around the castle. Eventually we found a bench and sat on it.

"We learn things here, like, you know, we should value all our moments," said Liam. "And live each day as if it were our last on Earth. Well, actually that's a bit strong. Let me rephrase that. What I mean is we should constantly be aware that we may die today."

I raised my eyebrows. Liam thought about it.

"Actually that's even *stronger*, isn't it? All I mean is: We must be aware that there is a distinct possibility that you and I may die today."

Bloody hell. I was in a secluded castle in a town called Deathmurder with a man who was repeatedly telling me there was a distinct possibility that I may die today.

"I mean, we may *not* die today," he said, raising his finger. "But . . . we *may*."

He wasn't making me feel much better, to be honest, but there was no stopping him now. We were on a path to existentialism.

"Both statements—that we *may* die today and that we may *not* die today—are ultimately true. But it's more meaningful to say we *may* die today, because we then value every moment."

"It's also a bit more frightening," I said. And it was. Fair enough, I'd be valuing every moment. But I'd probably be valuing them from under my bed.

"Well, maybe. But the thing is, Danny, it's very easy to become complacent. Samten says that being aware of our mortality makes us more open, and ironically, makes us feel more alive. Now, let's take a walk over here . . ."

For the next hour and a half, the *Richard & Judy* crew filmed me chopping celery with monks, cleaning toilets with monks, wandering around the gardens with monks, and generally just getting up to all sorts of monk-based mischief. And I was having fun. The monks had welcomed me with open arms and shaven heads, and I was slowly falling in love with their way of life. It's hard to explain, but everyone had a certain . . . glow. They were happy. And rested. I was taught how to meditate, and I was given a slap-up lunch, and I learnt about their teachings.

Eventually the director called for a break.

"Are you getting what you need?" I asked.

"It's fine," said Jim. "But we need something . . . *else*."

I nodded enthusiastically.

"What else do you need?"

"I'm not sure. . . . It's just that . . . at the moment it's all quite . . . *nice*."

"But monks *are* nice. That's one of the things about monks. Especially *Buddhist* monks. They're *renowned* for their niceness."

Which is true. Very rarely will you hear that a Buddhist monk has, for example, attempted a kidnapping or tried to carjack a pensioner. That's one of the main things about Buddhist monks—they possess a total and utter inability to carjack a pensioner. I call it a weakness.

"Monks are nice, yes," said Jim. "But I just wonder . . . well . . . You already seem pretty sold on Buddhism. . . ."

"It's lovely!"

"Yes, but . . . You see, if you decide that Buddhism is the way ahead for you, then there probably isn't any point in doing any more films with you. Because you'll already have decided. So, you need to take a deeper look at their way of life, I think . . . show them from another angle."

"Right," I said, determined to come up with a solution. Yes had given me a chance. I wasn't about to stuff it up.

"I'll leave that with you," said Jim, and he went off to do something important.

I was having a biscuit with Ricky. He said he'd known I was hungry, because even at a distance of thirty feet, he could hear my tummy rumbling through his headphones.

"I have to try and show them from another angle," I said. "Look at them in a deeper way. How am I going to do that?"

Ricky took a bite of his biscuit and thought about the situation.

"You could mess with them a bit," he said.

"Mess with the monks?"

"Mess with their Zen. They're supposed to be the calmest people on Earth. See if you can get one riled. It'll make for great telly."

"You think I should anger a monk?" I said in disbelief. "It'll never work! They're too laid-back!"

"Well, you could give it a go. It'd just give them some options in the edit. You know . . . you could spice it up a bit. You could show the darker side of monks."

"But monks don't *have* a darker side. Do they?"

I can honestly say that if there was one thing I wasn't comfortable with, it was this. After all, Robin had said I'd be getting under their skin, not getting on their tits. But it was a *suggestion*—from a television professional! Plus I knew why I was there, and I didn't want to be a primadonna, and so I nodded and said that was a good idea. Well. It was the *only* idea.

Rather reluctantly I set about finding a way of severely vexing a Buddhist.

I wandered around the grounds, looking for potential ways and means.

I'd be meeting Samten later on, and I didn't really want him to think I was some kind of maverick monk-baiter. But suddenly I noticed a pond. If all else failed, I could always push a monk into the pond. But somehow that seemed too harsh. It seemed to me that it would be a shame if at some point in the distant future, when scores of young people take up the lessons of Yes, all they did was get drunk and push a couple of monks into a pond.

"So you're going to be meeting with Samten later on?" said a monk on the bench.

I'd sat myself down for a moment to compose myself.

"Yes," I said. "I think so."

"Oh, that's great. You're lucky. He's amazing. You'll love him. He's amazing."

"Is he?"

"Yes. He's amazing."

"Why?"

"Why? Because he's *amazing*. He makes you feel like the only person in the world when he talks to you. He's the most spiritual man you'll ever meet. He just *knows* things. You can ask him anything, and he *just knows things*. And he's patient, and he sets a pure example to all he meets."

"He sounds brilliant," I said, genuinely convinced.

"He is. He's brilliant," he said. "He's *amazing*."

Suddenly there was a voice from one of the windows behind me. It was Jim.

"Danny! You ready?"

I signalled that I was and began to collect my thoughts.

"So . . . ," I said to the monk on the bench. "I was just wondering— not that this has anything to do with anything, really—but what *annoys* someone like you?"

The monk breathed in through his nose, and thought long and hard.

"War," he said.

"War?" I repeated.

"War," he said, and he turned to face me and nodded, grim-faced.

Jesus. If I was going to have to start a bloody war before I could vex a monk, this was going to be a very long day indeed.

"Okay, Danny," said Robin. "Samten is ready for you now. We'll just do a general interview with him, okay?"

"Okay," I said. "I'm ready."

Ricky winked at me and gave me a little thumbs-up. And then the tallest monk in the world walked into the room. He smiled and shook my hand.

"I'm Samten," he said.

"Wow!" I said, genuinely impressed. "You're the tallest monk in the world! You should be *King* of the Monks!"

"Well . . . thank you," said Samten, who had taken it as a compliment, when I'd actually meant it as a fact. "Why don't we sit down in the lounge and have a chat?"

Samten had the kind of voice that made *anything* sound peaceful and appealing. He could have said, "Why don't I tie some bacon to your face and bring a wolf round your flat?" and I'd have said, "Definitely! Let's go!"

So I did as Samten asked, and while the crew set up cameras and microphones, we sat in the lounge of Dobroyd Castle and had a bit of a chat. I instantly warmed to Samten. He had a kind face with round glasses and short, neat hair. His smile never seemed too far away.

"I should warn you," I said, "I've never done this before. So I might be a bit rubbish."

"You're going to be fine," said Samten, and I believed him.

"Have you ever seen the *Richard & Judy* show?" I asked.

"No," said Samten. "We don't have televisions here. But this will be very good for us. We rely on donations and on people coming to visit us and lending us their skills. So, rather than giving us money for staying here, people can help out. If they're an electrician, they can help make sure our wiring is safe. Maybe they're good at gardening, in which case they can help maintain the garden for a bit. Or, like, in your case . . ."

Samten looked at me, but then stopped. It was clear he was struggling to come up with a way of someone like me being of any use whatsoever to a castle full of monks. I tried to help him.

"I usually make radio shows," I said. "Maybe I could, you know, come up with a half-hour light-entertainment radio programme about monks and monk-based issues."

"Mmm," said Samten.

"A programme *by* monks, *for* monks."

"Maybe."

"We could call it *Monky Business*."

He nodded. "Yeah. Or . . . are you any good at cleaning?"

The interview began minutes later.

The venerable and very tall Samten Kelsang, I found out, has been a Buddhist since 1983.

"I first met Buddhism when I was at college," he told me.

"What were you studying?"

"Well . . . I started out doing maths and statistics. And then I realised that wasn't quite right for me, so I moved toward zoology."

"So you studied zoology?" I said, impressed. It seemed quite a leap from maths.

"Well, yes, I did. But then I decided that wasn't quite right for me, so I moved on to psychology."

"Psychology? Wow. So, you're a psychologist?"

"Well, I didn't do that for too long. In the end I moved from that as well."

"Oh. To what?"

"Um . . ." He coughed. "Pottery."

I was amazed. "You went from maths to *pottery*?"

"Via zoology and psychology."

Which, of course, is the *classic* route.

"The good thing about this was that after all that, I didn't get the chance to apply for university, because it was so obvious I just wasn't going to make it. So I got out of the machine. Usually you're pushed straight into university, and then you're pushed straight into a job . . . but I wasn't. I had time. I could figure out what I wanted to do with my life. I think everyone should take a year out between school and university. It's important to have time to figure out what you want to do. Because there are key points in life, times when one decision will affect the next twenty years of your life. And only then will you have the freedom to make another choice, which could affect the *next* twenty years."

The words struck a chord. My decision to take the new BBC job was one such moment. It represented the end of jobs . . . but the start of a *career*. A career which could very well affect the next twenty years of my life. Instinctively I thought of Jason and the bitterness that that reality had brought him. I had to make sure I didn't fall into the same trap.

"Yes," said Samten. "You have to be very careful with your decisions in life."

"Well . . . there's always the *next* life," I said, which was quite a good joke about reincarnation.

My Buddhist friend thought about it. "Yeah. I suppose so."

"Okay," said Jim. "And cut there for a second. Danny . . . could you ask Samten what usually brings people to a place like this?"

"Yes," I said, still quite pleased with myself for the reincarnation joke. Jim started the camera rolling again.

"Samten, what usually brings people to a place like this?"

"It can be anything. I often talk to people about what led them here, what milestone in their life it was that brought them to us. Sometimes it's a feeling. Sometimes it's pure chance. Sometimes it's a passing comment made by a stranger. Sometimes an encounter with an inanimate object or animal."

My heart leapt for a second.

"Hang on—go back. What was that about strangers and passing comments?"

I could sense Jim looking at me oddly from beside the camera.

"You'd be surprised," said Samten. "Sometimes people end up here because of something someone had happened to say. Something that clicked with them or just seemed to make sense. Something that struck a chord. Often the person who said it has no idea of the reso-nance of their words. But sometimes it can be the work of, well, an *enlightened being* . . ."

I was shocked. *What* had he just said?

"An *enlightened being*?" I asked.

"Yes," he said.

"Like . . . *Maitreya*?"

Samten nodded. "Yes. You *know* about Maitreya?"

Did I know about *Maitreya*? I couldn't quite believe what was going on here. My head was spinning.

"Yeah, I know about Maitreya! I know *all about* Maitr—"

"And cut there," interrupted Jim. "Um . . . I've a feeling that might be a bit obscure for our audience, guys. Let's ask the same question again, but let's keep it more general. . . . And action . . ."

I was confused. And frustrated. Suddenly, it seemed Maitreya was everywhere these days. Which is handy, I suppose, when your busi-ness is in omnipresence. All I wanted to talk about right now was Maitreya and the stranger on the bus and what all this could mean. All the things that had seemingly been random led me here, to Samten. But Jim was right. There was work to be done, and so Samten and I continued to chat about the courses on offer as we wandered around the grounds of Dobroyd Castle. It was great here, and I was beginning to really like my lanky pal. He showed me round the different rooms, told me a few stories, introduced me to more monks, and it was only when he explained that he needed to change a bandage on his thumb that filming came to a halt.

"What did you do to your thumb?" I asked.

"I fell down some stairs the other day. Stupid, really. I'll be back in a little while. . . ."

The crew went off to scout for some new locations. I realised I was rather enjoying myself. TV was quite easy. It was just talking to people.

"Remember, Danny," said Jim as the crew wandered off. "Try to challenge him soon. Get a reaction out of him. Dig deep into Buddhism. TV's not easy. It's not just talking to people."

Ricky smiled. Clearly he was looking forward to the bit where I tried to annoy the Buddhists. I ruefully nodded at Jim and just stood there, wondering how I was going to achieve my unlikely mission.

Seconds later I spied Liam coming round the corner.

"Hey, Liam," I said.

"Hello. How are you enjoying things?"

"It's great," I said, and we started to walk through the gardens.

"Have you ever thought about being a monk, Danny?"

I smiled. "Well . . . when I was a kid, I had a few martial-arts videos," I said. "There were all these Shaolin monks who spent half their time meditating and the other half jumping over tables and smashing bricks over their heads. It looked like brilliant fun. I suppose that's as close as I ever came to joining up."

"That's not what it's like in real life," said Liam, but to be honest, I'd guessed that.

Liam stooped to look at a flower, and I continued.

"I had this one video called *Shaolin Monks Versus the Ninja*," I said. "In it, all these Shaolin monks took on a mighty warrior ninja."

"Really? What happened?"

I shrugged. "There was some fighting and stuff. Someone jumped over a table and smashed a brick on their head."

"Who won?"

"I don't remember. Either the ninja or the monks. But I think that by the end of it all, they at least had a newfound respect for one another."

Liam looked pleased at this.

"That's good. A good moral."

I turned to face him. "Liam . . . have *you* ever fought a ninja?"

"No."

I was back with Samten and keen to finish the interview, so I could ask him about the vital issues now dominating my mind. We were in the World Peace Café on the grounds of the castle, and we were waiting for the crew to finish setting up for the final interview.

I wasn't really saying much. I was nervous. This was my last chance to do what I had decided in my head the *Richard & Judy* people *wanted* me to do. To vex a Buddhist.

But then Jim said, "Okay, we're rolling," and Samten sat up.

"So, Samten . . . would you say that since you got in Buddhism," I said, "you've become a much calmer person?"

"Well, yes, I would . . ."

"Good, good. Because that's the thing about Buddhists, right? You're very calm people, aren't you?"

"Yes, I suppose that's true. . . ."

"So, does anything annoy you?"

"Well as a Buddhist, one learns to cope with situations and realise that what goes on around us is . . ."

And then I did it. I don't know why I thought this would work, but it was all I had.

I started poking Samten.

Tap-tap-tap-tap-tap on his arm . . .

He looked slightly startled and stopped midsentence.

"Er . . . I mean . . . does *this* annoy you?" I said. "If I poke you?"

Samten looked at me, confused. I didn't stop poking.

"Because that *is* quite annoying, isn't it?" I said. I'd gone red. I could tell. I was poking a monk.

"Well," said Samten, finding his composure somehow, "no, it's . . ."

"It's *quite* annoying, isn't it? How about if I up the pace?"

Tap-tap-tap-tap-tap-tap-tap.

Samten's eyes widened. I looked up. Jim's eyes were even wider. Robin's jaw had dropped.

I was, indeed, tapping him very quickly now.

"Are you annoyed? Come on—say you're annoyed!"

I was virtually pleading with him. I really, really wanted him to be annoyed, but I couldn't tell whether it was working. I couldn't tell whether I was messing with his Zen. I couldn't tell whether he was getting annoyed or not. All I knew was, I felt dreadful.

I looked up, hoping Jim would shout "cut." But he didn't. He was just staring. Even the cameraman had stopped looking through his lens and was peeking round the side instead, his eyebrows arched. There was perfect silence, save for the sound of a man poking a monk on the arm.

"Danny," said Samten eventually. "There's something I think you should know."

My poking slowed.

He looked me deep in the eye.

"I am a very violent man, Danny . . . and I have a very short fuse."

I stopped poking him.

"So," I said. "Tell me a little more about the centre . . ."

"Was that okay for you, Jim?" I said. "I think I got him a *bit* annoyed."

"Well, I suppose so, Danny, but to be honest, what I meant for you to do was challenge him *intellectually*. You know? Probe him on his beliefs. Not . . . *poke* him."

"Oh."

Samten had been joking, of course, when he'd said that he was a very violent man. It was his way of dealing with a very odd situation.

We'd finished filming for the day, and the crew started packing up the gear. I'd be travelling with Ricky and Robin back down to London, and urgently wanted to talk to Samten about certain things. I found him, facing the pond, and resisted the urge to tap him on the shoulder.

"Samten," I said. "Could I have a word about something? In private?"

I don't know why I said that last bit. We were already totally alone.

"You're not going to start poking me again, are you?"

"No, the poking is over. And I'm sorry about that. I promise not to poke you or any other monks. I realise now that poking a monk is highly irresponsible behaviour."

Samten nodded slowly, and then beckoned me to follow him inside. Eventually we came to a door, and he pushed it open to reveal a room full of sunlight.

"I'll put the kettle on," he said as he hitched up his robes and started to take off his shoes. I was slightly surprised. They were huge hiking boots. But I'm not actually sure if this is unusual or not. Perhaps hiking boots are standard monk issue. I think I'd probably been expecting a couple of flimsy mocassins. It struck me that perhaps Samten was a fan of Extreme Monking. Perhaps he kept a hang glider under there too.

He flicked the kettle on and opened up the fridge.

"Do you take your tea white?"

"Yes, please."

"Right. Well . . . oh. You can either have it black or with yoghurt."

"Um . . . what flavour yoghurt?"

Samten bent down to take another look in the fridge and stood up again.

"Strawberry."

I thought about it. "Black, please."

Samten brought the tea and sat down on the chair next to mine. He settled into his seat, fixed me with a friendly grin, and nodded to me, letting me know I should say whatever it was I wanted to say.

"Samten, when I was downstairs, we almost started talking about . . . Maitreya."

Samten nodded gently.

"Well . . . I mean . . . who *is* he? Because I've . . . heard of him."

"Maitreya is the buddha of love. He's the next World Teacher."

"Right, well, what I'd like to know is . . . Is it possible that I could have met him on a bus recently?"

I cringed. Maybe I'd got to the point a little too quickly, there. But Samten didn't seem to mind.

"Well . . . I suppose it's *possible*. Why?"

"Because in a roundabout way, that's why I'm here, talking to you. This is the first bit of presenting I've ever done. I'm not a TV presenter. But someone offered me an opportunity, and instead of saying, 'No, I can't do that' or 'No, I've never done it before' . . . I said yes. And I only had the chance to say yes to that because I'd ended up at a party I probably wouldn't have gone to six months earlier. I took a chance. *Lots* of chances. And if some of the people I've met along the way are to be believed, it's because I met Maitreya on a bus."

Samten nodded as if he understood. But I listened to the exchange in my head and decided that he probably didn't.

And then Samten said, "I'm not sure I fully understand."

And so I let it all pour out. I explained everything. I explained about how earlier in the year I'd been living my life in a more negative way. About how I'd been saying no to the little opportunities in everyday life, and how I'd become scared that that was all I'd ever do. About how I'd started to regret not knowing how much I'd missed out on. And about how one night, on a bus in the East End, a stranger uttered a sentence that would change all that.

Samten thought about what I'd said. In his presence, the silence felt heavy, but when it was there, it was like it was *supposed* to be there. And eventually he smiled, and a moment later he spoke.

"It sounds like you've found your path to enlightenment."

The crew had finished packing up and were grabbing some food before the long trip home.

Samten and I walked around the grounds of the castle and talked more about Yes. It was still sunny and, save for the odd monk cycling to or from the town, we were alone.

"What I think is interesting," said Samten, "is this idea about giving up control. Letting what you call your Yes moments lead the way. Because actually we don't even have control in the first place. It's a myth. In life absolutely *anything* can happen."

"Like you hurting your thumb."

"Exactly. I didn't know that was going to happen."

"No. Neither did I."

I probably didn't need to say that.

"But I *did* hurt my thumb, and I had to accept it and adapt. If we have faith that some higher powers—some enlightened beings—are helping us to develop spiritually, then you begin to relate to life completely differently. And I suppose life starts to become a little more magical. Every opportunity must be seen as a chance to learn. We have to be open to whatever happens, good or bad. Because anything that happens is a chance to increase our wisdom and to walk farther down the path to enlightenment. So, if you miss the bus, that's an opportunity to learn. If you become ill, that's an opportunity to learn something new, like compassion, maybe."

"What did you learn from hurting your thumb?"

"Not to trip down the stairs."

I laughed.

"But in reality . . . hurting my thumb limited what I could physically do, and so it gave me plenty of time for meditation. It presented me with a valuable opportunity."

"You should hurt your thumb more often."

"I don't think that would help."

We found a bench and took a seat.

"I suppose it's like you discovering you didn't like maths," I said, "and ending up doing pottery instead. It may have meant you couldn't go to university, but that was for the best, wasn't it? It meant you could do something you really cared about."

"Exactly."

"And I imagine you can also make your own mugs now, too."

"Well . . . I wasn't much good at pottery, either."

"Oh."

A breeze picked up. We both took a moment to listen to it.

"So, tell me about some of the things that have happened to you, then. As a result of saying yes."

"There was this scratch card, right? And I never normally play scratch cards. But the card told me I should, and so I did. And I won twenty-five thousand pounds."

"Wow," said Samten.

"But then I lost it again."

"Ah," said Samten.

"But the thing is, that just proved to me that what I was doing was right. It didn't matter that I'd lost the money. The important thing was that I'd won it in the first place. I didn't have twenty-five thousand pounds when I found the card, and I didn't have twenty-five thousand pounds when I'd finished with it. I hadn't actually lost anything. But I *did* feel like I'd *gained* something."

"You should lose large sums of money more often."

"I don't think that would help."

I waited for Samten to say something else. I was keen to hear what his reaction to my scratch card tale would be. But he was far away, lost in thought. When he finally did speak, it was to say a sentence that, under any other circumstance, would probably have lead to a brief scuffle and a broken nose.

"You're a peacock."

Huh?

"I'm a what?"

"You're a peacock. You see, if you're open to a situation, you can transform it. You can be like a peacock. Apparently they can thrive on poisonous berries, when other animals would get sick. If you have the mentality where you can't open up to things, you can get into situations where you feel down or depressed. If you have this ability of openness, you can actually thrive on difficult situations."

"Like hurting your thumb?"

"Or losing that money. What have you learnt so far? As a result of saying yes?"

"Well . . . lots, really. Men can have babies. Aliens built the pyramids. No man should walk a cat. And that I'm a peacock."

Samten looked a little uncertain about the valuable lessons I'd learnt along the way. And to be fair, I could see what he meant. If this were an episode of *Quantum Leap* or *Highway to Heaven*, you'd be a little upset if those were the only morals to the story. The fact was I wasn't *sure* what I'd learnt yet. Not exactly.

"Well . . . whatever," he said. "What I'm saying is, there's so much we can learn from just accepting the way we are rather than being attached to the way we'd *like* to be."

Samten was right. His words made sense. He was a wise man. While I'm not a religious person, if I ever do decide to be, I think it might be alongside people like him. Plus I'd save a fortune on conditioner.

"Can I ask . . . ," said Samten as we headed back to the crew. "Did you find that more coincidences happened when you let go of a controlled life?"

"Well . . . I suppose so," I said. "I mean, the very fact that everyone's been talking to me about this Maitreya fella, and then thanks to Yes, I end up here, and you know all about him . . ."

"Yes, we should talk about Maitreya."

We stopped walking, and I asked him my question.

"Samten, do you *really* think it's possible that the man on the bus— the one I met that night—was Maitreya?"

"Your guess is as good as mine. But yes. It *is* possible."

Now it wasn't just Brian telling me this was possible. Or his friend Pete. Or even Elias Brown. It was someone else, someone *new*. There were now four of them. That's more or less a *group*!

"The thing you must be asking yourself," said Samten as we reached the front of the castle, "is what on Earth inspired that man to say that to you? What made him utter the words 'say yes more' to a man who needed to say yes more?"

I heard Ricky call my name. They were ready to go, now, and I waved to say I'd be there in a second. Samten continued.

"From a Buddhist point of view, we talk about inspiration coming from the enlightened source. Sometimes we can feel inspired to say something, and then think: Where did *that* come from? In reality it came through the inspiration of enlightened beings."

"Enlightened beings like . . ."

"Maitreya, yes. Any enlightened being, like Maitreya, is constantly working for all human beings. He walks among us. He's present in this world, working to help all human beings."

"Like Superman?"

"Yes. Kind of. But he helps us, whether we know he's there or not, just as the sun shines equally on all human beings. Now, a blind person won't necessarily *see* the sunshine, but that doesn't mean the sun doesn't shine on them. . . ."

Robin tooted the car horn.

"If that *was* Maitreya on the bus," said Samten, "then, to be honest, he's a bit early. He's not supposed to turn up for another few thousand years. . . . But maybe this is a sneak preview. It could have been him. And you may find as you progress down your own path to enlightenment, that you receive more help from enlightened beings. Or maybe more help from the people around you. People you wouldn't expect it from. Listen to what they tell you. Sometimes inspiration comes from the strangest places. Even the ordinary can be magical. Be open to it."

I said, "Okay." And I meant it. I would.

"I think you're going to be all right, Danny. You seem to be quite a free spirit in many ways. There is a lot to be said for childish innocence."

I smiled warmly. And then I realised that, in effect, Samten was calling me a simpleton. I nearly said something, but then I remembered what he'd said about being quite a violent man, and I bit my tongue, just in case.

Sometime on the motorway home, we stopped the van and made our way into a faceless, peeling service station. Ricky wanted a milkshake, and Robin needed a pee. It was his third pee in as many hours. The man appeared to have the bladder of a moth.

I sat down at a table, and Ricky joined me moments later.

"So that was fun," he said. "I'm quite into all that Buddhist stuff, now. Peace and joy, you know. Did you like it?"

"Yeah, definitely," I said. "And thanks for your tip, by the way. I think the poking went down really well."

"No problemo," said Ricky, stirring his milkshake. "So, this was your first go at presenting? How did you get into it?"

"I just said yes. I met Gareth at a party, and we got to talking about this and that, and then there was a meeting, and they asked me if I wanted to have a go, and I just said yes again."

"Simple as that."

"Yup. I just said yes."

Ricky smiled and muttered something under his breath.

"What was that?" I said, and he repeated it, louder.

"*Si!*" he said. "*Si a todo!*"

I blinked a couple of times. "Eh?"

"*Si a todo*. It means . . . oh, what does it mean again? 'Yes to everything.' It's Spanish."

"It means 'yes to everything'?"

"Yes. *Si.*"

He sucked at his milkshake. It made a horrible noise.

"But where does 'yes to everything' come from? I mean, is it a phrase or something? Or a proverb?"

"I dunno. A couple of years ago, I was helping make this holiday show for BBC2. We were in Barcelona, and we met this guy, called Marc or Marco or something. And that was his motto. Yes to everything! *Si a todo!*"

"*Si a todo*," I said, again.

"Yeah. He was running this tapas bar or something, and he lives his whole life by that maxim."

"He's . . . a *Si* Man . . . ," I said.

Ricky looked confused.

"What, like . . . a sailor?"

"No, no. A *Yes* Man. He's a bloody *Yes Man*!"

I couldn't believe it. I thought I was the only one.

Ricky smiled and said, "Yeah, I s'pose so."

"And is this bloke . . . *happy*?"

"The happiest man I've ever met."

I glanced back at Ricky, who was scooping out the last of his milkshake with his fingers, and I shook my head. Sometimes inspiration comes from the strangest places. Sometimes even the ordinary can be magical.

"Have you ever been to Barcelona?" he said, licking his fingers.

"No," I said. "Never."

"You'd love it. It's great this time of year."

He stood up as Robin arrived back at the table.

"You should go there sometime," Ricky added.

CHAPTER 21

In Which Daniel Meets His Match

I was on the bus, and my phone was ringing.

"Hello?"

"Danny? Hello . . . It's Gareth from *Richard & Judy*."

"Hiya, Gareth!"

"Just thought I'd keep you updated on things."

"Okay."

"We had . . . well . . . an *unusual* reaction to your piece, after it went out on Monday . . ."

"Unusual?"

"Yes. We had . . . er . . . well . . . an *abnormal* number of complaints."

"What? Really?"

"We think it might be because you spent a large portion of the main interview poking a monk."

"Ah."

"Where are you now?"

"I'm on a bus."

"Give me a ring when you get home. We'd like to start planning the next VT to film . . ."

"Oh. Ah. I won't actually be home until tomorrow night. . . ."

"Okay, well . . . give us a call then . . ."

"Will do. And listen—can you tell Ricky something?"

"Sure. What?"

"Tell him I'm on my way to Barcelona."

It was three days since I'd poked a monk and such a lot had happened.

I had found it quite incredible that somewhere out there, there was someone else, like me, saying yes. Not as an option, but as a way of life. From what Ricky had told me, this man wasn't an amateur like me. He wasn't just doing it until the New Year or because he felt he

needed to or because he couldn't get out of it. He was doing it, it
seemed, because that's just what he did. He said yes. To everything.

Even if Ricky hadn't suggested going to Barcelona, I would've
wanted to meet this man. But now that I'd said yes, I couldn't *not* meet
him. And so Ricky had given me an e-mail address he thought might
work, and I had tried it.

I told Marc the truth. That I wanted to speak to him about *si a todo*.
He was the Yes Man of Barcelona; I was the Yes Man of London. . . .
It seemed only right that we should compare notes.

He wrote back the same day.

It was, of course, to say *si*!

> querido danny,
>
> in this moments i'm in la riviera (italy), over a mountain
> surrounded of a full power nature; clear days you can see cor-
> sica from here, and the cinghiale come into the garden to eat
> fruits . . .
>
> after two thunder trips it is now possible for me to be in
> barcelona this thursday—we could have a shock proteico de gam-
> bas and seafood in taller de tapas and burn a part of
> barcelona . . .
>
> si a encontrarnos, si al shock proteico, y SI A TODO
> ! ! !
>
> it would be very elegant to meet with you . . . are you
> free to come on thursday??
>
> saludos cordiales, me parece atomico el encuentro,
> marc

What kind of Yes Man would I be if I said no?

So here I was, on Thursday morning, on a bus to the airport, and
excited.

Everything was sorted. One night in Barcelona—the flights cour-
tesy of the good people at Siemens, who, because they offered me a
new handset all those weeks ago, had also come good on their offer of
a free return flight to anywhere in Europe. I couldn't believe my luck.
It was like Yes was looking after me.

I didn't know what to expect from my trip to Barcelona. I didn't know what to expect from life anymore.

I was standing, as agreed, in the square at Plaza Del Juamo, waiting for Marc. I had no idea what he looked like, no idea what we'd be doing tonight, no idea what to expect. I didn't know how old he was, how he dressed—all I knew was his name, and that he worked in PR. I cast my eyes about the place . . . an old man in a hat with his hands in his pockets. Could be him, I guess. Over there—a middle-aged man with a pipe. Maybe. But none of them seemed to be looking for anyone. None of them seemed to be looking for me.

Another five minutes passed. Then another.

And then, on the other side of the square, a taxi furiously revved its way through the streets and came to an abrupt halt. A tanned and handsome man in his thirties, wearing a suit jacket and T-shirt jumped out of the back and gave the driver a high-five through the open window before leaning down to give him a little hug. He waved good-bye, and then looked up across the square. He was searching for someone. He was searching for me.

It was Marc.

"Come on, we go first to a friend of mine," said Marc, "and then we do full-power Barcelona! Atomico, Danny—come, we walk through here . . ."

Marc was marching me through the back streets of the Gothic Old Town, through narrow, dark streets, and he was a friendly ball of energy. He was also whistling. Not a normal whistle, either. A kind of . . . *chirp*. The noise a small, happy bird makes—in bursts of one or two seconds—and like no noise any other human being has ever made in my presence. It was happening a lot. Between every few sentences or whenever we rounded a corner . . . a short, sharp *chirp*. It was a pleasant noise, but not one that you could ever really say you'd been expecting.

"Come, it is not much farther"—*chirp*—"we find my friend in his shop."

I was struggling to keep up with Marc's pace. He was moving quickly, striding through the alleyways and streets as if there just wasn't enough time for everything we had to do tonight.

"Hola, Marc!" came a shout from high above, quite suddenly. I looked up to see a large, bald man, leaning out of his window, waving at Marc.

"Hola, Emilio!" shouted Marc, and we continued on just as quickly.

We pounded through a square, where teenagers were playing experimental music with keyboards, and smoking cigarettes. The walls were pockmarked with bullet holes that Marc—pausing for only the quickest of split seconds—explained remained from the Civil War.

"Barcelona is the finest city, I think," he said. "I have always lived here until recently. Now, I live in the quietest village in Italy, but Barcelona is always my home. . . . It is a special place, a mediterranean city in Europe . . ."

"Hey, Marc!" shouted another voice from high above, and Marc raised his hand and continued on, and chirped his chirp by way of an answer.

"You have been here before?" he asked.

"Never," I said. "But I like it . . ."

Then it happened *again*—someone else leaning out of a window, three or four floors up, and shouting his name . . . and then I realised. Marc was only chirping when we walked through residential areas, places where people would have their windows open and the sound could drift in. He was chirping for his friends. People here knew his chirp, and this was his way of saying he was back in town.

I tried a chirp of my own. It was rubbish. Marc laughed and was about to say something, when we heard a voice coming from the end of the alleyway. We looked up to see yet another someone waving at Marc. He'd heard the chirp, but he'd been late to react. He'd nearly missed us. Marc said, "Back in one minute," ran back down the alleyway, and in just three or four swift and impressive movements, scaled the front of the building and pulled himself through the appropriate window. A minute later he appeared at the front door of a building opposite and walked casually toward me. It was a little confusing.

"So," he said. "Now we continue . . ."

"Marc," I said. "You just scaled the front of a building and appeared from somewhere totally different."

"Yes," he said as if nothing odd had happened at all. "I had to say hello to my friend."

The next friend we had to drop in on owned an antiques shop, hidden away on another tiny street. His name was Oleos, and he didn't speak any English, but he looked delighted when he heard Marc chirping. Oleos shook my hand with vigour, and I can only assume Marc then told him why I was there, because suddenly he started saying, "*Si a todo!*" over and over again before running off to fetch three antique glasses and a bottle of whiskey. He dusted the glasses off, filled them, and handed them round.

"*Si a todo!*" he said.

"*Si a todo!*" said Marc.

"*Si a todo!*" I said.

An hour later and we were in a cramped but friendly bar in the Old Town. Amazingly everyone—customers and bar staff alike—had cheered when Marc the Barcelona Yes Man had walked in.

Since our whiskey in the antiques shop, we had been joined by Oleos and his little dog, Melvyn; a German photographer called Jonas; and a Spanish soap star called Isabel, who had come straight from filming another episode of the slightly depressing-sounding TV drama *The Town of My Life, It Hurts!*

Marc had once again explained what I was doing in Spain.

"So you just thought, yes, I will go to Barcelona?" asked Isabel. "Just like that?"

"Pretty much, yeah."

"Just because a man you met had met Marc?"

"Yup."

"And you just said, Marc, I will come to meet you?"

"That's right. And Marc said yes."

"And then you just got on a plane and came? All the way to Spain? To meet a stranger?"

"Yes. It was an odd coincidence. A man I only met because I said yes to a job had met Marc a couple of years ago, and it turns out that he only says yes too!"

"*La casualidad no existe*, Danny!" said Marc. "There is no such thing as coincidence! *Si a todo!* It is the only way!"

"*Si a todo,*" said Oleos, and everyone raised their glasses.

"It is good to say yes!" said Isabel. "Yes to everything!"

We were a small and happy group, and I felt incredibly welcome. There was such warmth in the air. Warmth toward me but also an overwhelming warmth toward Marc. It seemed to me that he was one of those people you meet in life who have an almost magnetic optimism. He loved life, and life seemed to love him right back. Maybe he seemed so comfortable in his own skin because he knew what was important to him—and right up there at the top of the list was friends.

"Marc . . . could I ask you something about, you know, *si a todo*?" I said. "How has it affected . . ."

But Marc wasn't listening.

"Danny!" he said. "An egg!"

Eh?

"Here—take this . . ."

Marc suddenly produced an egg. By which I mean he took one out of his pocket—not that he sat down and laid one.

"An egg?" I said.

"Here! For you!"

And then he slammed it onto the table, rolled it, and peeled off its shell in one elaborate movement.

"An egg for you!"

I didn't quite know what to say. It's not often men I've just met take eggs out of their pockets and peel them for me.

"*Si a todo,*" he said. "Take the egg!"

"Take the egg?"

"Take the egg!"

I could only imagine that this was some kind of proud Spanish tradition, and to refuse a boiled egg when it is both peeled and offered would be a major racial slur. I took the egg and raised it at the girl behind the bar.

"I am taking the egg!" I said, and then popped it in my mouth.

"So, is this a Spanish tradition?" I asked Jonas, the German, between chews.

"No," he said. "Sometimes Marc just likes to eat an egg."

"Come on!" said Marc. "We continue on . . . *si a todo*, Danny, we go somewhere else, now . . . a party for a new club, I have invitations for us both . . ."

"Great!" I said. A party! An exclusive nightclub opening, in a hip and slick city! I was filled with a new hope. Surely this was what being a Yes Man was all about. Marc knew it, and now so did I.

And so Marc and I left the others at the bar and set off in search of this brand-new party. For once it wasn't *me* chasing a Yes. . . . I was saying yes to someone *else's* Yes. It was like Yes squared!

"Hey, Marc," I said as we walked through a precinct and around a man on Rollerblades who appeared to be doing tai-chi. "Could I talk to you a bit now about saying yes, because I've been saying it for some months now, and while it's been great, there have also been downsides. I've done things I should never have done, and—"

"Like what?"

"Well, saying yes has been great. But certain things have happened. And"—I thought of Lizzie, and then of Kristen, but pushed the thoughts aside again—"I just want to make sure I'm doing this properly. I mean, did you ever . . ."

"Here we are! The club!"

Marc approached a bouncer and pointed at me and said something. The bouncer nodded, and we were ushered straight in.

I had been desperate to talk to Marc and seek his advice. But almost as soon as we'd entered the club, I'd ended up speaking to a friend of a friend of his friend, who seemed determined to tell me every last detail of her life.

"My ex-boyfriend," she said as my eyes darted round the room, trying to find Marc again, "he went to London in the summer."

"Oh, did he?" I said.

I couldn't see Marc anywhere. Just acres of suited, booted, ultra

smart and trendy Spaniards in Barcelona's newest—and most velvety—
club.

"Yes. He liked London very much."

"Good," I said.

A man in a black suit with his shirt unbuttoned to the waist walked
past me. He stopped at a mirror to check himself out. I think he was
wearing foundation.

"My ex, he is a liar," said the girl, and my ears pricked up.

"God," I said. "I'm sorry about that."

The man was still checking himself out in the mirror. He seemed to
be really enjoying the view.

"Why you say you are sorry?" said the girl.

"Well . . . it's not good to be a liar."

"It's good!" she said, a little offended. "He was liar, famous Spanish
liar!"

"He was a famous Spanish liar?"

"Yes. A criminal liar."

The man in the mirror had been joined by his friend, this one with
the most elaborately crafted facial hair I have ever seen and who had
now *also* locked eyes with himself in the mirror.

"He was a famous Spanish criminal liar? Are you sure that's good?"

Both men nodded at themselves, then at each other, and wandered
off, probably to find another mirror.

"My ex was a liar in the best court in Spain!"

"Oh," I said, realising what she'd meant. "A *lawyer*?"

"Yes. Liar. What did you say?"

"I said 'lawyer.' I thought *you* said 'liar.'"

"What is different?"

A more cynical man than I would say she probably had a point.

"Danny! *Si a todo!*" shouted Marc, when he was back by my side. He
had two glasses of champagne in his hand, and he now appeared to be
wearing a cravatte. He handed me a glass, and then slapped me on the
back. I laughed. I really, really liked Marc. It seemed like he had a passion for life that up until now I'd been trying to force. It just seemed
to come naturally to him.

"Come, sit up there," he said, pointing to a raised area near the dance floor. A few people sat there, sipping drinks and looking like the Barcelona elite. The man with the elaborate facial hair was staring into his glass, probably trying to catch a glimpse of himself in an ice cube.

"I will," I said. "And perhaps then you could talk to me about being a Yes Man . . ."

"Sure, sure, we will," he said. "But remember—this is only the beginning! We have plenty of time!"

It didn't feel like the right moment to remind Marc that I'd be returning home to London the very next day, so I took my drink over to the raised area, and took a seat. Marc made it halfway, but was whisked away by a glamourous woman who seemed to want to speak to him. A moment after I sat down, I was joined by a gentleman in a shiny, sequinned suit.

"Hola," he said.

"Hola," I said, and then there we sat, neither of us speaking, both of us staring at the dance floor, which was slowly filling up.

I decided I shouldn't be too fixated on asking Marc about his experiences of Yes. After all, I was seeing it firsthand, right now, and here in Barcelona. For Marc, saying yes wasn't as technical and regimented as I'd made it. It was just a general attitude of positivity and freedom, of going with the flow and of seeing what happens.

Some kind of announcement came over the speaker system, but as it was in Spanish, I couldn't make it out. Whatever it was, it must have been encouraging people to get down onto the dance floor and have a bit of a dance, because as soon as it finished, the five or six people sitting on the raised area with me got up and headed toward it. Only myself and the man in the shiny suit remained, and we looked at each other and smiled. I felt bad, though—what was I missing out on? Had I ignored a direct instruction? Had I missed a Yes moment? Where was Marc to translate? I looked out over at the dance floor, but couldn't see him. It was suddenly crowded. No one was dancing, though. They were all just standing there, chatting. I stood up to get a better view, and so did the man in the shiny suit next to me. He leaned over and said something to me in Spanish, and I masked the fact that I didn't understand it by just smiling. He said it again, and I shrugged and smiled. And then, suddenly, and quite without warning, I lit up.

A spotlight had swung around and was trained on the raised area. Some music kicked in. It got louder, and there was a cheer. What the hell was going on here? I went to tap the man in the shiny suit on the shoulder, but to my horror noticed he had just whipped out a microphone. Oh, good God. This man was a singer. A singer in a shiny suit. A singer, standing on a raised area, in front of a dance floor packed with specially invited guests. A singer, who had just started to sing a Spanish pop song while I—a hugely embarrassed-looking bystander—shared a stage with him.

I immediately tried to get off the raised area and into the crowd in front of me, but the man in the shiny suit had moved forward, effectively blocking off the stairs. Unless I physically tried to move him aside, I was stuck. I looked behind me. There was just a wall. I had no way out.

So, I did the only thing I could. I sheepishly sat back down on my chair and pretended I hadn't noticed a thing. I stared at my feet and prayed that the song would be over soon. Once, I managed to look up, only to see a vast sea of people staring at me like I was some kind of freak of nature or part of the show that they just didn't understand. Soon, people started taking photographs. In the corner of my eye, I noticed a news crew. I had no idea who this man singing this song was, but he was clearly someone a little more famous in Spain than he is in Britain. I realised with mounting horror, that any and all footage of this bloke's opening song would feature a bright red man with glasses sitting quietly in the background wishing to God he spoke Spanish and could have understood what can only have been a request for anyone who wasn't a Spanish pop star to leave the stage!

The song went on for an absolute age. It was longer than any song I have ever heard in my entire life. But it was probably the instrumental section that was worst. At least the singer could do a little dance while that was on—but me? I could only sit there. I glanced up once again and noticed that most of the people in the front row were fixated not on the celebrity gyrating in front of them—but on his backing group. Me.

I tried to affect a casual air now, tapping along in time with the music, like in some bizarre and very wrong way I was *supposed* to be there, and finally, thankfully, the song came to an abrupt and welcome end. The crowd went mad. The flashbulbs flashed all over the place, thus ensuring my embarrassing bit part in the history of this club was recorded forever, someone somewhere screamed, and one man shouted for an *encore*. The man in the shiny suit took a bow, raised his hand to the crowd, and backed away, casting me a suspicious look as he exited stage right. The spotlight faded, some different music started up, and I slowly and carefully stood up and tried to walk off the stage with as much dignity as a man who'd accidentally gatecrashed an important gig could muster.

"Danny!" said Marc, suddenly behind me. "Come on! I have just received a phone call. . . . A friend has invited us for a drink! A beautiful house! High on the hills! You will see all of Barcelona! Come, now, we go!"

Half an hour later I was standing on the balcony of the renowned Spanish artist called Gaspar, surveying all of Barcelona beneath me. I knew Gaspar was renowned because there was a shiny leaflet on his couch that said as much, and I knew he was Spanish because he had a huge glass of wine in each hand.

Marc and I looked out over a beautiful city while Gaspar fixed us some olives.

"Danny . . . ," said Gaspar, a bearded and important-looking man. "I feel I have met you before . . ."

"Do you?" I said. "I've never actually been to Barcelona before."

"Maybe in London? I was in London very recently. But we did not meet, I think . . ."

"I don't think so," I said.

Somewhere in the house—a grand, airy house—a phone rang, and Gaspar excused himself.

"Marc," I said, and he made his little chirping sound in response. "I find it incredible that I'm here. You know? I mean, I know that on paper, I'm just at some bloke's house in Spain. But at the same time, I feel like it's fate that brought me here. Because all I did was let things happen . . . and here I am."

"You *have* to let things happen," said Marc. "The world knows what it is doing. *Si a todo* is a very powerful expression."

"But what does it mean to you? Because I think that although we both say yes a lot, you do it slightly differently."

"For me, it is an attitude. People look at me strangely when I say *si a todo*. They say, you would say yes to war as well? To *terrorismo*? To bad things? Well, no. I like to live by a more positive way. . . . I don't say no to war. I say yes to peace."

"That's exactly what some other people said to me recently," I said. "I met some peace protestors in London, by chance. They wanted me to help them chalk for peace . . . and when I did, that's what they said. 'Yes to Peace' instead of 'No to War.'"

"*La casualidad no existe, Danny!*" said Marc. "The world knows what it is doing."

Just then Gaspar walked back onto the balcony.

"My apologies," he said. "I am preparing for a big exhibition. New ideas. No one has seen them before, and I am getting things ready. That was a friend of mine calling. A Portugese artist who lives in England."

"Oh," I said. "Whereabouts?"

"He lives in Bath."

I was shocked.

"That's where I grew up," I said. "My parents live there."

Marc made his little chirping noise.

"Coincidence does not exist! *La casualidad no existe!*"

"How strange!" said Gaspar. "But also . . . *this* is strange too. After I talked to him about my trip to England, I remembered where I know you from."

He stood a little bit closer to me.

"I saw you on television."

Oh. God. I knew exactly where as well. In the background of the nine o'clock news as I sat behind a man in a shiny suit as he sang a Spanish pop song. But then he looked concerned, like he was straining to remember something . . .

"You were doing . . . ah, what was it? Like this . . ."

Gaspar started making a poking motion.

Oh my God.

Gaspar had seen me on *Richard & Judy*!

"But . . . *how?*"

"I was in London. I had a TV in my hotel."

"But that was only the other day!"

"Yes!"

Marc started to laugh and laugh and laugh.

"*La casualidad no existe!*" he said. "There are connections every-where! Sometimes we are brought to certain points, and we do not know why. . . ."

I was amazed, and I thought of Samten. This was a *ridiculous* coin-cidence. And this wasn't some bloke off the street in London who'd seen me do my first-ever piece of TV presenting. This was a world-renowned artist—in *Spain*! I mean, *what* were the *odds?*

"It is incredible what can happen," said Marc, "when you allow it to. . . ."

I stood there on a balcony under a million stars.

The following morning I had a few hours to kill, and I started by killing one of them in an Internet café on La Ramblas—the most touristy of all Barcelona's roads. I wanted to tell someone—*anyone*—about the events of the night before. I wanted to e-mail Ricky and thank him for telling me about Marc.

I had been genuinely inspired by my short time with Marc. He was someone brave enough to just let things happen. To roll with the punches. To go where the wind took him. And he'd changed my atti-tude, somewhat. I slowly realised that I had been treating Yeses like they were against me. That they were challenges to be overcome. That they were things I could *fail*. In actual fact they were just part of life. And if I treated them like Marc did, they would *become* life.

It seemed to me that perhaps Maitreya was a red herring. It seemed to me that we could meet enlightened beings every day, if we just looked out for them. The ordinary could be magical.

There was another reason for coming to the Internet café. I'd found the magazine in the lobby of the hotel that morning. It was a general lifestyle magazine with all that that entails—fashion, music,

sport, travel . . . the usual. I'd flicked through it, taking no real interest, but there'd been one thing in it that really struck me. One sentence that I'd needed to translate, and then check out. And once I'd
checked it out, needed to act upon . . .

I'd be meeting Marc at a restaurant just down the road to say good-
bye and thank him—and to give him a gift as well. A special one.

I bought a can of Coke and sat down at a screen, logged in, and
headed for my e-mail. I had a few waiting for me, but one name leapt
out at me straight away.

Lizzie.

```
Hey, you . . .
    Guess what? I'm coming to London. I'll be there on
December 2, for nine days, for work . . . this might be a
little cheeky, but . . . can I stay at your place? Tell me
to get lost, if not. But it would be great to see you . . .
    L
```

It was the best news I could have hoped for. December 2. Ten days
away.

Amazing. Just look at what life does when you let it.

I was understandably buoyant when I met up with Marc.

"*Hola, hombre,*" he said, and we walked through the streets at pace
again. "Come, I show you some of the city that you didn't see. . . ."

And even though it didn't seem like we had time, we squeezed it in.
Marc bumped into more friends, of course, and said *si* every time they
told him about another event he had to come to.

"They have a party next week," he said after meeting one friend.
"He has a house to paint, I help him," after meeting another friend.

What struck me about this wasn't the way his diary was filling up.
It was the connections he had made. The friendships. The time he
had for people. *That* was what it was all about.

At a café someone had seen fit to call Colon, I ordered a sandwich
from the waiter and looked Marc in the eye.

"Marc . . . I want to thank you."

"Why?"

"For letting me hang out with you. I had a lot of fun."

"Hey—we are not stopping being friends. . . . This is only the beginning."

"No, but . . . you didn't have to agree to meet with me. I was a complete stranger, after all."

"*Si a todo*, Danny. *Si a todo.*"

"Well, thanks, anyway. And I brought you something . . ."

I delved into my bag and pulled it out. I'd brought it with me for God knows what reason—evidence to show Marc? Inspiration? A reminder of what I'd done, and what I still had to come?

It was my blue, embroidered Yes cap.

I figured Marc deserved it more than me. Marc was a man who lived his life with positivity and verve. Marc was a *real* Yes Man.

He was delighted.

"Atomico!" he said. "Thank you, Danny!"

And then to prove just how delighted he was, he popped it onto his head and did a little chirp.

"So . . . what is next for you? You go home today to London, and then you see what life brings you?"

"Well . . . not exactly. I mean, I wanted to ask your advice on this, but . . . what does this mean?"

I reached into my pocket and unfolded a piece of paper. It was an advert. An advert I'd ripped out of the magazine in the hotel lobby.

I pointed at the sentence I meant. It was big and bold and colourful. It was next to a picture of a plane and a smiling flight attendant and some palm trees and sunshine.

"It says, 'Fly away toward Singapore,'" said Marc, before looking up and smiling.

"What do you think?" I said.

"*Si a todo*," he said.

CHAPTER 22

In Which Daniel Goes Far Beyond the Call of Duty

I felt as free as a bird.

What I was doing was utterly unheard of—at least for me. This was blatantly a dive straight into level six. A once only-mythical level. A level I had never been in before.

I was going to Singapore . . . *because I could.*

That was it. That was all.

I had seen an advert, said yes to it, and now here I was . . . recovering from a lengthy flight to a whole new place for no reason whatsoever other than life had dictated that I should. Life had conspired to show me that advert. Yes had conspired to make me obey it. Marc had inspired me to simply sit back and enjoy it.

I was at the airport when my phone rang.

"Dan? It's Wag."

"Hey, Wag, how's it going?"

"Not bad. Where are you?"

"On my way to Singapore."

"Singapore? *Why?*"

"No reason."

Thirteen hours later and I jumped into a cab outside Changi airport and chucked my small bag onto the back seat.

I was happy. Living in total acceptance of my decision. I would be in Singapore for a little more than forty-eight hours. Forty-eight hours in *Singapore*! A weekend! Who has a *weekend* in Singapore? Who comes back from a trip to Barcelona, finds a credit card he should never have taken out, and books himself on the next available flight to southeast Asia?

"Hello! How are you!" said the driver, more as a statement than as a question.

"I'm incredibly fine!" I said. "How are you?"

"I'm fine," he said, putting the car in gear. "An' how are you?"

I balked. I was pretty sure I'd just answered that, but couldn't be entirely certain. Singapore is many thousands of miles away, and I'd been in the air for many hours.

"I'm fine!" I said, again rather cheerily. And that should have taken care of that, really. But despite the fact that I already knew the answer, I felt rude not then asking him how *he* was. It's force of habit, and I'm British.

"And . . . how are you?"

He looked at me happily. "I am fine."

Good. End of story. We're all fine.

"And . . ."

Oh no.

". . . how are you?"

He turned toward me and raised his eyebrows expectantly. Well, what did I do now? I'd *definitely* already told him how I was, and I'd *definitely* already asked him how *he* was, but he was looking at me, waiting for me to say something. I could hardly change the subject—we were locked in a battle of etiquette. Mine ingrained in me from childhood; his learnt word-for-word from some kind of 1950s textbook.

"I'm fine," I mumbled awkwardly, and then barely audible and toward the window, "You?"

"Fine," said the driver quickly, now evidently satisfied. "Very fine, thank you."

There followed a minute of silence, for which I thanked my lucky stars. I switched my phone on, and it beep-beeped, welcoming me to Singapore. It beeped again a moment later. A text message from Hanne.

HOW ARE YOU?

I texted back.

I'M IN SINGAPORE!

I waited for the reply. Within thirty seconds, it was mine.

WHAT? WHY?!

I laughed.

NO REASON!

It was hotter than I think I've ever been. The car's air-conditioning system wasn't the greatest in the world, and it blew hot, sickly air toward our faces. We were driving through downtown Singapore, past giant shopping malls and wide, tree-lined streets. I looked out of the window, drinking it all in, noting Serangoon Road and Little India, and gleefully revelling in what I was doing. Why was I here? Because I happened to see an advert, when I was in Spain, meeting a man who says yes a lot, and been so inspired that I'd almost been looking for a level six. I had made this happen. Samten the monk had effectively told me that in life, anything can happen. I took that to mean there was no such thing as destiny. And if there's no such thing as destiny . . . then I can make *life* happen!

"Where are you from?" asked the driver all of a sudden.

"London," I said.

"Ah," he said. "Nice. London."

Another pause.

"And how far is London from England?"

"Oh. Er . . . London is *in* England. It's a city."

"England or London is a city? Which is capital city of London?"

He looked at me with eager puppy eyes. I explained that *London* was the capital of *England*, and he said he felt silly, but I reassured him. After all, you can barely find a minicab driver in London itself who would've known that for sure. As it turned out he—Ong Chee Kieng—had been driving a cab for sixteen years, and he'd moved to Singapore from China to marry his sweetheart.

"We very happy," he said. "Two children, also very happy. Singapore is a good place for children. Very clean. Very nice."

Singapore certainly is very clean. And very nice. Mainly because it'll fine anyone for anything, and fine them heavily. Gone are the days when tourists with long hair would be turned away as they arrived at the airport or offered a short back-and-sides haircut by a burly customs official with a pair of blunt scissors, but it's still a place that looks down on scruff. There's little else you can get away with, either; you'll be fined for jaywalking, for smoking in a public place, for dropping litter. Eating a sandwich on the subway will considerably lighten your wallet, too. According to Ong, radicals used to urinate in lifts as a way of making a statement against the system, until they started putting cameras in lifts.

Either that or the radicals ran out of urine. And perhaps most famously: Chewing gum is expressly and forcefully forbidden. It seemed to me that Singapore was a little like a nation of rather religious aunties; you love them for their affable strictness and sense of fair play, but you just wish they'd overdo it on the sherry and try and get off with the vicar once in a while. Funny, how a life of Yes had led me to a place of No. Their chewing-gum fury is particularly harsh. Those found selling it, importing it, or even using it, face a one thousand dollar fine. It was as Ong was explaining this to me that I suddenly realised with some degree of horror that somewhere at the bottom of my bag was a half-full bumper pack of Wrigleys that Wag had given me one night. There were at least twenty sticks left. Twenty! Essentially, in the eyes of the law, I was now some kind of drugs mule! There are some things you know are going to happen when you decide to say yes to everything, but being arrested for smuggling isn't one of them.

"So, why you come to Singapore?" said Ong before repeating a phrase he'd obviously learnt off the telly. "Business or pleasure?"

I smiled.

"Neither, really," I said. "I'm just . . . here."

Ong looked confused.

"Pleasure," I said. "Just pleasure."

I thought about it. It actually really was. Even my other trips abroad had had a vague point—whether to win the Spanish lottery or meet a Yes Man. The travel was just a by-product of a Yes. But this . . . this was a Yes in itself.

Ong dropped me at my hotel, Traders, and gave me a small yellowing business card, saying that should I need driving anywhere, I should give him a call. I promised him that yes, I would, then checked into my room, flushed my Wrigleys down the toilet, and slept for a very, very long time indeed.

Later I wandered out of my hotel and into the kind of heat that quite instantly robs sweat from every inch of your body. I had no idea what I was doing or where I was going, and neither did I need to. I had nowhere to be, nothing I needed to do, and so instinctively I walked down the very stylish, very long Orange Road; a shameful celebration of capitalism and really nothing more than dozens of vast shopping centres linked together by underground tunnels and air-conditioned walkways.

I found a McDonald's and bought myself breakfast. I was slightly surprised to see that this month's specially featured dish of choice was called the Chicken Singaporridge. Porridge doesn't appeal to me at the best of times, and less so when it appeared to be chicken-flavoured porridge in a bap. I wasn't convinced by their slogan, either: For that breakfast taste. Yeah, in *prison*, maybe. Still, Singaporridge was at least a catchy name. Presumably over in Little India, you'd be able to buy a BK Whoppadom.

Relieved that I was under no direct orders to buy Singaporridge, I bought a Big Mac, said yes, you *could* SuperSize me (some Yeses are the same the world over) and studied my map. But it was just words and drawings to me. What should I do? How do you let the wind take you, when there's no wind? *Literally* no wind, in the case of Singapore. I sat there for a moment, and then realised the solution. I would have to *create* the wind. Ong. I would call Ong.

"So what you want to see? Tourist place or real Singapore?" he said. He had an apple, and he'd brought one for me, too.

"Well . . . ," I said. "What do *you* recommend? What should I do?"

"I drive you round some places first," he said.

I had booked Ong and his car for a couple of hours for an almost embarrassingly small fee. He'd drive me round, show me the sights, act as a guide. And so he took me round the classic tourist spots—the CBD, the statue of Raffles, the proud alabaster-white Merlion, a Chinese temple—and stopped at a supermarket to buy us both water. We wondered what to do next. But I had an idea. Yes was all about experiences. New experiences, at that.

"How about things I would never normally see?" I asked him. "Can you show me that?"

Ong thought about it.

"I show you paradise!"

I was glad Ong was married, or I might have got the wrong idea.

"Paradise?" I said. "What's paradise?"

"Paradise is *kampong*—Pulau Ubin."

"Sorry?"

"*Kampong* is paradise for people. Pulau Ubin is island of paradise. For me."

"But what's a *kampong*?"

"Traditional village. Very quiet. Lot of nature. No hurry, no hurry. Pulau Ubin is best island."

I scrutinised my map of Singapore to find Pulau Ubin. And there it was, north of the airport. It turns out that Ong, like 90 percent of Singaporeans, lives in a high-rise. There's little space in Singapore. Nowhere to relax around nature. Rapid urbanisation and a relentless onslaught of shopping malls made sure of that. And while much of rural Malaysia still has that traditional *kampong* feel, Singaporeans fear they've lost it forever. Pulau Ubin is their last chance. Their last glimpse of local paradise. The one place they've got that remains untouched.

"Business want it already," said Ong. "Not long now before it goes. Two year, maybe. Maybe one. So sad."

I put my map down, and Ong said, "So you want to see?"

"Yeah," I said. "I'd like to see."

Ong dropped me off by the harbour and told me to give him a call when I got back. No hurry, no hurry, he said. I sat on the hard wooden bench by what Singaporeans charmingly call the "bumboats." I sat there and I sat there and I sat there. And nothing happened. But it didn't matter to me. I was perfectly relaxed. Perfectly happy to just *be*. I was there with four other people, and we sat in silence, staring into the distance, just waiting for the captain to finally invite us on board. But after thirty minutes, I'd had enough of just *be*-ing and turned to the girl next to me.

"Excuse me," I said, slightly startling her. "This is the queue for the boat to Pulau Ubin, isn't it?"

"Yes," she said. "But we have to wait."

"What for?"

"We have to wait until there are enough people. There are only five of us. It must be twelve before we can go."

I'm glad that the British bus system operates in a far different way.

Imagine a coach bound for Swindon that needed twelve people before it could set off. It'd sit there for months.

We continued to wait in silence.

Finally, thankfully, from around a corner, we were joined by two elderly men. Presumably even the captain of the bumboat was bored off his tits by this stage as he decided that he'd cut his losses and take just the seven of us.

We set off for paradise.

Twenty-five minutes later, and we were there.

I stepped off the bumboat and onto a long, wooden pier. Ong had been right about the island's natural beauty. On first sight the place was virtually untouched. A sandy beach with lush green trees and bushes and just a few rickety wooden piers leading from small, neat houses to tiny, barely seaworthy fishing boats. I walked toward the island with the others until we passed a carved wooden sign, reading WELCOME TO PULAU UBIN. I stopped to look at it while the others overtook me, and then they were gone, and I was left deserted with no one around me and no idea of where to go. It felt good. It felt random and . . . *free*. Where would I be if I hadn't said yes all those months ago? Would I be at home, sitting in a dark flat watching *Trisha* as the winter evenings drew in? Wherever I'd be, I'd never have been *here*.

I considered just setting off, but noticed a sign reading VISIT THE TOURIST INFORMATION KIOSK and a big pointing hand, so I obeyed. It was a large wooden building that I imagined contained all sorts of useful information and handy hints on where to go and what to do. I walked through the door, however, to find one vast, virtually empty room. There was a desk to one side with a door behind it, but apart from that, nothing. I decided I'd probably found the wrong kiosk, but just as I was leaving, a man walked through the door. Wordlessly he tossed a leaflet onto the desk, looked at me, then turned around and walked back through the door. I picked the leaflet up. "Pulau Ubin: An Island Getaway, Just a Bumboat Away." There were a couple of pictures, but it was rather sparse as leaflets go.

"Er . . . excuse me?" I called out rather pathetically.

Nothing. I tried again, louder.

"*Excuse* me?"

The man popped his head back round the door.

"Yes?"

"Um . . . do you have any other information on Pulau Ubin? Any more leaflets?"

The man looked at me as if I were asking him to sing a little song for me.

"No."

"What—nothing whatsoever?"

"No. This is all we have. Everything you need is there."

I looked at the leaflet. There was virtually nothing on it. Just a few pictures, a tiny map and a couple of poetic paragraphs.

"Oh. Okay. Thanks," I said, and walked out. I decided it was slightly strange that in order to house one set of rather rubbish pink photocopied leaflets, they'd not only built an unnecessarily huge building, but also employed a man to sit there all day on the off chance that a tourist might arrive and fancy one. It was like buying a bus, just to use it as a pram.

Nevertheless I was grateful for what I'd been given and set about reading it.

LIFE ON PULAU UBIN

No need for alarm clocks here—the early morning crowing of roosters sets the day off. A chorus of birds descend on the fruiting trees for the first meal of the day. The jetty rouses itself and the revving of motorcycles fills the streets. All is set for an easy and relaxed start to the day for the islanders.

Oh, yes. What an easy and relaxed start to the day. Woken at 5 a.m. by roosters, and then tormented by motorcycle revving until breakfast or suicide. To be honest, the *end* of the day didn't sound much better, either:

As night settles upon the island and people come to rest, the sound of diesel generators floats through the air. The insect-eating

**Tomb Bats emerge suddenly from their roosts and may be seen as
flitting, silent shadows. And while you are gazing upward, keep
your eyes open for the lime-green Oriental Whip Snake reptile as
it slides through the grass underfoot.**

Jesus! Woken unnaturally early and harassed by motorcycle gangs,
then killed by bats and snakes by lights out. No wonder Pulau Ubin's
remained untouched for so many years. So long as the tourist office
kept doing such a sterling job of selling the place, I had no doubt it
would remain untouched for many years to come.

I wanted to see the island and decided that the best thing to do
would be to rent a bike. So I did, from a thrilled-looking bike rental
man who appeared never to have rented out a bike before and set off
for a cycle round what Ong had described to me as the Singaporean
idea of Utopia. I felt like an explorer, pushing bravely into the
unknown. On a small bike.

Even though it's just 1.5 kilometres wide and 8 kilometres long,
Ubin is Singapore's second largest island, and as Ong told me, it
remains the only true *kampong* left in existence; the only one not
replaced by shopping malls and Singaporridge shops.

I cycled down a small incline and around a winding road until I
faced rather a large hill in front of me. But I had the energy and the
willpower and set about pumping away at the pedals until I was
about halfway up and about to pass out. It was maybe thirty-five
degrees, and I was sweaty and my boxer shorts already appeared to
be trying to attempt an expedition of their own, exploring areas of
my body usually reserved for someone with a qualification. I
stopped to straighten myself out, hopped back on the bike, and continued on for a good few kilometres.

Two hundred people live on Ubin, relying on the land to support
them or the odd tourist renting a bike. I didn't see one of them. I
passed abandoned farms, and dogs playing around derelict shacks, but
not one single solitary person. Maybe this was why Ong liked it so
much. In a place where you are never more than a few feet from
someone else, an island like this must mean so much.

That said, it became creepy after a while. Particularly when I started to cycle up roads surrounded by high hedges and lush, overhanging trees, where my only possible route was forward or backward, and the' ambient noise suddenly and surprisingly became absolutely deafening.

It's no more than a buzz at first . . . then it sounds like someone's left a few whistling kettles on the boil . . . then it becomes as loud as, or louder than, a car alarm. And you just can't tell where it's coming from.

I began to feel paranoid. Here I was, totally on my own, far away from anyone, in the middle of nowhere for virtually no reason whatsoever, surrounded by screaming, unseen kettles. What on Earth would the authorities think if they found my body out here? How in God's name would they piece together my final movements? What kind of motives would they come up with?

Suddenly I felt slightly panicky. I cycled on as quickly as I could, but started to realise that, in the bushes to the right of me, something was noisily running along with me. I couldn't see it, but it was causing enough of a disturbance in the long grasses for me to know it was big, and it was fast. Oh, Christ, what *was* it? I couldn't stop now. . . . I pedalled on faster and faster, and now I could definitely hear it thundering alongside me. What was it? Was it after me? I felt more like a character in a Stephen King book than I ever have before, and despite the fact that I was going deeper into what was now essentially a jungle, I couldn't turn around and go back for fear of coming face-to-face with it—if it had a face—and whatever it was was still there, still pounding the ground, mere feet away . . .

I rounded a bend at speed, but so did my potential captor. I was panicking properly now. Was I being hunted? What if whatever it was decided to eat me? What did they have over here again? Did the leaflet mention crocodiles? Or rhinos? Snakes can't run, can they?

I cycled on and furiously on, not once looking behind me, and thankfully, the noise from the long grass started to fade until it wasn't there at all. I was knackered, but determined to continue, and when I was far enough away, I stopped and got my leaflet out. I scoured those hundred or so words for any mention of killer kettles or things that might run alongside an innocent British cyclist, but there was nothing. Which, if I'm honest, just added to the sense of foreboding.

Was Yes trying to get me killed? It was supposed to help me live! The other noises around me still hadn't settled down, and I was now on a road surrounded by huge trees that blocked out the sunlight and gave everything a musty evening feel.

And then I heard a scuffling sound behind me and the sound of leaves being thrashed about, and I whacked my shins against the pedals as I tried to get the bike going again, desperate fear taking over. But my balance was off and my feet suddenly too big, and the noise got louder and louder, and then a lizard the size of a tank rushed past me and thundered, low and muscular, through a gap in the bushes where it stopped moving completely. My heart raced. I was being stalked by a lizard. A bloody *lizard*! *This* wasn't paradise!

And, in fact, if this *was* paradise, how come so few people seemed keen to live here? I had yet to pass even one person. Where *was* everyone? Was everyone a lizard? Maybe David Icke had been right!

I pressed on, sticking to the road and without once looking back for fear of seeing anything else that freaked me out. The lizard decided the prey wasn't worth it and left me soon after. I was knackered and red and in the mood for sitting down, which is when I spotted something. A signpost. It told me that a place called Nualong Beach wasn't far away, and that sounded perfect for me. A beach. Safety.

Before too long I found it. It was becoming slightly overcast now, but it was still warm, and I parked my bike and sat down on the beach. I was exhausted.

The water was calm, and the sun warm. Despite my lizard-based shenanigans, I was suddenly inordinately pleased to be here. I felt farther away from London than I'd ever been—and farther away from anyone else. It was just me. Thousands of miles away from another life. I thought about what had brought me here. The chain of Yeses that had led to me to be sitting on a beach on Pulau Ubin. Of course, it began with the man on the bus, but my Singapore weekend was all thanks to saying yes to a dull, bring-a-fact party. To Gareth. Then Ricky. And Marc. Who knew how many other chains I'd started, who knew what else I'd set in motion? Where else could this lead me? What did a yes I'd said last week or last month have in store for me *next* week or *next* month?

It was late November. Soon it would be December. That left just one more month of Yes before a whole new way of life started. A more responsible life, with nine to fives, and spreadsheets, and overhead projectors. No more jetting off to Singapore on a credit card and a whim. No more ruthless spontaneity. Just calm. Like the calm around me now. But there were still treats in store. Lizzie, for one.

I sat there in the sun and smiled. It was drawing to a close. Just another few weeks. I was looking forward to them.

An hour later, at the end of the pier, a large group of people—who seemed to have come from nowhere—were sitting down in near-silence, waiting patiently for the next bumboat to arrive and take them off to the mainland. I floated serenely toward them and recognised one or two of them from the journey over. There were maybe fourteen of them in all. But the strange thing was, they were all sitting on the one bench. There were four benches, forming one big square, and yet these people had all chosen to sit on just one side. This one group of disparate people had chosen to sit *alongside* rather than *away from* one another and stare in the same direction—at me, the approaching tourist. But I didn't feel intimidated or embarrassed. Because *they* didn't. They thought it was completely normal to all sit wordlessly on one bench. This would never have happened in London. We would all have sat on separate benches, always chosen the one with less people on it, always kept ourselves to ourselves. I was heartened by this simple sight. I raised my hand as I approached and smiled. I had to decide where to sit. Well, I couldn't very well be the only person to sit on a bench of his own, could I? That would mark me out as a typically aloof, unfriendly Westerner. So I conquered my awkwardness and did what I would never normally do. I strode up to them and sat myself down right in the middle of them. I was suddenly feeling very philosophical. Yes had done that to me. Opened me up a bit more. I was just another stranger, after all. A white stranger, maybe, with unusual trainers, but really, I was just another person to have sat myself down on that bench, to share a view and wait for a boat. No one said anything at all. A few people glanced at me, and I glanced back and smiled. There was a feeling of deep mutual respect on that bench. Silent, wordless respect. Me, from a land far away, and they—simple Malaysian folk, calm and serene—regarding me with quiet wonder. I breathed deeply and thought about this unexpected sense of community. How we could come from places so far apart and still share this sense of unspoken, unthreatening togetherness. Maybe *this* was what paradise was all about, I thought.

And then they all started talking about me, and it became clear that they were one big family group, and *that* was why they were sitting together, and now they were wondering who on Earth *I* was and why the hell I was sitting right in the middle of them and not on a bench of my own like any *normal* person. And I went a bit red.

I pretended I needed to stretch my legs and stood up and yawned, strutted about, pretended to find something fascinating about one of the other benches, and then sat down on it and studied my feet. A year or so later, the bumboat arrived, and I made sure I was the first one on it. I didn't want that lot getting there first, and then taking bets on where I would sit.

Back at the hotel, I sipped on a cocktail and sent Marc a text.

I AM IN SINGAPORE. I WAS CHASED BY A LIZARD.

I received one back, ten minutes later.

ATOMICO, DANNY!

I laughed. I really hoped I'd see Marc again.

It was getting late, and I would be returning to London the next day, and so I studied my map and thought about how I should spend the remainder of my time in Singapore.

I needn't have bothered.

Because I was to spend the rest of my time in Singapore worrying. Fretting, stressing, and worrying.

I had made my way into the hotel's business centre and checked my e-mails. I'd planned to send one to Lizzie, telling her where I was and what I was doing and how much I was looking forward to seeing her again.

I hadn't reckoned that someone might have e-mailed me.

```
To: Danny
From: whoisthechallenger
Subject: Next . . .
Hello, Danny,
Enjoying yourself? Still saying yes?
So why don't you . . .
Go to Stonehenge 2 !?
```

My heart sank. I was thousands of miles away, and yet the Challenger was still like a shadow. Who was this? Everything was worthless while they were still controlling me. I was supposed to be in control! Master of my *own* destiny! If it was Jason, he was being remarkably persistent for a man who should have got bored and moved on weeks ago. But *was* it Jason?

But Stonehenge 2? What was Stonehenge 2? *Was* Stonehenge 2 an actual place? Or did they mean I should go to Stonehenge again?

Quickly I went to Google.com and typed in "Stonehenge 2."

A second later, I had my result.

Stonehenge 2 existed.

They intended to send me to Stonehenge 2!

But what *was* it?

The original Stonehenge, an ancient Druid monument located in England, is shrouded in mystery. But Stonehenge 2: The Sequel is more of an oddity than a mystery. This 92-foot diameter creation is made of hollow plaster and is accompanied by two . . .

My eyes darted around the site. Stonehenge 2 is a monument to a monument . . . but where?

And then I saw it.

Texas.

Stonehenge 2 was in *Texas*!

Suddenly my world seemed to collapse.

Just when I'd accepted that in order to survive the world of Yes, it was necessary to just sit back and enjoy the ride, someone else had reached in and grabbed the steering wheel . . .

CHAPTER 23

In Which Daniel Faces a Terrible Crisis

I returned home to London knowing one thing: There was no way I could go to Texas. Enough was enough. The Challenger had pushed me far enough when he'd sent me to *England's* Stonehenge. He had another think coming, if he thought I was about to let him send me to a *Texan* one, too.

This was it. It was time to take a stand. But by not going to Texas or ignoring his cryptic words, I'd be failing. Breaking the rules. Saying no to something I'd sworn I'd say yes to. And I couldn't do that.

I knew that by the time Lizzie got to London, this was something I would have to have dealt with. A battle I'd have to have won. She'd be here in little more than a week . . . I'd said yes to her and couldn't break that yes now, meaning if I obeyed the Challenger's whims, I would have to organise and make the return journey incredibly soon and incredibly quickly.

But how would I explain it to Lizzie? How would I tell her what I'd been up to? That I was, in effect, living a double life? Maybe she'd take it well (because yes, I would have to tell her). Sure, I was still the mild-mannered, bespectacled Clark Kent–style radio producer of old . . . but now I was something else, too. A man with more going on in his life. A man with more confidence, more openness. A man who'd recaptured his spontaneity. Maybe she'd take a shine to that.

Or . . . would she *hate* it? Would she, like Hanne, find it immature, and unnecessary, and *stupid*? And would she feel it devalued our relationship when I told her that I had bought her a ticket from Melbourne to Edinburgh not out of some grand romantic gesture . . . but just because she *asked*?

Either way I was going to have to tell her.

But no matter how she reacted, everything could still go wrong. Even if I went to Texas and got back well before Lizzie arrived, it would solve absolutely nothing. The Challenger would still be in the picture, meaning the threat of considerable trouble and awkwardness would always be a moment away. . . .

Desperately I e-mailed Thom once again. He wrote back the same day.

> Danny,
>
> Really, really sorry—not been able to get in touch with Jason. To be honest, we're not all that close as friends, but I have left a message with his sister asking her to get him to e-mail me asap. I do have these details, though . . .

And below that, Jason's place of work and mobile number.

Excellent! Now I *really* had him! All this man's power lay in the fact that I couldn't prove it was him. While he was an anonymous threat, he was able to make me do things against my will. But once I'd unmasked him, he'd be another Ian; another person who knew—and who I *knew* knew. By exposing him, I would rob him of all authority. By exposing him, I would be able to *ignore* him.

I launched an immediate and forceful three-pronged attack. . . .

First, a strongly worded e-mail.

> Jason,
>
> I have your mobile number, and I know where you work. And I'm not doing it. I'm not going to Texas. I know who you are, which means I know that you know, which means you can no longer do this to me. I want to speak to you to make sure you understand, though. *You are no longer eligible to make me do things because I know you know that I know you know.*
>
> I'm going to phone you now.
>
> Danny

I picked up my phone and dialled his mobile.

Frustratingly it went straight to answerphone.

"This is the Vodaphone VoiceMail Service for 07*** *** ***, please leave a message after the—"

"Jason, it's Danny," I practically shouted. "The jig's up. I have your number now. Read your e-mail and never get in touch with me again. We've all had a lot of fun with it, and I'm sure you've had a great laugh with your mates down at the pub, but the party's over. Good night and go to hell . . ."

I hung up and looked at my watch. It was four o'clock—well within office hours. I dialled the work number that Thom had given me. I was pumped up, ready for a showdown, ready to tell this bloke to piss right off.

"Welcome to the immigration and nationality bureau," said a recorded voice. "Please note that all calls are recorded . . ."

There was a click while the call transferred to an operator, and then . . .

"Good morning, Home Office, how can I help?"

"I need to speak to a man called Jason, please."

"What's the surname?"

"I don't have a surname. I've only met him once. He works in immigration, making decisions about people . . ."

"I'm afraid I can't place your call without knowing a surname."

"I need to speak to him. Urgently."

"All appeals must be in writing . . ."

"I don't want to make an appeal. . . . I want to speak to Jason. . . ."

"Did you receive an RFRL?"

"I don't know what an RFRL is . . . I just need to speak to a bloke called Jason. It's a personal call; it won't take but a minute . . . please, just put me through to someone in the department who makes decisions about things like that . . ."

"Hold on the line . . ."

My heart started to race. I was getting closer. My three-pronged attack was about to climax. I was closing in on the man who had been mocking me from afar.

"SEO."

It was a girl's voice.

"Hi . . . is Jason there, please?"

"Jason who?" she said.

"I'm not sure. He works there. Making decisions about people. Saying no a lot. I *have* to speak to him. . . ."

"Hang on . . ."

The phone is muffled as she asks someone about something.

"He doesn't work here anymore," she said. "There was a Jason here, but he's gone. I'm new here. Sorry."

"Well . . . where's he gone? Do you have a number? I tried his phone, but it's switched off. I need to speak to him. I need to speak to him *right now*. . . ."

"Hang on . . ."

Another muffled conversation.

"No, I'm sorry. We're not allowed to give out personal details."

"But honestly—I'm not a stalker or a lunatic. This man, he's been . . ."

"I'm sorry."

I sighed and rubbed my eyes.

"Well . . . if you see him . . . can you get him to call Danny?"

"Sure. I'll tell the others, too."

"Thanks."

I put the phone down, slightly dejected. I'd thought that was going to be it.

What would happen if I didn't get him? Never got him? What would happen if I could never track him down and grab him and shout "I know who you are!" at him? Then the Challenger would live on. And I'd have to go to Texas after all.

It wasn't just that I was tired. It wasn't just that I'd had enough of travelling and wanted to stay at home and see Lizzie and finish the last month of Yes in relative comfort. It was that I'd been all but ignoring another aspect of my journey up until now.

The cost.

Texas wouldn't be cheap to get to. I knew I'd have to fly to New York, then probably change and get a flight to Austin, and then a cab or a bus or a train to Hunt, where Stonehenge 2 was. And I'd have to do it in the way I'd been doing everything else: on credit.

I now had several more credit cards than was sensible, thanks to the various offers, suggestions, and invitations of the kindly people at Visa, Barclaycard, American Express, and everywhere else, and I'd used each of them. I'd used them early on only for smaller things, sure; things like a curry with Wag. Or maybe a round of beers with Nathan or Jon or Ben or Rich or any of the other friends who'd suddenly found me all too easy to coax out of the flat for a pint. But later, well . . . the bills had *grown*.

Buying the Yesmobile had eaten up my savings, and I hadn't exactly been working very much lately. I'd been putting work off, knowing that a new job was just around the corner, hoping that everything would sort itself out. Then there'd been Lizzie's flight to pay for. And the insurance and the road tax for the new car. The train tickets to Liverpool. And Cardiff. The thousands of stickers I'd had printed up. Up until a week ago, I could bear all that . . . but the next bill would feature a hotel in Barcelona. Meals. Hasty withdrawals for taxis and trains. Flights to Singapore and back. And maybe, now, even a series of flights and hotels to get me to Hunt, Texas, to look at a smaller version of a monument that was already pretty small and which, anyway, I'd seen just a month or two before.

And what would I have to show for it all? What would I have to show for all the effort and expense and debt? A *feeling*. Try telling *that* to the bailifs. Was all this worth so much money?

The problem began when I won that twenty-five thousand pounds. It had made me feel like a very rich man indeed. It had made me think everything was going to be okay, like Yes was going to look after me. But now, sitting at my desk, studying my bills, I suddenly didn't feel like it was. Yes just wasn't living up to its end of the bargain.

So I did what any man sinking slowly into debt would do. I shoved the bills into a drawer and went out instead. In January I'd be turning a corner. Starting again. I'd pay it all off when I chained myself to that desk, where I'd stay for the rest of my life. I only had a month to go. *I only had a month to go.*

So, tonight I would drink. The problem was, I'd have to do it with Paul.

I was on my way to meet the man who'd called me for a polite conversation for a second time. So far, he remained the only person who had taken me up on the offer. I was not in a good mood. And I was not in the mood (and I hope he will forgive me for this) for meeting Paul. I needed to be with someone who understood me; not with someone who understood Border terriers.

We met at the Yorkshire Grey. The polite conversation was stilted, at best, but I don't think Paul had noticed. He was off on another monologue, while I just sat there, scowling.

"Musically," he said, apropos of virtually nothing, "my interests are varied. I'm probably *most* into Sarah Brightman. Do you like Sarah Brightman?"

"She is a very talented entertainer," I said, downbeat and downtrodden, when what I really wanted to say was "I can't *stand* Sarah Brightman." But this was a polite conversation. That was the deal.

"I think she's touring early next year, if you're interested in seeing her," said Paul.

Nope. I am not interested at all.

"That is excellent news," I said.

"I've loved her stuff ever since *Phantom of the Opera*. That's what first brought her to my attention. And then some friends in Brazil sent me an album of hers, called *The Songs That Got Away*, and I was so glad that they *hadn't* got away, because that was me hooked! I'll let you borrow that CD if you like."

"Oh yes, please."

"Since then I've been to see her in concert a few times. I saw her in Edinburgh in '97. I had tickets for the seventh row, on the right of centre, and that was fantastic, even though Sarah was standing to the left of centre, but it was still good, you know."

"Right," I said as if I'd been making mental floor plans in my head. I had finished my pint and was waiting for Paul to finish his. I didn't want to add yet another round to my Yes bill.

"And then I saw her again on that same tour in Norwich, and it was a bigger crowd this time. . . ."

And please, *God*, make this *end*. Make him talk about Border terriers again. Anything.

". . . and basically I started the standing ovation at the end of that gig, so if you ever meet her, walking around the BBC, you should say, 'I met the man who started the standing ovation in Norwich in 1997' and see what she says!"

"I will certainly do that," I said, playing with my glass. My very *empty* glass.

"Do! Do that! She'll love that. Yes, as I say, I think she's touring again next year . . ."

I put both my thumbs up.

"Hey—if you work for the BBC, Danny, you could probably get me an autograph."

I looked at him blankly.

"Couldn't you?" he said.

"If I bump into her," I said.

"You could fax her and ask for one."

What did he want me to fax? "Dear Sarah, the BBC would like an autograph"?

"Would you do that for me?"

Sigh.

"Yes."

Paul looked at his watch.

"Oh. I should probably get going . . . I'm going to the cinema tonight."

"The cinema?" I said, partly out of relief that the subject was changing and partly because, despite all this, I now wanted to extend the conversation.

"Yeah," he said. "Oh, God, I would invite you, but someone else got the tickets. It's kind of a date."

I nodded, a little relieved that my days of gatecrashing dates were at an end.

"Is she nice?" I said.

"I hope so," he said. "Friend of a friend."

I nearly told him about Kristen, but caught myself. I still didn't want to talk about that. And with Lizzie getting ready to come back to London, it just didn't feel . . . right, somehow.

"Well, good luck," I said.

"Cheers. My friend Simon set this up. He knows I'd never say no to a redhead. My own personal weakness. Your mates know your vul-nerabilities."

I was pleased for Paul. And I felt slightly guilty, too. Why had I been so grumpy about meeting with him? I suppose, in the back of my mind, I'd thought I was doing him a favour. He seemed lonely. But look at him: a successful man with friends who thought highly enough of him to set him up on dates. An active social life. We'll brush over the Sarah Brightman fixation, but the fact was he was fine. Life was sorted. If anything, he must've thought he was doing *me* a favour. Me, who never seemed to have anything to talk about. Me, who'd put stickers all over town, which essentially said, "Please call me! I am a sad and lonely oddball who craves the polite conversation of strangers."

Paul put his jacket on, and as he shook my hand, said, "I meant to ask . . . I'm in town again tomorrow night. I could bring you that CD. Do you fancy a quick drink, then? Save you sitting here all on your own."

I put my thumbs up again and said quite gratefully, "Yes."

And that, I'm afraid, was my big night out. Those were my efforts to drown my sorrows. Don't get me wrong; I rang around. I rang Wag, and I rang Ian, and I rang Nathan, Jonesy, Ben, and Rich. I even rang Cobbett. But each had an excuse. Each had somewhere else they had to be or something else they had to do. Each had the power of No. I found myself growing jealous of those freedom-loving bastards.

I trudged to the Tube and walked heavily down the steps of Oxford Circus station. Two stops later, at Holborn, I was forced to get out. There was trouble on the line. Some kind of power failure. We were instructed to find other means of getting home, or to hang around and wait for the bus replacement service.

It was a common enough occurence, but it had real resonance with me. Maybe, I thought, this was a sign of hope. This was how it had all began, after all. Perhaps it was a sign. Maybe Maitreya would come to me. Maybe I'd bump into the man on the bus. Maybe all this meant something. Maybe it *wasn't* all pointless.

The buses arrived soon after. With genuine hope in my eyes, I looked around me. Scoured the faces of the other affected, moody commuters and travellers, but I didn't see him. I moved upstairs, but to no avail. There were no men with beards. No men who looked like they might be enlightened.

The journey was long and the stops many. By the time the bus was running parallel with Roman Road, minutes from my flat, I was completely on my own.

As the bus slowed at a junction, I walked downstairs and jumped off. I would walk the rest of the way home. The last half an hour had confirmed a lot of things for me. I knew, once and for all, that I was on my own. That Maitreya did not exist. That the man on the bus had just been a man on the bus. That I'd done all this myself. That there was *no* grand plan.

And so I stopped at an off-licence, bought a bottle of wine, and went home, the pit of my stomach churning as I realised that at some point this evening I'd have to investigate how much a flight to Texas would be.

Oh. And to fax Sarah Brightman's agent.

That night, I had a bath. A long, long bath. I didn't want to get out. As long as I was in the bath, I felt protected. I wasn't near my phone or the Internet. No opportunities or favours or requests could sneak in through the locked door. It was a steamy, warm cocoon. Things really had changed since my Yes heydays . . . I'd only had time for showers, then. I'd always wanted to be out there on the other side of the door, searching for Yeses and grabbing them with both hands.

I'd brought my diary into the bath with me. I wanted to see what I'd been through. See whether, with a month to go, it had been worth it. Whether it could inspire me to want to travel to the other side of the world just one more time. I flicked idly through from page to page, through July and August and September, wondering what Ian would make of it all at the end of the month, when it would be me and him on New Year's Eve in the same pub we'd been in when I'd told him about the man on the bus.

There were things he knew about, sure—the scratch card, Amsterdam, the undeserved promotion, my newfound status as both respected minister and (failed) inventor—but there was so much more he *didn't* know about. So many experiences I'd had—people I'd met or places I'd seen. Things I'd done. Little changes in habit. Little efforts I wouldn't normally have made. No matter how well Ian knew me, much of this would surprise him. A lot of it surprised *me*. I suddenly felt rather proud of Ian. He'd been a constant support. A constant friend. Someone who *could* have used his special knowledge to teach me a lesson I'd never forget, but who *hadn't*. He'd seen the worth of this project. I guess it was like Paul had said: The people who know you well are the people who know your vulnerabilities. They know your weaknesses. But you trust them not to pounce on them; not to take advantage. And they don't, because they care. It's the strangers you've got to watch out for. The people like Jason. The people who sense weakness and for whatever reason, feel they have to crush you.

And as I flicked through the diary some more, and I thought about that, I nodded to myself, impressed by my own wisdom . . . until I was struck by one aspect of the diary in particular. One set of Yeses . . . one single chain of events . . . one idea that turned into a feeling that wouldn't go away . . .

The people who know you well are the people who know your vulnerabilities. . . .

But I pressed on. Reading through the diary. Taking it all in. Reading who I'd met and when, and what had happened before and after, and then I just couldn't help it. . . . I started to feel less and less well, and more and more nervous. I couldn't put my finger on why, exactly, but it had something to do with the thought that was slowly creeping up on me, slowly forming somewhere . . .

It was an uncomfortable thought—one that made the back of my neck prickle, and my heart start to beat a little faster. I pushed it to one side, knowing that it just couldn't be possible, that there could be no truth in it, that I was just being silly . . .

But the more of the diary I read, the more I started to understand . . .

I pulled my shirt and boxers on, walked into the living room, and turned the computer on. There was an e-mail I had to check. One I'd received a little while ago from Thom . . . It had been a throwaway sentence and had not really struck me as odd until now. . . . But now it struck me as *very* odd indeed. . . .

I uncorked my bottle of wine while the Mac started up. . . . This was stupid. What was I doing? But I had to check . . .

Finally the computer was ready. I clicked into my mail, and there it was . . . the sentence . . .

```
What's your address?
```

If Thom didn't have my address, how did Jason find it with such ease?

Maybe Jason had nothing to do with this at all.

I picked up my phone and started to dial . . . but then I put it down again.

I couldn't just phone someone up and accuse them of having a hidden identity. Of being the Challenger.

Could I?

I poured a glass of wine and paced the living room. A stupid idea. It couldn't be true. But the more I tried to force it out of my head, the more control the thought seemed to gain.

The people who know you well are the people who know your vulnerabilities. . . .

Was I being paranoid? Was I going mad? I mean, I already *knew* who the Challenger was, didn't I? It was Jason, the man who'd taken an active stand against the way of Yes. The man who'd sworn at me and made me feel like a little boy with a stupid hobby. The grown man who said no for a living.

But . . . *what if?* What if it was . . . a friend? A friend who knew what I was up to and where I lived and exactly what I'd been doing with my life?

Maybe there was a way of finding out. Or maybe not exactly finding out, but at least setting my mind at rest. It was a long shot, sure, but at least I could take that long shot and be done with it.

But it couldn't be a friend . . . the hat . . . the book . . . the T-shirt . . . the trip . . . it *couldn't* be a friend. . . .

I went to Hotmail.com.

Would this work? Could it?

In the log-in box, I typed an e-mail address. One that had become rather familiar to me. "Whoisthechallenger."

Below that, it asked me for a password.

What was the password? What would be the Challenger's password?

Slowly, and with two fingers, I typed in one familiar six-letter word, and then looked at it.

The computer whirred. And there, in the blink of an eye, it appeared. An in-box.

I stared and stared, and I still couldn't believe it. I was looking at an in-box. The password *worked*.

There was one e-mail. It was unread. It was from me. The angry e-mail I'd sent only a day before, telling Jason that the game was up, that I was making a stand, that he could go to hell.

I was stunned. The only reason I'd been able to guess the password was that it was a password I knew all too well.

Which meant that it was a *challenger* I knew all too well.

My head spinning, I picked up the phone, and I dialled.

Eighteen hours later I pulled the car up near the Horse & Groom. I tried to make it screech to a halt, but the braking system of the Nissan Figaro is annoyingly well-designed.

I got out and slammed the door shut.

"I wouldn't park there, mate," said a street cleaner. "There's traffic wardens all over the place. They'll have you fined within five minutes."

Oh, *would* they? I wasn't in the mood to be messed with today.

I opened the door of the car again, leaned over to open the glove-box, brought out a small laminated sign, and fixed it to the window.

MINISTER ON OFFICIAL BUSINESS.

Sod 'em.

It had been my suggestion where we would meet, and I wanted to do it on *my* turf. The Challenger, of course, hadn't realised they'd been found out yet. They assumed this was a social call—a normal day in a normal place, just as we'd done thousands of times before. I was calm on the outside. But on the inside I was full of adrenaline.

We sat down, and I spoke first.

"Well . . . it's nice to see you again," I said, making sure to pause dramatically before saying, "It's always nice to see . . . *the Challenger*."

There was a silence. I remained like that on purpose, trying to force a statement from someone who was now looking very embarrassed indeed.

"How did you find out it was me?"

How did I find out? I found out the same way they knew I was the Yes Man. Because those who know you best know your vulnerabilities.

I took a deep breath, and said one word.

"Norway."

"Sorry?"

"N-O-R-W-A-Y. Like the country."

Something dawned on Hanne.

"You used the same password on your fake Hotmail account as you've used for everything else for the past five years," I said. "Including your mobile phone account."

I imagine that after she reads this book, she probably won't be using the word "Norway" for passwords quite so much. But it serves her right.

Her pin number, by the way, is 4626.

"Oh . . . well. Right. I should probably apologise," she said.

"Yes, you probably bloody should! When did you first know, Hanne?".

"Early on. I mean, I *assume* it was early on. God knows how long you'd been doing it by then. But at that restaurant, you ordered fish. You never ordered fish before. You never even *ate* fish before. You said they were too creepy. You said you were sure they were looking at you funny, even when they didn't have heads. But as soon as the waiter recommended it, you just said 'yes.' *That's* how I first knew something was up."

I suppose the lesson here is that you should never underestimate an ex-girlfriend's intuition.

"And then there was the fact that you came to dinner at *all*," she said. "I mean, that was *odd*, Danny. You'd done some odd things before, but that was *really* odd. I was fuming. I was fuming for days. I knew you were up to something, and every time I met you or heard from you, you did something to confirm it. *Yes*, you minded if I started seeing someone new. *Yes*, you were going to help the murdered son of a sultan. *I've* had those e-mails, Danny. And *then* . . . sponsoring a small African child for me, Dan. Do you think I haven't seen those leaflets too? And the flowers? At first I thought you were just being easily influenced by advertising, but then I put two and two together and got . . . well . . . an idiot. An idiot who says yes a lot."

"But why not just *tell* me you were on to me? Why all this Challenger business?"

"You'd never have stopped if I just told you! And this way, it was like . . . a prank or something."

"A *prank*? You were going to send me to bloody *Texas*!"

"Texas? No, I wasn't!"

"You said, 'Go to Stonehenge 2'! That's in Texas!"

"No, I wanted you to go to Stonehenge—for the *second time*! I wanted you to go to Stonehenge, *twice*! When I texted you and you were in Singapore, I thought, right, well, for some reason he obviously wants to bloody travel. So I was going to keep sending you to Stonehenge until you'd had enough! It was going to end up like *Groundhog Day*! It would've been 'Go to Stonehenge 3' in another few weeks!"

"But why *Stonehenge*?"

"Because you hate theme parks. You always have."

I put my head in my hands.

"Stonehenge is *not* a theme park! Shelf Adventure—*that's* a theme park! Stonehenge is a . . . you know . . . a . . . *thing*. A monument. An attraction. But it's not a *theme park*! You set me up on a *date*, Hanne!"

"And again I didn't expect you to actually say yes! It was a blind date, Danny! Set up by your ex! How much more creepy did you want me to be? Or did you expect me to gatecrash *your* date, like you'd gatecrashed mine? You should have just said no!"

I didn't say anything. I was still reeling slightly from my lucky escape. I didn't want to think about how close I'd come to booking a ticket to Texas; about sinking even deeper into debt. And all because I'd got carried away with this evil Challenger figure. The evil Challenger figure, sitting before me now, looking not particularly evil at all. I had invented a motivation for them. My mind had exaggerated their intent . . . but why? As another way of making life more exciting? I had become a fantasist.

"I thought you were a bloke called Jason," I told her, for what I can only hope was the first time in our relationship. "I thought *he* was the Challenger."

"I didn't want to call myself that," she said. "That wasn't my idea."

Hang on.

"Well, whose idea was it, then? Seb's?"

"No, what I mean is . . ."

Something started to dawn on me.

"You had *help*, didn't you? You weren't doing this alone, were you?"

"No, no, I . . ."

"You didn't get all this from fish at all! That *wasn't* the starting point! You made that up!"

"I was worried about you! I thought I was helping!"

"And the T-shirt—the 'Just Say No' T-shirt—it's a little convenient that that arrived just when I was thinking how much I missed the word 'no' . . ."

"We were trying to help. We were both trying to help. . . ."

"It was . . . my God, it was *Ian*, wasn't it?"

Hanne looked at the table and nodded silently.

Treachery! Ian had *betrayed* me!

"He said he just wanted you to stop," said Hanne. "We felt it was our fault. You were going mental, Danny. Ian told me. He said we had to break your new habit. He said it was important that we got you to say no."

My eyes nearly popped.

"He thought it was important I said no? Well, of *course* he did! He wanted me to say no, so he could punish me! He's wanted that all along!"

"Punish you? No . . . *help* you . . ."

My head was spinning. All this time I thought I'd been battling a dark, brutish presence, a challenger intent on my demise. I'd blamed it on a man I hardly knew, when in reality the enemy walked alongside me. Two mates. Playing a trick on me. A trick they thought would *help* me! I needed to calm down. Maybe she was right; maybe I'd been taking this far too seriously, attaching too much importance to it all. Maybe I'd been doing that all along, right from the start. Maybe all this was the greatest waste of time ever committed in the name of self-help. . . .

"I'm sorry, Danny . . . It was just supposed to be a bit of fun. . . ."

"But it's . . . *devalued* everything somehow . . . ," I said.

"It was only supposed to be a bit of revenge for all the stupid boy-projects you put me through when we were going out. But you know what? I got quite *into* it. It was like a stupid *girl*-project. I used to go to sleep at night, giggling about all the things I could make you do! I'm sorry, Dan. I can kind of see what you saw in those projects, now. . . ."

"That is highly immature," I said. "I am glad I am past all that, and I hope that one day you grow up as I have."

Hanne watched me as I started to stand up.

"Where are you going?" she said.

"Don't tell Ian about our meeting, okay?" I said. "I have to go and think of a suitable punishment for him. I am sure that he must have contravened the rules set out by the Yes Manifesto in *some* way . . ."

Suddenly there was a none-too-subtle cough from my right, and I remembered something I'd completely forgotten to do.

"Oh, God, I'm so sorry. Hanne, this is Paul. He's a new friend of mine. I gave him a lift here. We have polite conversations."

Paul had been sitting there in confused silence for the last fifteen minutes. In the rush to expose Hanne, I'd forgotten to introduce him, and as I'd already said yes to having a drink with him, I'd had to bring him along.

"Hello, Paul," said Hanne.

"Hello, Hanne," said Paul.

"Hey . . . *Hanne's* got a dog," I said, a thought suddenly coming to me. "Don't you, Hanne?"

"Er, yes . . .," she said. "A poodle."

"A *poodle?*" said Paul, and he let out a little laugh. "I can tell you a thing or two about *poodles*. . . ."

And, much to Hanne's horror, I left them to it.

As I drove through London, I laughed. I was relieved. There was no one after me anymore. There was nothing anyone could do to stop me. The Challenger had challenged. And the Yes Man had prevailed.

I would get Ian back for this—make no mistake about it. But that would come later. Later, when I'd thought of something suitable. Something that would *really* make up for the deceit and the pranks . . . but not today.

Because today I had to get home and clean the flat for Lizzie, happy in the knowledge that life was now a good deal simpler.

December was going to be *easy*.

CHAPTER 24

In Which Daniel Is Content

I was content.

Lizzie was asleep in my flat.

I'd picked her up a few mornings after my victory over the Challenger, sleepy and fragile, a little the worse for wear after twenty-four hours on a plane. I was in the kitchen, making a cup of tea, when I heard her wake. Moments later I turned around and there she was: a brunette ball of hair and sleep.

"Hello, you," she said.

For a second we just smiled.

"Tea?"

"Be rude not to," she said. "You can't go turning tea down the minute you arrive in England."

I flicked the kettle on again, and her eyes scanned the flat.

"Nice to see the place again," she said. "You've tidied up for me, haven't you?"

"No. It's always like this. It is always very tidy."

"Mm-hmm, I'm sure it is. And you always have fresh flowers on the table, do you?"

"I walked past a stall on Roman Road. The man was shouting out loud about how it was a bargain not to be missed, so I . . ."

"Sure, sure."

She smiled and started to slowly walk around the flat, looking at my shelves, studying my books. I made the tea while she peered out of the windows at the trains going by outside. It felt good to have her around again.

"What's that thing?" she said, pointing at something odd and plastic in the corner.

"That," I said, proudly, "is the new Easy Steam Cleaner. It is both brilliantly simple *and* simply brilliant."

"Have you used it?"

"Twice. The first time I nearly scorched myself. And the second time too as it happens."

She raised her eyebrows and continued her casual meander. She picked up a book that was facedown on the table and studied it.

"You're learning Flemish?"

"*Ja.*"

"Why *Flemish*?"

I shrugged.

"*Spreekt du Engels!*" I said with some degree of jollity.

She looked impressed.

"What does that mean?"

"It means 'Flemish is a complex and enigmatic language.'"

It doesn't mean that at all. I don't know *what* it means.

She smiled, and said, "Is it okay if I have a shower?"

"I'll get you a towel."

Twenty minutes later, with her shower over, she walked back into the living room, drying her hair and smelling of mint. She looked lovely. And she was carrying something.

"What on Earth is *this*?" she said.

It was a neatly framed certificate. One of three I'd hung up in my bathroom.

"That's my nursing degree from the University of Rochville," I said.

"Rochville? Where's *Rochville*?"

Good point. I had no idea.

"It doesn't matter where Rochville is," I said with all the authority of a man who'd bought his degree off the Internet. "All that matters is that I am now a fully qualified nurse. Based on my life experience and television-viewing habits."

"Full of surprises. What are the other ones on the wall in there?"

"One is my certificate of excellence, the other is my certificate of distinction. I did very well. I imagine I was probably top of my class."

"Why didn't you tell me you had a nursing degree?"

"I am not a boaster."

She started to walk backward. I assumed she was going to put the certificate back, but she stopped and pointed down the hallway.

"There was something else I noticed. In the hallway?"

I wasn't sure what she meant.

"You appear to own a large portrait of yourself with a dog."

"Oh. Yeah."

"So?"

"Um . . . well, y'see . . ."

I didn't really want to tell her about my psychotropic mindbomb. It might give her the wrong idea about me. But how else to explain it?

"I entered my local newspaper's pet-personality contest, and the prize was a lovely portrait of me and my dog."

"But you haven't got a dog."

"That's right. I actually entered Stuart, my cat, but the artist got it wrong."

"But you haven't got a cat, either."

"No. Correct. Look . . . it's probably best if we don't discuss that portrait."

This was all getting too weird for her. I could tell. I took a step closer to her. "But it's probably best if we *do* discuss something else. . . ."

She looked concerned. So did I.

"Sounds a bit serious," she said. "If you don't want me staying here, then it's cool, I can—"

"No! No, it's not that. It's something else. Something about me. And I think I need to tell you sooner rather than later, because I've made that mistake before, and I'd rather not make it again. Maybe you should sit down. . . ."

It was time to tell her. To get it out in the open and out of the way. To reveal my hidden identity.

And so she sat down. And I told her. I told her what I'd done. I told her everything, right from the start, the whole story. The man on the bus, the Yes Manifesto, Ian's threats of punishment, my determination to succeed. I told her about Jason, and about Hanne and Seb, and about hanging out in Wales with a hypnotic dog that I thought could cure all my worries. And she nodded, and she smiled and frowned and nodded some more, and she looked like, despite it all, she understood. So I told her more. I told her about how sometimes it had all gotten too much for me, that sometimes I thought what I was doing was pointless and worthless and stupid, and how for a moment I'd looked for meaning in the arms of Maitreya until I realised that *I* was to blame for all this, and how when I thought I'd just had enough, something else would happen to pull me back in. And then I held my breath as I told her about Edinburgh—about how buying her a ticket was something I never would have had the confidence to do, but how by blaming it on Yes I'd made it okay somehow. And she nodded quietly again, but I couldn't gauge her reaction this time, so I just pressed on and told her about Ian and Hanne conspiring against me, and how I'd defeated them, and how now, here she was in London, in front of me, and maybe if I'd never said yes to a ticket, and she'd never said yes to that ticket too, we wouldn't be where we were now. In short I told her everything. Or *nearly* everything. The only thing I left out, in fact, was my time with Kristen.

It was a lot for her to take in.

Eventually she collected her thoughts and exhaled heavily.

"Well, thank *God*," she said.

It wasn't quite the reaction I'd been expecting.

"Eh?"

"Well, I'm hoping that you saying yes explains the Amazing Penis Patch I found in your bathroom."

I went a bit red. Shit.

"No," I said. "That's Ian's."

As it turns out I was pretty pleased that I'd told her about the whole Yes thing.

We were in the Royal Inn on a cold and dark winter afternoon, and I was telling her more about what I'd done. She loved the sound of Marc and said she too wanted to be stalked by lizards on Pulau Ubin and expressed amazement that I'd dropped the Geese for Peace campaign so early in its development. Part of her was humouring me, sure. But another part of her seemed genuinely intrigued by the idea. The Yes idea, I mean—not the geese one.

"There's one thing I need to know, though . . . ," she said, tracing a short line on the table with her finger. "Me coming here and staying with you . . ."

"No. That's not part of it. That's a Yes I would *always* have said."

"Because I understand the Edinburgh ticket. . . . Things were different then, but now, if I felt that you . . ."

"No. Lizzie. Honestly."

"Cool."

But I didn't want her to think I was just being polite.

"Seriously," I said, "I never . . ."

"Shh. I believe you."

And from the way she looked at me, I think she really did.

The next few days flew by just as they'd done in Edinburgh. Lizzie attended her meetings, and I picked her up afterward, and we ran around town together. We met Ian for lunch—he had never before met the mystical Lizzie—and she said all the right things and made all the right noises.

Ian had come clean and admitted his part in the whole Challenger debacle the moment I'd confronted him about it. He'd tried to persuade me that it was for my own good; that he'd been worried I'd get bored; that he thought it best if I said no, anyway; that as I hadn't technically said no yet, I was still winning. I was stern with him, but the truth was, it was fair enough. There was nothing in the Yes Manifesto which expressly forbade him from confirming Hanne's suspicions. So I told him I forgave him. But only—and this is between you and me—because I had something rather special planned for him.

Anyway, Lizzie had treated the two of us to an ice cream afterward, and laughed graciously at all of Ian's jokes. I think she felt sorry for him because of the whole Amazing Penis Patch thing.

"She's fantastic," he said, when she'd popped to the bathroom, and I nodded, because she was.

We piled into my little car and drove to the cinema near Canary Wharf that night, the three of us, and despite Ian's protests, we agreed to go to the first film the man behind the counter recommended. Afterward we sat in a Docklands pub, and Lizzie chastised Ian for taking such pleasure in my trials and tribulations, for encouraging Hanne, and for keeping his mysterious punishment a mystery.

"The punishment still stands, by the way," he said. "You may have won the battle, but you haven't won the war. You can still fail. And I can still unleash my punishment."

"So what *is* the 'punishment'?" asked Lizzie for probably the third time that night.

"I am not at liberty to divulge it," said Ian. "But rest assured, it's a good one."

"It's only fair to punish Danny if *you* experience life as a Yes Man . . . ," she said. "So you know what you're talking about and can tailor the punishment accordingly."

I smiled. I knew what she was up to.

"That way you can come up with a really *suitable* punishment."

"*I'm* not bloody saying yes to everything!" said Ian. "Talk to the Yes Man over there! I'm not the one spending all my money on degrees and potions from the Internet."

Lizzie and I exchanged a conspiratorial glance. We knew *exactly* what he was buying from the Internet.

But she charmed him and charmed him, and eventually he agreed to say yes—if only for the rest of tonight. He ended up buying drinks for the three guys behind the bar, texting yes to an eminently dull colleague who wanted to have dinner the following night, and having a lovely conversation with a blonde girl at the next table. At one point we had to rescue him from the arcade machine in the corner. Every time he finished a game, it read PLAY AGAIN?, and it was forty minutes before we noticed.

The next morning Lizzie drove back with me to Bath to see the city and meet my parents and Sammy the cat. And back in London one rainy Saturday afternoon, I took her for a curry of chicken dansak at the Madras Valley, and then on to spend a few hours on Great Portland Street, where she sat and laughed with me and a few hundred of my very closest friends.

We were . . . *becoming* something, her and me. No. Scratch that. We *were* something. And that was great.

But it was sad, too.

One afternoon she came back to the flat with a small gift.

"I found this on the Tube. I thought you might like it."

It was a flyer. I read the top line.

"An Invitation to Tim Miller's Gay Men's Performance Workshop."

"It's a chance for gay men to express their personal stories through performance and dance," she said. "I know you're not gay, but that's an invitation, and anyway, I imagine you like dancing, don't you?"

I laughed. She didn't think it was stupid.

"Also," she said. "I thought *I* might try it."

"Try what? Expressing your personal stories through dance?"

"No. Saying yes. So I went into a travel agency. I asked them where would be a good place to spend Friday night. They said Prague. So I got us two tickets."

"You did *what*?"

"I got us two tickets to Prague. So what d'you say? Do you want to go with me to Prague on Friday night?"

"You . . . *wow* . . ." It was the first time a girl had done something like that for me. I didn't know they *could*. I'd found a Yes Girl! I wanted to tell her she was brilliant, that *this* was brilliant, that *Prague* would be brilliant, but all I could manage was "Yes!"

It was an incredible trip. Spontaneous, carefree, fast, and fun. We'd flown out for one night in the late afternoon, and by nine o'clock we were walking through the Old Town Square. It was a bitterly cold December night, but crisp and fresh, and we bought hot chocolates to keep our hands warm. We walked to St. Nicholas Cathedral, and we kissed on Charles Bridge. And just after ten o'clock, we looked up at the sky, because instinctively we knew that something was changing. I couldn't tell exactly what at first, but then, slowly and gently, it started to snow. We laughed, but there was something different about Lizzie's laugh. And then I realised—this was the first time Lizzie had ever even *seen* snow. Here. Now. This. I was amazed. Saying yes had done this for her; given her a present. In the prettiest city in the world.

The day that Lizzie had to go, neither of us wanted to talk about the future.

We skirted around it. We'd had two great weeks together. One in

Edinburgh. And now one in London. That's what I tried to focus on.

I'd woken early and watched her sleep, and although I felt calm, I felt uneasy, too. I knew she was going. And I knew something inside me was going to have to change.

I cooked breakfast while Lizzie ordered her cab to the airport. When she'd finished packing, she came into the living room, where I was sitting quietly with a carton of juice.

"I've got a Yes for you," she said quietly.

"How do you mean?"

"Something for you to say yes to."

"What is it?"

She smiled.

"How about you come out to Australia for Christmas? Meet everyone? You could spend New Year's there. With me."

I didn't know what to say. It was a lovely idea. But my head felt heavy. I mean, technically, yes, I could clear it with my parents and sort out a flight and spend Christmas in a country I'd never even come close to before. But was it the right thing to do? This wasn't a normal Yes. This was a *big* Yes. Because it was a Yes that could and probably would end up hurting me.

"Look . . . let's say I did come out. What would happen afterward?"

"Afterward? Well . . . I guess we'd see."

Yeah. We'd see. But I could already see it. Afterward, I'd come home to London. And I'd be here alone. On my own again. Back in precisely the same situation that I'd been in exactly one year before, effectively throwing all my good work away. If I got any closer to Lizzie than I was already, I'd be setting myself up for the biggest fall of my life. And I was scared.

"Well, if you can't make it out at Christmas," she said, "how about January? Or February?"

"I'm starting that new job in January," I said, slightly more coldly than I'd meant. "I'm not going to be able to do the things I did anymore. I've got to move on from all of that. Get responsible. Make sensible choices. And anyway, I don't think they'd give me time off so soon just so I could fly out to Australia and see you."

"Oh. Right. So . . . it's kind of now or never, then?"

I shrugged and looked at my feet, feeling terrible. Don't get me wrong: I wanted to go. I really, truly did. But I just couldn't.

If I allowed myself to hope that this could work, that we had a future, that somehow distance didn't matter . . . then I'd be making the inevitable far worse. The fact was this *couldn't* work, and the longer this went on, the deeper it would cut me. It was a part of my Yes life, and my Yes life was almost over. To drag it into the *next* life would be unfair. Sometimes you have to make a decision to protect yourself. Sometimes it's better to lose a foot than risk a leg.

"I can't . . . ," I said before realising that there was something else I could say. Something that might make all this so much easier. "The other thing is . . . I kind of recently met someone. And . . . I don't know, maybe it'll lead nowhere, but you know . . . at least she's in England, and . . ."

Lizzie looked hurt, and I hated myself, but she nodded. I avoided her eyes.

"So, thank you, Lizzie," I said. "But it's a No."

She touched my arm and said she understood.

"A pity your first No had to be to me," she said, and I smiled sadly.

And an hour later I carried her bags to the cab, and she left.

CHAPTER 25

In Which Daniel Makes a Terrible Admission, Searches His Soul, and Finally Accepts That He Must Be Punished

Two nights later in the Yorkshire Grey, Ian seemed nearly as upset as I was that Lizzie had gone. Far more upset than when I'd told him the grand Yes adventure was over. I was stopping. That was it. I'd said no.

"I just can't believe she's gone," he said, shaking his head. "She really livened up the place, didn't she? Such a *special* girl. And funny, too. And down-to-earth. And with a really cool accent."

He really wasn't helping matters. But I nodded along.

"Well . . . here's to Lizzie . . ."

He raised his pint and took a sip. We sat for a few moments in silence.

"I did the right thing, didn't I?" I said.

"Oh, absolutely. Definitely. You did the right thing, yes."

"In saying no to Australia, I mean."

"Yes. You did. No doubt about that. Remind me why you said no again?"

"Because sooner or later we'd have to say good-bye again. And if it's sooner, I'll be less hurt than if it's later. Sometimes it's better to lose a foot than risk a leg. And she lives in *Australia*, for Christ's sake. Australia! That's, like, twice as far as *Singapore*!"

"Ah. Yes. You did the right thing. You can't be going over to Australia every weekend just because your girlfriend lives there."

Girlfriend. It was the first time anyone had called her my girlfriend.

"But you know . . . it's not too late," he said. "I mean, technically, you *could* still go. It wouldn't be a No, then. It would be a Yes. Which would mean you were still in the game."

"Ian . . ."

"No, you're right. About that whole foot thing in particular. Taking a risk is definitely overrated. I remember thinking that when you said 'sometimes the biggest risk is never taking one.' I remember thinking, 'No. What about kayaking?' You're *right* not to take the risk. It *is* better to be safe than sorry."

"Yes. Because I wasn't just saying yes to a trip to Australia, was I? I was saying yes to letting myself get possibly very hurt. That must be, like, a level seven or something. Totally unacceptable."

"*Totally* unacceptable, yes. But you know . . . still *possible*. All I'm saying is you haven't definitely said no until you definitely haven't done something. And you haven't definitely not gone to Australia yet. Your No to Lizzie is still in the Maybe stages. It could still be a Yes, it depends how it evolves. You've still said yes to everything *else* so far . . ."

And as if on cue, the barmaid was suddenly by our table.

"Hello, lads," she said, picking up our empty glasses. "Another pint?"

I opened my mouth to speak, and Ian raised his hand, trying to stop me . . . trying to stop me from saying . . .

"No. Thank you."

The barmaid walked off, and Ian looked furious.

"You fucking *idiot*!" he said. "You *threw it away*! You threw the whole thing *away*! You could have done it! You could have still gone to Australia! But oh, no, Danny doesn't want another pint, and what Danny doesn't want, Danny doesn't get. All that work, Dan! All for *nothing*!"

"That's not true," I said. "Not true at all. Yeah, okay, so I failed. But look at what else happened to me. Look at the difference in me now. I'm alive. I'm having fun again."

"Fun? You're back where you started. In the pub, with me. You don't have Lizzie anymore, you're seriously in debt, and you're about to start a job I'm not certain you truly want."

"I *do* want it. Yes has been good to me. I'm moving on."

"And Kristen? Where does Kristen fit into all of this? You can't just transfer what you feel for Lizzie to some girl you happen to have slept with along the way. . . ."

I looked Ian in the eye and held his gaze.

Gradually it dawned on him.

"Oh, my God . . . you didn't sleep with her, did you?"

I couldn't look at him, now.

"You didn't, did you? You said no! You *already* said no! This is a travesty! This has been a sham! You said no to a girl, and then no to a pint! You haven't just broken the Yes Manifesto! You've virtually broken the *law*!"

He threw his hands up in the air and sat back in his seat with a jolt. He said nothing for maybe ten or fifteen minutes. He went and got himself a pint—but for the first time in our lives, not one for me (I had, after all, said no). Maybe this was his punishment.

Turns out it wasn't.

"Be here on Tuesday night," he said, "for . . . *the Punishment*."

And he drained his pint and left.

I know. I'm sorry. I should have told you. But I was worried you wouldn't like me as much. I was worried you'd think I was a failure. I hadn't done anything I shouldn't have done with Kristen. And that's precisely why I didn't want to talk about it. Had I said yes, of course, I'd have been discreet, sparing you the gory details, but I would at least have ticked it off as another fantastic Yes in a very odd period of my life.

But I couldn't do that. It wasn't a tick. It was a big, red cross over my head.

I'd thought if I ignored it, it would go away. It wouldn't count. I'd never have to think about the fact that I'd failed. And so I'd kept schtumm, kept it out of my diary, said nothing—not even to myself. Saying yes to Kristen would have been a Yes too far. I didn't want to do something like that. I couldn't. It wouldn't have just affected me, but Kristen too, and—if I ever stood a chance of seeing her again— maybe even Lizzie.

But ironically my No had just made me Yes even harder. It was only then that I truly threw myself into the fight, determined as I was to make up for lost ground. So I jetted off to Barcelona. And then, just when I was starting to remember again, I found a way to push myself farther, and I booked a flight for Singapore. Subconsciously I can't have just *stumbled* upon that advert . . . on some level, I must have been *looking* for it . . .

• • •

So that was that. Ian was right. I'd said No to a girl, and No to a pint. Two things that if as a teenager I'd known I would one day do, would have utterly horrified me.

My Yes adventure was over. I had failed, and Ian knew all about it. I'd never before imagined the moment would be like this. Failure just hadn't seemed an option. It was only saying yes, after all. I'd wanted to make it all the way to New Year's Eve and be standing underneath a sky full of fireworks with my friends by my side as I reclaimed my right to say no.

But tonight the sky was dark and dull. Nothing was lighting it up. Just a clouded moon and the odd passenger jet, flying off to who knew where.

Ian was right, of course. Sometimes you *do* have to say no. I knew that now, and I knew it more than anyone. It's part of the human experience, and I'd been wrong to deny myself of it. But it had been fun, and I'd learnt a lot. And it wasn't as if I was alone, was it? Not *really*. All over the world, right now, people were making their decisions. Millions were saying yes to their friends, to new experiences, yes to themselves. And millions more were saying no, too. No to opportunity, to chance, to life.

Maybe that's what I needed to do for a while. Just for a while. Start saying no again. Stay in. Rest. Maybe that would be good for me. I was exhausted, physically and emotionally.

I got home to the flat and found my diary. I hadn't bothered to update it since Lizzie had left. Maybe now was the time. It's funny, writing a diary. We assume that all the experiences are our own. That we're unique, and they're unique to us. But every thought we've ever had, everything we've ever said, every time we've surprised ourselves with a new experience or idea, every memory we've made, every story we've heard or told or been part of . . . it's already happened before. Somewhere and somehow and sometime, someone has shared our experience without us even knowing.

Maybe there were other diaries out there, just like mine. People who'd been through things like I'd been through.

I was on-line, now, but rather than check my e-mails or read up on the news, I headed for Google. I'm not sure why I did it, but I typed the phrase "I wish I had said no" into the search box, and clicked Search.

I expected to get a million results. But I didn't. There were very few corporate sites, very few business pages coming back at me. I suppose regret doesn't sell. But what did come back to me was an Internet we only see when we look for it. The personal side of the Web. The people's side. The side I suppose I wanted.

There were blogs and diaries and entries in guestbooks and the odd celebrity interview. But the blogs were the most revealing. The innermost thoughts. The diaries tucked away in Tulsa or Peckham or Moscow, by people who have something personal to say and want to say it to an unseen world. A diary to be read by people they'll never meet. A way of being brave, sharing every aspect of their daily lives— the dull, the meaningless, and the meaningful.

I read my way through dozens of different pages that night, searching for God knows what. Advice? Guidance? Instead I found just what you'd expect. People who'd said yes when perhaps they ought to have said no.

A girl in Oklahoma wished she'd said no when a guy called Ryan asked her out, because he ended up taking Stacey to the party instead.

A man in France wished he'd said no to playing basketball that night, because he'd sprained his wrist and now couldn't type "prolpery."

A guy called Ken wished he'd said no to bringing inexperienced bird-handlers to a summer falconry event, because it was "just plain embarrassing."

But oddly it all seemed quite trivial. Apart from the crack users or the drunk drivers or the people who'd done something so obviously bad and wrong that it should never have been an option in the first place. But what I found next was different. What I did next seemed important. What I did next was type in "I wish I had said yes."

There were eighty-five results.

At first things seemed to be just as trivial. "*I wish I had said yes*, when he offered to go Dutch."

But slowly I started to find themes developing. Sure, there were people out there who wished they'd said yes to certain things, and it

had been no more than a casual annoyance. There were people who'd
kicked themselves once or twice over the years, and probably uttered
the odd "tsk" when the memory shot back to them and disrupted a
lazy afternoon. People who'd probably lost a few hours sleep over a
careless no . . .

But there were also people who knew . . . *pain.*

The pain of missing something; the pain of not knowing what *could*
have happened; the pain of discovering that sometimes, opportunity
really will only knock once; the pain of knowing where a No had
brought them and realising too late when a Yes in its place could have
led them.

The pain not necessarily of having said no, but of not having
grabbed a Yes.

**We gave the PlayMobil away today. I wish I had a penny for
every time Harry had asked me to sit with him and play. *I wish I
had said yes* and sat with him every single time he asked. Now he
is older, and he never asks his dad to play. I miss that so much.**

**"Yes, oh yes!" would have been the easiest answer. And why I
did not say those words, I do not know, and even today, *I wish I
had said yes.***

**I will never be able to explain just how much *I wish I had said
yes*, because then at least we could have stayed where we were,
and we could have held him in our arms until he was gone. *I wish
I had said yes.***

**I miss her, I miss her. *I wish I had said yes* to her, because I
miss her so much now.**

***I wish I had said yes* every time he wanted a hug. But I was
always too busy, and now I just can't . . .**

I didn't know these people. I didn't know their lives or their back-
grounds, and I'd never know why not having said yes to one moment

in time meant quite so much. They were just voices in the dark. But I could see their sadness.

Sure, it's a case-by-case thing, but I was starting to realise that regret could always be with you. And maybe there's a real difference between doing something we regret, and regretting not having done something. And it seemed that difference could be . . . well . . . *sadness*.

Take the stupidest thing you've ever done. At least it's done. It's over. It's gone. We can all learn from our mistakes and heal and move on. But it's harder to learn or heal or move on from something that *hasn't* happened; something we don't know and is therefore indefinable; something which could very easily have been the best thing in our lives, if only we'd taken the plunge, if only we'd held our breath and stood up and done it, if only we'd said yes.

If only.

If I went to see Lizzie and it didn't work out, would I regret it as much as I would regret never having done it? Would knowing be better than not knowing?

But suddenly I snapped out of it. I switched the computer off. I was being stupid. I had done the right thing. The only thing I could. This wasn't a film. This was my life. A part of me—and maybe even you— had hoped that by reading those random people's experiences and seeing their grief, something would snap inside me. And I'd realise that I wouldn't want to be like them, wouldn't want to regret like them, realise that it wasn't too late, that I could still take a chance . . .

But it didn't.

It just made me feel like there were other people out there who would understand; who would know exactly how I felt. And right now that was enough for me, somehow.

The following morning I would cut up my credit cards. I would book an appointment to get a haircut, during which I would lose my mullet and regain my old self. I would look into the best ways and means of selling my car. I would go back to how I was, in preparation for how I *would* be.

Soon it would be Friday. I still had a couple of days to brace myself for whatever punishment Ian lined up, and I would undertake his wishes with a smile and good humour. *You want me to dance around the pub in little blue pants?* Fine. *You want me to dress like a pirate and call myself Mr. Shitler for three weeks?* Done. I'd do whatever he wanted.

And so I got on with life. I went to the supermarket. I rented some DVDs. I started thinking about what I was going to do in January at the BBC. I played a few video games, replaced all the batteries in all my remote controls, and fixed a broken pen. I stayed in and watched telly. Lizzie left a message, saying she'd gotten back safely and wishing me a happy Christmas. I couldn't face phoning back.

And just when I thought that any hope had gone and that the course of my life was now more or less set, I received a postcard.

And that postcard, my friend, changed *everything*.

CHAPTER 26

In Which Something Remarkable Happens

It was Tuesday afternoon and time to face my punishment.

I drove through central London on my way to Langham Street and the Yorkshire Grey, where Ian would already be waiting for me.

I parked my car outside the Yorkshire Grey, popped my MINISTER ON OFFICIAL BUSINESS sign on the dashboard, and walked through the doors. He was sitting at a small table by the fireplace. He smiled when he saw me. Of course he did. The bastard. He'd been looking forward to this since the summer, and the fact that I'd lied to him about Kristen had only doubled his venom.

I had my diary in my hand—the result of nearly six months of intensive Yes-saying, the proof of my decision to live my life religiously by the power of Yes—and yet the very document that also confirmed I had failed. I set it down on the table and saw that Ian too had brought something. A long, red envelope, with the words THE PUNISHMENT written across the front.

"Is that the punishment?" I said slightly unnecessarily.

"It certainly is. It's a good one. I think you'll like it. I have put a lot of thought into it, Danny. A *lot*. You did far better than I thought you would," he said. "I'm sorry it had to be this way. But a deal's a deal. As we have established, you have failed on three counts, averaging out to roughly one failure per two months. Not an impressive record."

The fact that all three Nos had happened in the last six weeks apparently meant nothing to Ian. And he'd conveniently forgotten about his role in the dastardly plot to make it all so much harder, too.

Luckily I hadn't.

I would still have my revenge on Ian. But not today.

"So . . . let us count the ways in which you have said no."

"Well, hang on. What about the ways in which I said yes?" I said.

Ian considered the point, and with a theatrical wave of his hand, signalled for me to explain. I felt like a serf being granted an audience with the king.

"Well . . . what I mean is . . . I've tried really hard at saying yes to things. Yes to everything. And what I've learnt is that Yes is a powerful word. It's a word that can set us free and let us open our hearts and fly like the wind. It's a word—"

"Oh, Jesus, shut up, mate. Yes. It's a word. But the point is, it's a word you failed to say three times. To a pint. To a girl. To Australia. And now, by the power vested in me by the Yes Manifesto, I . . ."

"There's something else I haven't told you."

Ian put his head in his hands.

"If I've got to rewrite the bloody punishment . . . ," he said. "What is it? What haven't you told me?"

"Well, what you're saying isn't strictly true. I mean, yes, I did say no to those things, and so *technically* I failed, but . . ."

"Oh, here we go," said Ian, throwing his hands up in the air. "You're going to find a loophole, now, aren't you? Or some kind of last-minute twist. Well, that isn't fair. You said no. That's the end of it. You failed."

"That's just it," I said. "I *did* fail. I *didn't* say yes to everything. But I only said no to two of those things. I only failed on *two* counts."

Ian looked at me suspiciously.

"Have you been round Kristen's house? I *thought* you were looking a little tired. . . ."

"No. I'm tired because I've been up half the night packing."

"*Packing?*"

"I'm going to Australia. To see Lizzie. See how things go. Take a risk. I'm saying yes."

"*What!?*"

"I'm flying out tonight. I'll be there Christmas Eve. I'm afraid your elaborate and well-thought-out punishment will have to wait until I get back."

"But the punishment is *brilliant*!" he said, holding up his little red envelope with some degree of desperation in his eyes. "You can't do this to me! I worked long and hard on this!"

"I'd better go."

I started to stand up. Ian looked at me pleadingly.

"But . . . what changed your mind?"

I picked up my diary and flicked to the last page.

I found the postcard—the glorious, glorious postcard—that had arrived mornings before. I put it on the table and slid it toward him.

"Read this," I said, and I watched him while he did.

"Oh . . . ," he said. "Wow."

And then he handed it over, I put it back in my diary, left the pub, and got back in the car. I was driving to the airport. But there was one thing left to do.

I got my phone out and dialled Wag's number.

"Wag?"

"Hiya, Dan."

"Where are you?"

"I'm in Italy."

"Right. Well. This'll sound a bit odd, but there's a big favour I need . . ."

Many thousands of feet up in the air, I thought about what I was doing. It was a risk, yeah, but it was a risk I was glad I was taking. Lizzie had been delighted when I'd phoned her up to ask if the offer still stood and to explain my behaviour the last time I'd seen her. And like Ian, she'd wanted to know why I'd changed my mind; what could possibly have happened to make me decide to find the one credit card I hadn't cut up—the one credit card I'd saved "for emergencies"—and book myself on the first available flight to Melbourne.

I opened up my diary and took out the postcard. It was battered, and bruised, and smudged, and it was all the way from Thailand.

Danny,

How's it going? It's Jason here, I met you a while back at Thom's party in Liverpool. Sorry for being a bit of a dick that night—methinks one too many. Well, a few days later I realised that I really did want to go travelling with my brother. Work was getting me down anyway, dunno if you could tell! So here we are in Thailand; dunno where to next. We're having an amazing

time. **Thom gave me your address and said you wanted to chat with me. I'm back home in a few months, how about then? My new e-mail address is *******@hotmail.com or call me on 07*** *** ***. Gotta go, the beach is calling . . .**

Jase

I smiled. Jason had said yes.

I had no idea whether his decision to give up his job and do something that made him happy had anything to do with me. I suspect that on the whole it didn't. But a part of me still hopes that it did.

It's incredible how a few words from someone you hardly know can have an impact on your life. Of course some would call this divine intervention. That maybe Maitreya *did* exist, and it had been him that had done this. But I knew something. A stranger can affect your life in a thousand different ways—with a new thought or idea . . . or suggestion. I had my man on the bus—perhaps Jason had his stranger at the party. And maybe right now, he was on some beach in Thailand, telling a local girl (who one day, I like to think, he might marry), all about the night he met the stranger at the party, and all about those few words he'd said that had made him change his ways.

It was actually more likely that he was on some beach in Thailand, getting drunk, but it's a nice thought all the same.

The fact is saying yes hadn't been a pointless exercise at all. It had been point*ful*. It had the power to change lives and set people free. People like me or Jason. Maybe even you. It had the power of adventure. Sometimes the little opportunities that fly at us each day can have the biggest impact.

And now as I sat, cramped and sleepy, in a passenger jet high above the ocean, I would see what else Yes had in store for me.

This was it. This was *life*.

I leaned against the window and fell asleep in an instant.

SELECTED EXTRACTS FROM THE DIARY OF A YES MAN

December 26

On Christmas Day we had a barbecue with the family and drank beer with all the various cousins and brothers and stood around and baked in a thirty-degree heat. I feel it is important to stick to as many international cultural clichés as is possible in life, so as well as the barbie, I also had someone lend me a hat with some corks in it. Plus, despite my lack of tan and muscles, I really fit in here. Australia is the *land* of the mullet! I feel that at last I am among my own people.

Lizzie's just made me a cup of tea. She's looking after me. I am pretending to be more jetlagged than I am. I get a lot more tea that way.

December 28

This morning Lizzie woke me up to tell me we were going on a journey in her little red Nissan. We set off in the direction of a place called Glenrowan. She wouldn't tell me why. It took three hours to get there, and when we arrived, there didn't seem to be much of it.

And then I saw it. Towering high into the sky, with a gun in one hand and a bucket on his head was . . . a Big Ned Kelly! A Big Thing! *My first-ever Big Thing!* It must have been a hundred feet if it was an inch! A true Australian hero, lovingly re-created in concrete and fading plaster. Okay, so it was no Big Prawn, but it was *brilliant* nonetheless.

When we got home, I sat down with a map and enthusiastically attempted to plot the most efficient route round Australia with a pen. A grand, epic journey that would take in the Big Rock, the Big Lobster, the Big Cow and the Big Oyster. Me and Lizzie. On the road, in a tiny red car. For months and months and months.

December 29

It appears that the map has mysteriously disappeared.

How curious. Lizzie seemed just as shocked as I was and gave me a look that some would have mistaken for guilt, but which I know was of a genuine disappointment.

December 31

It's New Year's Eve.

Exactly one year since the last one.

And the night I was supposed to have finished being the Yes Man, in a pub, with Ian—either triumphing as the Yes Man, or receiving my punishment with humility. But here I am instead, on the other side of the world, having said the biggest and most unexpected Yes of my life . . . and happy.

Melbourne is ablaze with fireworks.

Lizzie and I hug. And at one point she looks at me, and she says something along the lines of "We can make this all work out, can't we?", and I look at my watch, and I see that it's 12:04 in a brand-new year. And I realise that for the first time in months, I feel like I can say whatever I want, with no restriction, and no regrets. *Anything* I want.

And so I turn to her.

And I say "Yes."

EPILOGUE 1

In Which Ian Gets His Just Desserts

To: Danny

From: Ian

Subject: Help me!

Dear Danny,

In the last forty-eight hours I have received more than one hundred calls on my home telephone. Each one of these has been from a confused Italian looking for someone named Charlie. One of the more persistent callers is a teenage girl who, as soon as I pick up, spends upwards of a minute simply screaming at me.

I did the sensible thing, of course, and switched my answerphone on. However, I forgot that my outgoing message contains my mobile number, and consequently I woke up this morning to find thirty-two texts and forty voicemails—one of which was just a minute and a half of screaming.

I take it that all this is not just coincidence.

You bastard.

Your former friend, who wishes he had helped the Challenger even more now,

Ian

P.S. Enjoy Australia

EPILOGUE 2

In Which We Must Finally Say Good-bye

Well, then, there you have it.

I am fully aware that technically, I failed at being the Yes Man. I'm sorry about that, and I hope you don't feel too cheated. But I hope you'll agree that, in the end, I probably won something a little more important.

Nevertheless, my Yes adventure was at an end. I hope, maybe, that at some point today, or tomorrow, or next week, even, *you* might say yes to something you'd normally say no to.

Not necessarily to psychotropic mindbombs, mind you, or big blokes in pubs who think you're looking at their girlfriends, or random trips to tiny islands in South East Asia. But little things. Yes to a friend. Yes to a drink after work. Yes to a stranger. Yes to yourself. You'd be amazed at where they can lead.

In other news, there are a few things I should probably fill you in on, if you've time.

I never did track down the man on the bus. But I kind of like it that way. Because that way, perhaps Maitreya really *is* walking the streets, looking after each and every one of us. It's quite good not knowing for sure. Although it does mean I can never look at a bearded stranger without a quick double-take, which one day could potentially land me in some trouble.

Jason returned from Thailand a few months after I got back from Australia, and we met up in Liverpool for a pint. He seemed far happier this time. By complete coincidence, it turned out that he'd been in Melbourne on New Year's Eve too—though neither of us had known that at the time. It's strange to think that if a Tube train hadn't broken down one night in London, it's possible neither of us would have been there, under the fireworks at Federation Square, welcoming in a new year and a fresh start. Samten the monk might say it was an inevitable coincidence. Marc would say there's no such thing. Who knows what the Hypnodog would say, so I'll leave the deciding vote with you.

Ian's punishment, it turned out, was an old-fashioned one. He handed me the prized red envelope on my return. I opened it to see the words "Go to Australia." It seems he was determined that if I didn't do it myself, he would send me to Lizzie anyway. I thought that was incredibly sweet, though, when I told him that, he blushed, and called me a tosser, and said he was only sending me there because "that's how they used to punish the criminals in the olden days." And then his phone rang, and he had to go off and answer it.

And since you're probably wondering, yes, me and Lizzie are still together. Though I should tell you that Lizzie isn't her real name. She chose it, when I started to write down everything that had happened, because she said she'd always wanted to be called Lizzie. And even though it's her middle name no one ever calls her that, and if she was going to be in a book, then that's the name she'd like to have. Which is a very Lizzie thing to do.

Anyway, a few months after New Year's Eve, Lizzie got a job offer in London. She moved a week later, and she's behind me right now, watching as I type this. She says hello.

She also thinks you should know that a few months after she moved in, I decided it was *my* turn to ask *her* a question. A big question.

She said yes.

ACKNOWLEDGEMENTS

Danny would like to thank Ian, Hanne, Wag, and Lizzie; Jake Lingwood and all at Ebury; Simon Trewin; Sophie Laurimore; Jago Irwin and everyone at PFD; Ryan Fischer-Harbage and all at Simon & Schuster; Daniel Greenberg; Sarah Bennie; the award-winning Stine Smemo; Di Riley; Claire Kingston; Dawn Burnett and Little Hannah Telfer; Bob Glanville; Dr. Frank Cottrell Boyce (who wishes he was Swiss); Mike Gayle (for being Mike Gayle); Howie and Liz at UTA; Andrew Collins; Espen Tarnesvik; Dominant Joly; Marc Gehring; Ricky the sound man; Jonathan Davies; Karl Pilkington (keep existing); Paul Lewis (who I must point out for legal reasons has not bullied since 1995); Xavier McMahon and family; cheeky Kieran Harte; Gareth Jones; Dan Glew and everyone at Cactus TV (thanks for giving me a break); Daisy Gates; Lisa Thomas and all at Karushi; Lee Phillips and LeafStorm; James @ Two Associates; Charlie, Matt, and James from Busted (!); my wonderful joinees (making the world a better place one Friday at a time!); the venerable Samten Kelsang and everyone at the excellent and very good value Losang Dragpa Centre; Hypnotist Hugh Lennon and Murphy the Hypnodog; Arlene for the wonton; Dean the soldier; Ian Critchley; Myfanwy Moore; Graham Smith; John Pidgeon; and all at the BBC (still the best place to work in the world).

Special thanks to my mum and dad and to Greta Elizabeth McMahon—between the three of them, they make everything brilliant.

ABOUT THE AUTHOR

DANNY WALLACE is a cult leader, a producer, and a comedian. He is the author of the number one British bestseller *Join Me*, which is currently being adapted for film. BBC America recently and bizarrely dubbed him "one of Britain's most respected journalists," but perhaps *Playboy* had a more accurate description of him: "F***cking brilliant." He is twenty-eight and lives in an old match factory in London.

HAPPY NOW?

an invitation to

Tim Miller's
GAY MEN'S PERFORMANCE WORKSHOP

This workshop is for gay men and queer boys to
gather together and explore some performance stuff.
Jumping off from a warm up, we'll tell

Is this you?

★★★★★★★★★★★★★★★

THE STARBU...
GROU...

Would like to invite a...
everyone to our third lo...

Come along if you are...
Aliens, Telepathy,...

Blind Begger, Whitechapel

Wednesday 6pm

Ask for Brian

★★★★★★★★★★★★★★★

HYPNOTIST
HUGH LENNON
& HIS
HYPNO-DOG!

DOG HYPNOTISES PEOPLE
A TWO-HOUR COMEDY SHOW